THE CHINA READY COMPANY

USING THE CHINA READINESS ASSESSMENT
TO PREPARE YOUR COMPANY FOR CHINA

THE CHINA READY COMPANY

STEVEN H. GANSTER
WITH KENT D. KEDL

CHINA PATHWAYS, LLC
AURORA, ILLINOIS

Published by China Pathways LLC
Aurora, IL 60502

Publisher's Cataloging-in-Publication Data
Ganster, Steven H.

The China Ready Company: using the China Readiness Assessment to prepare your company for China / by Steven H. Ganster with Kent D. Kedl. – Aurora, IL : China Pathways LLC, ©2005.

p. ; cm.
ISBN: 0-9772086-0-5
ISBN13: 978-0-9772086-0-9

1. Investments, American-China. 2. New business enterprises-China. 3. Economic development. I. Kedl, Kent D. II. Title.

HG5782 .G36 2005
332.67/3/0951-dc22   20055932118

Set in 11/14pt MetaPlus
Cover design, layout and graphics by Yaean Design Ltd.

Visit our China Readiness Assessment online at
www.chinareadycompany.com

Visit Technomic Asia at
www.technomicasia.com

Printed in the United States of America
09 08 07 06 05 • 5 4 3 2 1

This book is dedicated to the Technomic Asia staff -
past and present

Contents

Acknowledgments

The perspective in this book stems from years of consulting work in China, and from collaborating with many fellow Technomic Asia associates as well as many clients. I owe a great deal to the insights and experiences of these people. They are too many to name, but I would like to highlight those who lent particular input or support to getting this book together. Foremost, my senior partner, Kent Kedl, who has directly helped write the book as well as contribute ideas and his own experience to the mix. Also my compatriots at Technomic Asia: Qi Tang, Andrew Liu, Zhu Yi-Cun, Jackie Liu, Eileen Liu, George Jin, Michael Ding, Daniel Wang, Joe Qiu, Amanda Liu, Angellia Boey, Koh Swee Kee, Hayes Zhang, Clara Hu and William Wang.

There are past associates who have moved on to new things, as well as extended family of Technomic Asia, who I would like to acknowledge: Tom Oakley, who has been a strong supporter of our practice; Duane Glader, who helped birth the China Readiness Assessment concept; Bob Horn, who participated in the early development of the concept; and Nikunj Javeri, whose team developed the engine behind the original model. I owe particular debt to my consulting mentor, Aaron Lebedow, my Asian mentor, Joe Champagne, and long time partner, Mark Cleaver, who kept the ship moving as we traversed troubled waters.

My experience in China is a reflection of the pain, sweat, and tears of our clients and industry peers. I would particularly like to note some of those who have directly contributed to insights in this book: John Breitenstein, Jay Hoenig, Peter Ellefson, Phil Murtaugh, B. K. Chng, Terry Fry, Chip Chaikin, Craig Allen, Jeff Mei, Kevin Dempsey, Tom Gougarty, and Dominic Seto. A special mention to some of the early contributors to the model's development and structure: Richard Stanley, Raymond Tsang, Richard Garston, William Keller, Charles McIntyre, Jay Gmerek, Jock Holliday and Peter Han.

Thanks goes to Barbara Bohn, our editor; Arlyna Blanchard, who did the design and graphics work; the team at the Jenkins Group who helped get the book produced and released; and Al Maruggi and the team at Provident Partners, for their marketing support.

A very special acknowledgement to my wife and family for putting the insights in this book in proper context, and enabling me to apply fundamental life and relational principles to doing business in China. Also, to my brother Dan and sister Nancy, who helped keep me going when the going was tough, and good friend and advisor Jack Lavin.

Prologue

The Road to Readiness — Development of the China Readiness Assessment

 I suggest that the only books that influence us are those for which we are ready, and which have gone a little further down our particular path than we have gone ourselves.

E.M. Forster

The numbers don't lie. From 1994 to 2004, U.S. companies alone invested more than US$43 billion in China, exported $200 billion of goods to China and imported a staggering $1 trillion from China. During this time, many U.S. and European companies reconfigured their manufacturing and sourcing from the West to China. Jobs have migrated out of the West and business with longstanding customers has disappeared to heretofore unheard-of Chinese competitors. These dynamics have put China at the center of attention for Western businesses. From large companies looking to stay profitable by lowering their manufacturing costs or seeking new markets, to smaller firms reluctantly following their shifting customer base—the *pull* of China is very strong today.

For many Western firms, China is no longer simply an untapped opportunity or a grand vision of 1.3 billion consumers with their wallets open; rather, it is a fire-breathing, consuming dragon. Opportunities exist, but these are mixed with overt and covert threats as China becomes a legitimate competitor for jobs, markets, customers and even product innovation. We are at the early stages of this competition and are now settling in for a long-term marathon. For many, it will be a race of attrition, and for others it will change the very structure and culture of their company as they recondition their organizations, discovering muscles and flexibilities they never knew they had. Some will win and some will lose, but all will need to run hard to survive.

Some companies have profited from being among the pioneers of new business relationships with China; others have experienced significant disappointments. Erroneous market assumptions, changing government policies and an often uneven playing field have no doubt contributed much to failed China initiatives. However, equally damaging has been the absence of a clear understanding and awareness of the cost, stress and risk to a company's organization when doing business in China. In the early 1990s, management often did not do the necessary homework before launching into a complex and dynamic marketplace—and the carcasses of many of these firms are littered across the landscape. What have we learned from these past 15 years of doing business in China? How can these painful lessons be applied to companies entering or expanding in China today? What are the key challenges companies will face? Are there core characteristics and competencies that a company needs to successfully address these challenges? If so, is there a way to identify and nurture these success factors in companies *before* investing in China?

After a flurry of investment in the 1990s—the results of which were generally unsatis-factory—we felt it was time to step back and evaluate what happened. As managing director of Technomic Asia, one of the first foreign market strategy consulting firms in China in the early 1980s, I and my colleagues have been active participants in and front-row observers to the China growth strategies of many Western companies. The insights presented in this book are based on the experiences of myself, my partner Kent Kedl and other associates at Technomic Asia as we assisted more than 170 multinational firms in developing their China strategies over the last 17 years. In order to get a hind-sight view, we catalogued these experiences and interviewed dozens of managing directors of companies that had invested in China in the 1990s and early 2000s. We probed them about what they would have done differently had they been armed with a crystal ball: What issues did they miss? What mistakes had they made? What do they know now that they wished they knew then?

DEVELOPMENT OF THE CHINA READINESS ASSESSMENT

The result of this evaluation and reflection was the development of the China Readiness Assessment, a process to assist senior management to think through their approach to China effectively and thoroughly *before* making an investment. The past 15-plus years of doing business in China have been a battle, with winners and losers on both sides. Although many developments have made it a bit easier or at least more understand-able, the war has just begun. Successful companies think carefully before walking into oncoming fire: Would you go into battle without proper preparation and planning, taking inventory of weapons and defenses, taking stock of resources and supply lines?

Without evaluating the experience of your commanders? Without understanding the strengths and weaknesses of your enemies?

The China Readiness Assessment clarifies the key attributes of a China-Ready Company. It presents both a *descriptive* model and a *prescriptive* methodology to assist companies in better grounding their strategic growth efforts. The assessment will help company executives and stakeholders take an objective and probing look at both the reasons driving their proposed expansion into China and their organizations' abilities to succeed there. Its primary aims are to help management focus their strategic intents and identify the core competencies and resources which need to be cultivated in order to support a China initiative. By considering both its Motivations to pursue a China strategy as well as its Organizational Preparedness to execute that strategy, a company's state of *readiness* can be described. The process provides a constructive learning environment wherein executives can think more effectively and plan strategically.

The China Readiness Assessment can help all types and sizes of foreign companies in their China strategic planning. The process is especially useful for management of companies with limited experience in China, but it is also an effective tool for more seasoned China executives trying to enlighten staff from their home office as well as gain consensus among the management team. Small to mid-sized companies will find the assessment particularly valuable as they typically have more limited resources, thinner management depth and less international experience than multinationals. For them, the cost of failure can have devastating consequences, not just an unsuccessful project to be written off.

We have filled the book with true stories of companies, many of them clients, which struggled to succeed in China. We relate the good, the bad and the ugly of these companies' experiences. The reader will be able to identify with many of these issues and will benefit from the stories told by veterans who wistfully say, "I wish we would have known this before we started." These experiences will offer both warning and advice on how you can wrestle with many of the same issues and challenges. I am grateful for the input (sometimes unintended) of these clients. They have borne the brunt of our learning curve in China. While we reference a number of their experiences in this book, we have taken care to retain their anonymity.

Finally, a word of perspective: This process is more art than science, more experiential than deductive. When your company prepares to do business in China, you are not preparing to enter a static state for a single moment in time; rather, it is dynamic and constantly changing.

To use another metaphor, let me quote that great philosopher from Universal Studios, the ogre Shrek. His description of himself—"Ogres are like onions ... they have many layers"—may also be applied to China. China has many layers and, to succeed there, it is necessary to peel them away, one by one, to get to the center of what it means to be truly ready. We hope that this work will contribute to the peeling of a few layers in your understanding of doing business in China.

Book content map

This book provides a practical guideline and framework to help management address China's challenges. While nothing can replace the "six Ds" of doing business in China ("due diligence, due diligence, due diligence"), the process described in this book can provide you with a helpful tool as you wrestle through your strategic planning process. A company can use the China Readiness Assessment flexibly to suit its specific needs, from comprehensive implementation of the entire process to digging more selectively into some of its components.

While the chapters are organized to move sequentially through the China Readiness Assessment, feel free to skip around to areas that are of particular interest or concern to your company. If you are struggling with understanding your primary motivations for expanding in China, start with chapter four. If you are more concerned about risking intellectual property, go to chapter five.

To help you navigate the rest of the book, listed below are the main themes of each chapter. The book also includes comprehensive chapter summaries providing further description of the content.

CHAPTER ONE: THE GOLD RUSH

The first chapter reviews the history of U.S. investment in China over the past 20 years. Through the metaphor of a gold rush, we highlight the key lessons learned by these companies, some of them leading to hard-won success and others to abject failure. These lessons provide the rough framework for the China Readiness Assessment and offer important insight to executives today on what not to do as they approach (or re-approach) doing business in China.

CHAPTER TWO: THE CHINA CHALLENGE

Chapter two highlights the difficult and unique characteristics of China's market environment. This characterization provides a necessary backdrop to better understand specific hurdles a company will face when doing business in China and further highlights the need to be well prepared. The principles to address these and related challenges successfully form the core content of the China Readiness Assessment.

CHAPTER THREE: OVERVIEW OF THE CHINA READINESS ASSESSMENT

Chapter three describes the key dimensions of the China Readiness Assessment. We provide an overview of the concept and how it applies to companies investing in China today. It describes the relationships between the key dimensions of the model and establishes a readiness matrix showing the implications of a company's positioning as it measures its Motivation against its Organizational Preparedness. With the overall process defined, we will then be ready to examine more deeply each of the model's components.

CHAPTER FOUR: UNDERSTANDING YOUR MOTIVATION TO GO TO CHINA

Chapter four characterizes the first of the two core dimensions of the China Readiness Assessment, the motivation to enter or expand in China. It outlines the five motivators driving a China expansion and the importance of clarifying the rationale behind each one. The chapter concludes with a methodology to measure the nature and urgency of a company's composite motivation to pursue a China initiative.

CHAPTER FIVE: OPERATIONAL PREPAREDNESS — TRANSFERRING YOUR KEY COMPETENCIES TO CHINA

Chapters five through seven characterize the three sets of indicators which comprise a company's Organizational Preparedness, the second overall dimension of the China Readiness Assessment. Chapter five leads off with a company's operational preparedness, addressing the key issues surrounding transferring or replicating core company competencies to China to support a local operation. It discusses three important and related issues surrounding this transfer: protecting your intellectual property, establishing the right business structure and working with local partners.

CHAPTER SIX: MANAGERIAL PREPAREDNESS — SUPPORTING YOUR CHINA OPERATION

This chapter covers the human resources side of establishing and operating a China business. It reviews the need for a combination of strong and ongoing management support; sufficient management depth to staff your China team while maintaining a capable organization in your core operation; enough China-related experience and resources to jumpstart your local China operation, and a flexible and responsive management style to deal effectively with China's unique and dynamic business environment.

CHAPTER SEVEN: FINANCIAL PREPAREDNESS— MAKING IT HAPPEN

The last aspect of a company's Organizational Preparedness comprises the key elements of being financially prepared to both explore and execute a China strategy. We review four primary aspects to measure: your company's financial health, its willingness to spend the necessary funds to fully explore and evaluate the market and your options, your tolerance for risk, and expectations on returns on your investment.

CHAPTER EIGHT: THE CHINA READINESS ASSESSMENT IN ACTION— A CASE STUDY

The last chapter introduces the ABC Company and describes its experience going through the China Readiness Assessment, providing a real-life and complete picture of the process and its benefits. Here we put flesh on all elements of the China Readiness Assessment through the eyes of ABC management.

APPENDIX: ON-LINE CHINA READINESS ASSESSMENT

The appendix briefly describes the China Readiness Assessment On-line (www.chinareadycompany.com) and an accompanying workshop that can provide a format to help you begin to implement the China Readiness Assessment within your company.

Chapter 1
The Gold Rush

 Neither law nor order prevailed, honest persons had no protection from the gang of rascals who plied their nefarious trade," wrote mounted police officer Sam Steele, describing the scene at the base of the treacherous Chilkoot Pass in Alaska during the Klondike Gold Rush of the late 1890s. "Might was right; murder, robbery, and petty theft were common occurrences. [1]

Many Western executives whose companies invested in China in the early to mid-1990s would echo these words spoken about the plight of many prospectors rushing to the Yukon in the late 1800s to strike it rich in gold. In those days, avalanches, drownings, typhoid, spinal meningitis, murder and scurvy claimed many lives. Of the tens of thousands who actually made it to the Bonanza, only a handful found fortunes. Sounds a bit like China as the last decade came to a close.

In the Yukon gold rush, most stampeders knew little to nothing about where they were going, so pamphlets were available from slick "marketers" to help them on their way. Most contained no real information and made outrageous claims of wealth to be had by everyone. Those who survived the perilous journey mostly found only disappointment once they reached Dawson City and the grossly exaggerated claims of "gold for the taking." Many stampeders headed home, empty-handed and financially ruined. Some China veterans reading this can feel their pain.

The 1990s marks a key evolutionary phase in Western firms' investment history in China and offers important insight to executives today on what not to do as they approach (or re-approach) doing business on the mainland. The experience of the last decade, much of it disappointing, sheds light on many of the characteristics needed to be a China-Ready Company.

---

[1] Courtesy of the Adventure Learning Foundation, "The Klondike Goldrush"

HOW WE GOT HERE

A BRIEF HISTORY OF FOREIGN INVESTMENT IN CHINA

Over the course of the 1990s, China pulled away from its regional rivals in terms of foreign business interest and investment. The Asian Tigers[2] retreated to their cages after the financial crisis was ushered in by the plunge of the Thai baht in the summer of 1997; Japan remained in a "hollowed-out" economic state from the late 1980s, and China's chief mega-country rival, India, simply never got going after similar economic liberalization noise in the beginning of the decade.

FIGURE 1.1: UTILIZED FDI (FOREIGN DIRECT INVESTMENT) BY SELECTED ASIAN COUNTRIES, 1991-2000

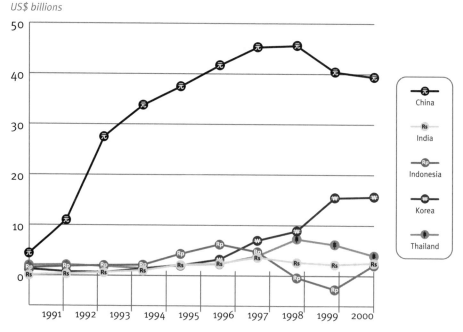

US$ billions

SOURCE: VARIOUS GOVERNMENT STATISTICS

While I use numbers cautiously in this book because they are rather perishable as reference points, some basic trend data tell a convincing story. Compared to the stop-and-go growth rates of other Asian countries over the 1990s, China maintained a steady 7%+ real gross domestic product (GDP) growth level. Figure 1.1 portrays the foreign investment activity in these countries over the same period and shows how China dominated the region. Cumulatively, China consumed more than US$325 billion in foreign direct

---

[2] Various definitions of countries are included but commonly comprise Hong Kong, Singapore, Korea, Thailand, Malaysia, Indonesia and Taiwan.

investment (FDI) from 1991 to 2000, and the gap with other Asian countries continued to expand after 2000 as China's FDI consumption climbed even higher.

This figure contrasts with US$56 billion in Korea and less than $20 billion in India over the same period. There is a similar story in terms of total trade, with China expanding from US$136 billion in 1991 to almost $475 billion in 2000 (as with FDI, this figure has continued to climb, topping $1 trillion in 2004). In sum, China satiated Western management's investment appetite for the region as the last decade came to a close.

PROSPECTING

Investment opportunities in China essentially began in 1979, when the Chinese government started its "Openness and Development" program. Previously, several large, primarily European firms had minimal investment, but this was based on longstanding ties to China from before the 1949 Communist revolution and did not result in significant activity. China has been open to U.S. firms only since the early 1980s, when increasingly close political ties between the two countries were solidified. This period saw some tentative investment by large companies such as General Electric Co.

At that time, the only entry structure available to foreign companies in China was a joint venture with an existing Chinese state-owned enterprise that had little to no experience with multinational businesses. This period presented an often murky investment environment for foreign firms. There were no transparent legal or banking regulations. The government, as well as investors, was somewhat blindly making its way through then-Premier Deng Xiao-ping's admitted policy of "crossing the river by feeling for the stones." Economic growth was not very impressive despite the latent potential of the large population. Chinese officials began talking of entering the General Agreement on Tariffs and Trade, or GATT (the predecessor to the World Trade Organization) in 1987, while the social landscape began to erode due to high inflation, government corruption and increasing social unrest. The decade culminated in the Tiananmen Square tragedy on June 4, 1989.

Our consulting company was one of the early entrants, having set up a joint venture in Guangzhou in 1985. But we, like many of our clients, were only dipping our toes in the water to gauge the temperature. We kept our key assets—and money—outside the mainland in Hong Kong. To those of us who were in China after Tiananmen Square, it seemed as if nascent investment and development had suddenly come to an early and bitter end.

THE GOLD RUSH

However, contrary to just about everyone's misgivings, the 1990s actually saw explosive expansion of China's GDP and a liberalization of market-entry conditions. Rather than reject China's ruling authorities for their role in the events in Tiananmen Square, the developed world generally increased its interest in China as an investment target, believing that closer ties would spur positive change in social, economic and political spheres—not to mention some commercial rewards. The result was a massive inflow of foreign investment. The Chinese government, seizing an opportunity to regain favorable world opinion, loosened entry requirements and opened many sectors. Concurrently, it made attempts to privatize unprofitable SOEs (state-owned enterprises) while slowly dismantling the "iron rice bowl" that guaranteed a living wage for workers despite the poor financial performance of their employing organizations. Deng Xiao-ping made his famous "to get rich is glorious" speech in South China in the spring of 1992, unshackling the Chinese people from the oppressive binds of the state-planned economic system—and the economy took off. The first half of the 1990s was not unlike the Yukon gold rush.

During this period, multinational companies scrambled for position in China to participate in the anticipated boom. CEOs flocked to Hong Kong, touting big plans for their companies in China as they made the executive cocktail circuit on the yet-to-be-handed-over Island City. It was not uncommon to hear Western CEOs make public statements such as, "We'll be $1 billion in China in five years." When they jetted back to the U.S., locally based management scrambled to put together deals to fulfill these grand visions while the gold still glittered. Most of these investments were through 50-50 joint ventures, often the only option at the time.

In their rush to enter China, Western firms often "married their first date." In many cases, these agreements were essentially arranged marriages orchestrated by the Chinese government. The promise of access to a market with double-digit growth and a population, at that time, of nearly 1.2 billion proved too seductive to resist. Like

American George Carmack and his friends Dawson Charlie and Skookum Jim in 1896, they "dreamed of salmon with gleaming gold nugget eyes in blue-green water."

FIGURE 1.2: FOREIGN INVESTMENT AND ECONOMIC GROWTH IN CHINA, 1981-2004

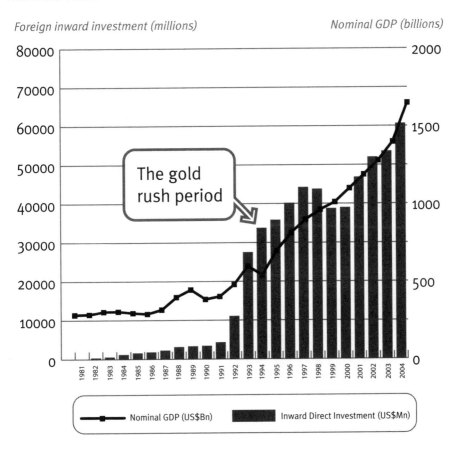

SOURCE: CHINA STATE STATISTICS BUREAU

FOOL'S GOLD

In the second half of the 1990s, however, the tide began to turn as the Chinese government attempted to put the brakes on an economy growing out of control. The continuing migration of the Chinese rural population into the cities created social problems, unemployment and major infrastructure strain. As the economy slowed and the poorly structured JV marriages made in the early to mid-1990s started to fall apart, the gold began to lose its luster; for many, it was indeed only fool's gold. As a result, initial investments began to look dubious, the flow of money into China slowed and many executives' initial enthusiasm turned sour. Some "stampeders" headed back home, hat in hand, their pockets significantly lighter.

REFINING PROCESS

This changing tide compelled many Western firms in the late 1990s to re-assess their China strategies and take corrective steps such as shutting down unprofitable ventures, buying out partners and rethinking their overall approach to the market. In this process, the flaws in their strategies came to light. They discovered the true identities and intentions of their joint venture partners—who ended up being the ugly stepsisters, not Cinderella. Management expended an enormous amount of time and money during this time, essentially undoing their efforts of the previous few years. Though painful, this re-assessment period resulted in significant benefit and a renewed, though more sober, confidence in China. While many executives now walked with a limp from their initial foray into China, they were at least walking and were a lot wiser for the experience. Others never returned.

COMMERCIALIZATION

Since the early 2000s, companies have again begun assertively addressing the China market but often with a more deliberate and measured approach. China's continued economic emergence is materially affecting the global economy. Chinese companies are beginning to crack Western markets, improving their quality to more accepted standards and offering much lower prices (some Chinese companies are even aggressively acquiring Western companies in industries such as mining, steel and even computers[3]). Foreign firms are using China as a low-cost manufacturing base for other markets and are setting up local supply chains, either on their own or through contract manufacturers. Western companies are seeing their main customer base migrating to China, compelling them to respond—or lose longstanding accounts.

China still offers significant opportunity but it is also becoming a serious threat to many Western manufacturing firms. Today, China must be viewed as an integral part of a company's global strategy, not a discrete planning initiative. The option of not addressing China is no longer on the table for many companies.

---

[3] Citing Lenovo's acquisition of IBM's PC business in early 2005.

LESSONS LEARNED

The gold rush years of the 1990s resulted in many painful lessons for Western firms. "I certainly had rose-colored glasses on at the time," lamented one U.S. executive who invested big in China in 1995 and then watched the operation crumble before his eyes as the forecasted market bonanza turned out to be a mirage. Highlighted below are some of the more salient lessons learned.

FIGURE 1.3: PHASES IN FOREIGN INVESTMENT IN CHINA

Door opening 1980s	Liberalization ~1990-1995	Stabilization ~1995-1997	Normalization ~1997-EARLY 2000s	Modernization 2004...
• SOEs dominated • Many investment and trade restrictions • Limited foreign investment— a select few pioneers • Not on MNCs' radar	• Major GDP expansion— key sectors boom • Borders open—easy entry • Multiple new players enter • FDI investment significant	• Economy overheats— money tight • Oversupply exists in many sectors • Government slows economy • JVs falter and many die	• Economic growth more controlled • Restructuring of early investments • Emergence of successful MNCs—some exits • WTO a major issue	• China becomes a leading world economy • Evolves as "workshop" of the world • Emergence of China-based global players
PROSPECTING	**GOLD RUSH**	**FOOL'S GOLD**	**REFINING PROCESS**	**COMMERCIALIZATION**

A STILL PICTURE VIEW OF THE MARKET

Many executives took a snapshot view of market characteristics, as well as the competitive structure, which led to grossly inaccurate planning assumptions. The frenetic pace of change in China throughout the 1990s made long-range plans highly perishable. Companies frequently overestimated a market's potential, particularly in terms of value, due to unrealistic pricing assumptions. As new supply was dumped on the market, often from unexpected sources, domestic market pricing rapidly deteriorated, and with it went acceptable margins. It was not unusual for local Chinese government and private groups to enter a new market based on the seeming success of an operation in a neighboring province—the leap from a state-owned hairy crab restaurant to a quasi-private fiberglass plant did not seem very broad to many local entrepreneurs and government officials with the means to make things happen in their locale. Western firms tried to compete—or, even worse, partner—with such firms on the basis of the growth and prospects touted by the new and inexperienced owners of these Chinese companies.

RELIANCE ON PARTNERS

As most foreign investment during the gold rush years was in the form of a joint venture (often a 50-50 share), troubled marriages were common for Western investors. Executives often seemed to leave their common sense at home when they came to China, choosing partners based on casual due diligence or simply accepted at face value when offered up by ingratiating government officials, with little knowledge of their venture partner's capabilities, contribution and motives. For example, relying on their partner's local market expertise and *guanxi*[4], foreign stakeholders did not provide enough sales and marketing support. But many of the local partner companies were still mired in—or recently emerging from—a state-run, command economy mentality based on scheduled production quotas rather than market demand, and had little Western-style marketing experience. As a result, brands were poorly developed, sales forces lacked punch and the business plan had more value as scrap paper.

GETTING MORE THAN YOU BARGAINED FOR

Western firms often inherited the baggage of their venture partner in the form of excess, even off-the-book employees, retirees, family pensions, hidden liabilities and non-performing assets. Naively accepting the venture partner's description of their operating structure, foreign firms did little of their own due diligence to ferret out the skeletons in the closet—they were just excited to have found a partner, and they were in a hurry. After the deal was signed, run-down plants appeared out of nowhere and an army of unproductive employees suddenly appeared on the books. These liabilities forced operating costs well beyond expectations against a backdrop of often shoddy financial planning. The weight of this excess baggage often put a stranglehold on the local venture, making it impossible to meet financial targets.

LACK OF STAYING POWER

Operational and partner problems aggravated what already was an inherent weakness in Western, and particularly U.S., management approach: short-term financial perfor-

---

[4] *Guanxi* (pronounced gwan-shee) is a Chinese word that broadly means "relationships" and refers to the vast network of social connections so common in Chinese personal and business cultures.

mance pressure. When the gold's luster started to dull and the pressures of Wall Street hammered down, many stakeholders ran for the hills. In some instances, companies bailed out of China altogether; in other, perhaps more insidious, cases, corporate management abandoned their local partners to face China's market challenges on their own. Many a China-based Western manager struggled to salvage the operation when no one from corporate answered the phone or returned faxes. "For a while, we were in the spotlight. Then, it became dark," said one U.S. chemical company executive who ran the China operation in the latter 1990s. The shame is that much of the pain of poor and delayed investment returns and significant disenchantment regarding future opportunities in China was self-induced as management ignored or misconstrued China's challenges.

Taking a fresh look

Today, corporate executives tend to waver, being pulled in one direction by the voluminous press on China and in the other by the pain of their past wounds. For many executives, the scale teeters back and forth as China presents its two faces. Like the Chinese philosophy of yin and yang, two principles that oppose and balance one another in their actions and represent all the opposite principles one finds in the universe, the reality is that China's profile is also neither black nor white but encompasses both. Western companies need to exploit the upsides while effectively dealing with the downsides.

Figure 1.4: China's opportunity-risk scale

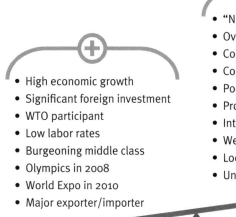

- "No one making money"
- Overcapacity/price wars
- Counterfeit products
- Corruption
- Poor infrastructure
- Protectionism/nationalism
- Intellectual property infringements
- Weak legal system
- Looming banking crisis
- Unpredictable risks (e.g. SARS)

- High economic growth
- Significant foreign investment
- WTO participant
- Low labor rates
- Burgeoning middle class
- Olympics in 2008
- World Expo in 2010
- Major exporter/importer

A balanced view of China comprises a mix of characteristics:

- China's economic growth is real
- U.S. manufacturing is migrating to China
- While there is still a lot of junk produced in China, production quality can be top-notch
- China is not mystical, but it is complex
- Western company failures have, in large part, been the result of ill-conceived strategies, lack of due diligence and poor implementation, not unfair play
- Overcapacity does not mean you can't make money in China; it does mean that you have to plan more effectively where and how you will participate
- China is a strategic market that should be viewed in a global context
- A China strategy today often has both offensive and defensive implications
- It is tough to do business in China

Despite the poor strategies and failures of the 1990s, many Western firms that did their homework and structured their business models appropriately are making money in China today. Successful companies conduct rigorous due diligence of their investments and seek to control the operation in most key management functions. When setting up joint ventures, they contract for only selective assets whenever possible. Most importantly, they start with a clean company (vs. equity acquisition) whenever possible to avoid inheriting unwanted baggage.

Executives work closely with local government on setup–optimizing benefits and aligning objectives with local interests. Instead of burdening the local operation with too many expatriates, they localize human resources as soon as feasible and prudent. Smart companies are designing their operational model to make money in China, not merely transplanting the market approaches and structures they have used in the West. Leading companies are looking at China in creative ways, not limiting their participation in the value chain to their roles in developed markets. These companies recognize that China is in a formative stage of development, where roles by market players have not yet been defined and offer opportunities to be unique. Lastly, successful firms are giving their China operations the needed support and attention from the home office, providing the necessary staying power to weather the inevitable storms to come. We will look at many examples of successes and failures, as well as the reasons behind them, as we proceed through subsequent chapters.

Successful Yukon prospectors found that most of the gold was not at the surface, but rather 10 or more feet below. To reach it, the miners had to dig through a layer of permanently frozen ground. The ground had to be thawed before it could be dug, then the dirt sluiced to separate it from the gold. It was incredibly difficult work.

The "gold" that China offers is no different and requires a similar level of hard work, good planning and perseverance as the business climate changes. For those willing to dig in for the long haul and take some risks, they can echo the anticipatory shouts of some of the first Yukon prospectors: "There's gold in them thar hills!"

CHAPTER SUMMARY

In this chapter, I set the backdrop for our evaluation of a China-Ready Company. We compared China's opening up in the early 1990s to the gold rush in the Yukon Territories in the late 19th century. Just as many stampeders met a gloomy fate in their rush for gold, so did Western companies clambering to make their claim in China.

Over the course of the 1990s, China separated itself from the rest of Asia, dominating foreign investment and trade growth. Indeed, just as buildings sprung up in Dawson City, so too skyscrapers seemed to emerge overnight in major cities across China. But as the prospectors experienced in the Yukon, the going was extremely tough and the prizes few–so, too, for Western companies in China as the economy overheated in the mid- to late 1990s. China's prospects were looking like fool's gold to international executives who had thrown caution to the wind and invested heavily in China in the previous few years. Most of these investments were in the form of joint ventures with weak partners whose façades often masked unprofitable, unproductive and poorly managed organizations. The next few years were spent cleaning up or shutting down these ventures. At the end of this difficult period, those companies that survived and had the stomach to go on renewed their efforts in China, but with a more cautious and careful approach.

In the last several years, interest in China has accelerated once again. Not only has China's domestic market continued to expand but its economy has made a significant impact in global markets. Chinese companies have migrated up the value chain in their exports to the West, and foreign firms have shifted manufacturing to China to serve both local and overseas markets. As a result, China now presents both opportunity and threat to Western companies.

As is often the case with lessons learned, there was a lot of pain and anguish over this period, as Western companies struggled to deal with China. These experiences offer important lessons for companies as they venture into China today, providing warning signs to avoid making the same mistakes. China is a tough place to do business, but the rewards can be great if you are well prepared.

Chapter 2
The China Challenge

 Now the general who wins a battle makes many calculations in his temple ere the battle is fought. The general who loses a battle makes but few calculations beforehand. Thus do many calculations lead to victory, and few calculations to defeat.

Sun Tzu, 'The Art of War'

As we have seen in the last chapter, many multinational executives in the 1990s did not have a very productive time "in their temple" before launching their attack on China. They should have heeded the advice of Sun Tzu, the renowned Chinese general who wrote *'The Art of War'* more than 2,000 years ago. Much of his treatise addressed the strategies of conducting warfare, and most importantly, on the preparations for battle. He considered all aspects of the fight, from the environment and each side's resources, men and commanders, to human nature itself.

These same elements, in a commercial context, are worthy of attention by Western management as they plan their China strategy. In this spirit, I will lay some basic groundwork on the nature and scope of China's market and the key challenges it presents. These challenges warrant specific attention and preparation and will help you to lay successful plans for "war."

I cannot hope to capture in one chapter the complexity of doing business in China; rather, my aim is to bring to light particular challenges for a Western company expanding in China. These insights will help us to better appreciate the character and requirements of a China-Ready Company, which will be described in subsequent chapters.

The main challenges are:
- Addressing the rapid pace of change
- Defining your addressable market
- Understanding the value chain

- Being cost competitive
- Dealing with corruption
- Finding and retaining human resources
- Implementing effective relationship management

I will also weave into the discussion some key characteristics of China's market landscape to further establish a point of reference for the China Readiness Assessment, which will be presented in chapter three. This background perspective will help you be a better general and have a more fruitful time while in your "temple" making preparations for battle.

ADDRESSING THE RAPID PACE OF CHANGE

As I described in chapter one, China's economic evolution over the last 10 to 15 years has been nothing short of remarkable. Because of this rapid change, a major challenge for Western firms is to hit a moving target. New buildings and roads seemingly appear overnight, to the point that some expatriate executives have trouble finding their way home from the airport after an extended overseas trip.

The figures below provide a compelling picture of the pace of this change since China more widely opened its doors to the West in the early 1990s: [1]

- Growth: China's GDP expanded more than 270% from 1993 to 2004, growing at an annual average real rate of ~10%
- Trade: More than US$1 trillion annually in total trade places China third or fourth in the world
- Investment: Foreign investment has grown five-fold since 1992 to almost US$60 billion today, ranking it second in the world behind the U.S.
- Cell phones: More than 300 million subscribers by yearend 2004, the biggest cell phone market in the world
- Web users: With more than 80 million subscribers at yearend 2004, China trails only the U.S. for the most Web surfers
- Autos: Annual car production raced from 230,000 to ~2.3 million, mostly in the last three to four years
- Big Macs: the number of McDonald's restaurants jumped from 1 in 1993 to ~600 by yearend 2004

[1] A reminder that any data points on China are subject to debate—these figures are illustrative of real changes in China's landscape.

With this blistering pace of development, it is no wonder that many foreign companies have had blurry long-term visions of their China market opportunity. Though in a different league than Sun Tzu, Yogi Berra also made some sage remarks appropriate to our purposes. "You've got to be very careful if you don't know where you're going, because you might not get there." This dynamic market can make it very difficult to know where you are going when you can't get a clear fix on the target destination. Like a dragonfly dancing over the water, China presents an often-fleeting market that doesn't hold still long enough to grab it.

In this context, China presents a transition from a command to a market-based economy. This transition has profound implications for doing business there yet is sometimes difficult to measure as the nature and pace of development vary by geography, company, industry and business situation.

FIGURE 2.1: CHINA'S SHIFT TO A MARKET ECONOMY

COMMAND ECONOMY	MARKET-BASED ECONOMY
• Centrally controlled access to resources • State-owned means of production • Capital flows based on policy directives • Regulating by subjective Party policy • Welfare in the form of state subsidies to society • Target-based production rationale • Centrally controlled cost-basis pricing • Government-regulated markets	• Resources allocated according to forces of supply and demand • Private ownership of production • Investment flows based on efficient employment of capital • Regulation by objective law • Welfare in the form of direct government transfer • Demand-based production targets • Market-driven pricing • Competitive markets • Entrepreneurship

In many sectors, the shift to a market-based economy is almost complete, such as in consumer goods, where most companies have a free hand to develop and market their product portfolio, while other sectors remain in more of a command economy—media and publishing, for instance, are still tightly controlled by the central government.

Most markets lie somewhere in between. Pharmaceuticals and automotive are open to foreign investment but still have tangible government participation in ownership rights, price controls, etc., as well as intangible involvement including protectionism, nationalism and bureaucracy. Western management needs to anticipate further progression to a more market-based economy, whether in assessing addressable market, qualifying prospective partners or analyzing competition.

China officially entered the World Trade Organization (WTO) in 2001, which heralded another milestone in development and its participation in the global economy. However, the benefits of China's WTO entry are still unrealized in many areas. WTO promised to level the playing field by reducing duties, increasing transparency and protecting Western firms' intellectual property rights. Indeed, gains are taking place but in many cases the process is painstakingly slow. Still, given time and patience, China's market *will* become more open to foreign investment across virtually all industry sectors. Foreign firms *will* receive more national treatment and benefit from a more uniform and rules-based system. Regulations *will* become more transparent and consistent with international norms and practices. The government *will* attach greater importance to the protection of intellectual property. The Chinese currency *will* eventually become fully convertible and more free-floating.

FIGURE 2.2: EVOLUTION OF CHINA'S MANUFACTURING SECTOR

Characteristic	⟨··· 1990	Today	2010+
Industry breadth	Low-tech, basic, heavy/light assembly	Very broad, mid-tech	Mid- to high-tech and services
Government vs. private	SOE dominant	Rapidly emerging private sector	Emerging global players
Infrastructure	Very poor/inefficient	Semi-developed/ spotty	Regionally developed
Labor skill	Unskilled	Semi-skilled and emerging entrepreneur	Skilled and highly entrepreneurial
Management capability	Unsophisticated/ bureaucratic	Emerging but still weak in the middle	Mature and able to fully localize
Foreign manufacturing	Niche and highly controlled	Broad and emerging independence	Limited state involvement

But these changes *won't* happen overnight. While it is difficult to anticipate the timing of China's WTO compliance, it could drastically change a company's strategy–and even its interest level—in China. Constant vigilance is required. In another wise quip by Yogi Berra, "You can observe a lot just by watching." For instance, China's manufacturing environment has shown dramatic change in the last 10 years, with the likelihood of continued evolution in the next decade (Figure 2.2). These changes have occurred at a pace far exceeding what many Western countries experienced in the twentieth century.

In considering China's manufacturing environment as a backdrop to potential investment in a local facility, some key characteristics should be kept in mind:

- China will be a world leader in certain industries (low-cost, large-scale, good quality) and the Asian manufacturing center for many multinational firms.
- China's huge domestic market will provide stable demand to support the evolution of the manufacturing sector, independent of world demand and export potential.
- Chinese imports and exports will have significant global and especially regional impact.
- China will become increasingly self-sufficient in intermediate raw materials, manufacturing equipment, labor skills and even management competence.
- Imports will continue to lose cost competitiveness to local operations, despite WTO.
- Multinational companies with major manufacturing in China will continue to localize their supply chains aggressively.

In short, China's manufacturing environment will have a global impact, often causing a cascading effect as a market's supply chain shifts its priorities to East Asia. This point is evident now as senior manufacturing and supply chain management are playing an integral part in a company's strategic planning process for China. Companies are rethinking their global manufacturing footprint as their supply chains migrate to Asia. In one way or another, a China facility will directly impact a firm's operations in the West. The timing of this impact can be hard to predict but, in our experience, Western management has more frequently erred in underestimating the rate of change.

This dynamic environment can present a particular challenge to Western management teams that suffer from a cumbersome decision-making process. Opportunities or threats can emerge quickly and need rapid response. Deals have disappeared while locally based foreign management waited for the next board meeting back at corporate headquarters. Competitor plants have been built while multiple management teams and committees deliberated about a possible investment. Yet, despite this need for speed, careful due diligence must be done on any China investment, making the decision process even more challenging.

This shifting market landscape also calls for flexibility and adaptability: The best-laid plans should be uprooted if circumstances change. Sun Tzu offers some good advice. "According as circumstances are favorable, one should modify one's plans." Of course, building in this flexibility from the beginning is the best approach but often all contingencies cannot be foreseen.

DEFINING YOUR ADDRESSABLE MARKET

Many executives have done the fantasy math of calculating how much money they would make if each person in a country of 1.3 billion bought their product. Indeed, despite the fallacy of this formula, China is a large actual market for many companies and a massive latent market for others.

Marketers like to measure the number of middle-income Chinese consumers as a benchmark of opportunity. This figure is a bit elusive and dependent on definition, but is sizable under any formula. Some estimate 50 million to 100 million, while others target 250 million to 300 million. Even at the higher figure, the addressable market represents less than 25% of China's total human potential.

Whatever the number, these wealthier consumers are concentrated on the Eastern seaboard. Despite encouragement by the Chinese government to go inland, FDI, trade and higher disposable income levels are still geographically concentrated along the coast, as are the top cities receiving foreign investment, such as Suzhou, Shanghai, Shenzhen, Wuxi and Guangzhou. To get a sense of this economic concentration, imagine putting 70% of the total U.S. economic activity along the east coast, from Boston down to Miami.

FIGURE 2.3: FDI IN CHINA BY REGION

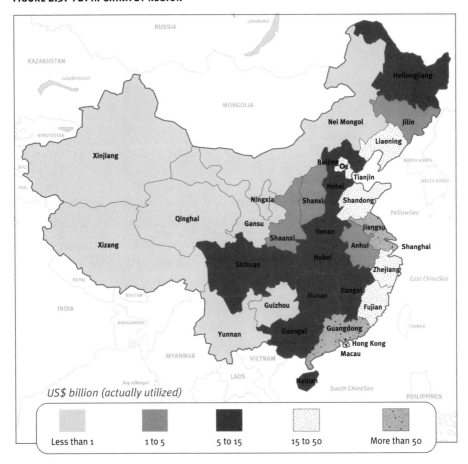

China's 1.3 billion people make it the most populous country in the world, accounting for one-fifth of the global total, though its land footprint is about the size of the continental U.S. Urban population comprises 35% and continues to grow as rural residents continue to migrate to cities in the coastal areas where investment and economic prosperity are stronger. Currently, more than 170 cities register over a million inhabitants.

China's buying power is concentrated within the top 30-35 cities, but even then, there is a wide disparity between the disposable income level of the top city, Shenzhen (more than US$3,300 per capita) vs. Chongqing, near the bottom of the list (only ~$1,100 per capita). In rural areas, where 600 million to 700 million people still reside, income levels are less than US$400 per capita.

FIGURE 2.4: SEGMENTATION OF CHINA'S URBAN MARKETS

	1985	2003
Total cities	324	660
Urban population		
More than 2 m	7	33
1 to 2 m	8	141
0.5 to 1.0 m	34	274
Less than 0.5 m	275	212

SOURCE: CHINA CITY YEARBOOK; CHINA STATISTICAL YEARBOOK

China represents a vast and regionally oriented market landscape in other ways as well. Required product features, brand positioning and marketing approach all must be examined to comply with differing cultural preferences, business practices, diet and even language between regions (while Mandarin Chinese is the standard spoken language, there are thousands of regional dialects, each sharing a common written script). Market channels are regional in scope with few nationally oriented distributors. Local and provincial governments can also change a company's opportunity and market access. In the end, marketing and distribution strategies in China are typically regionally based. However, this condition will change over time as more national players evolve in a number of markets. You need to accurately forecast the pace of this development in your market space in order to establish effective channel strategies.

These and other factors make defining an addressable market—where you can make money—very tough. This challenge is especially important when positioning a product. From a relatively simple two-tier product pricing structure 10 years ago, most of China's markets have fragmented considerably and become more complex.

The historic price structure was often simplistic with a wide gap in price—as well as performance and features—between imports and locally made goods (Figure 2.5). If customers needed the imported product features and had the money and an import license, they bought it. The mass volume market, however, often included low-end, poor-quality product made in China by state-owned enterprises or small private firms, and buyers were very cost sensitive.

FIGURE 2.5: CHINA'S CHANGING PRICE STRUCTURES (INDEX BASIS)

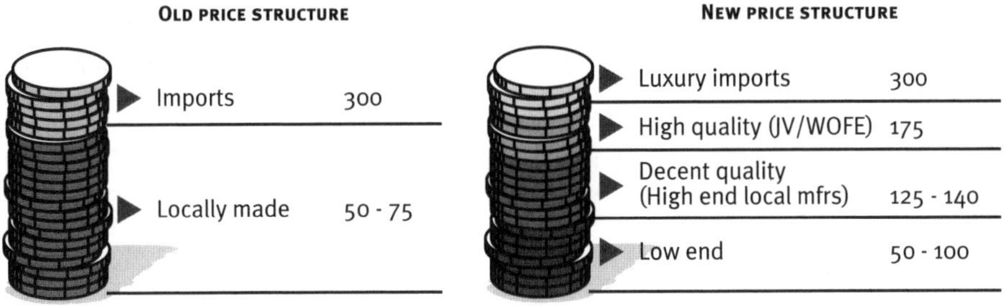

OLD PRICE STRUCTURE   NEW PRICE STRUCTURE

Imports	300
Locally made	50 - 75

Luxury imports	300
High quality (JV/WOFE)	175
Decent quality (High end local mfrs)	125 - 140
Low end	50 - 100

Today, many markets have or are moving to a more fragmented price tiering. As foreign companies localize manufacturing and scale down product features and specifications, they have been able to expand their addressable market vs. an imports-only offering. Local firms have also migrated up the quality chain to compete for these larger middle-tier markets.

It is imperative to understand not only today's market tiering but its future evolution. As companies attempt to expand their addressable markets to encompass a larger customer base, cost pressures will grow, especially with the emergence of local competitors whose cost structures will make them very tough opponents (I will discuss this more in chapter five).

UNDERSTANDING YOUR VALUE CHAIN

The migration of manufacturing to China is changing the global value chain of many industries. As requirements for local sourcing, product development support, after-sales service and just-in-time delivery grow in intensity and complexity, it is important to consider very carefully what your company's China value chain looks like today, how it will evolve and at what point in it you will participate. China's less developed value chain may require that you carefully balance your resource deployment between China and the West (what we call the power loop). China's value chain may also have different players not present in the West—players that have access or power to influence customers. This market immaturity can offer opportunities to redefine and enhance your role in the value chain by playing at different levels than you do in your home market. Simply transplanting your Western structure and value offering may not be the best strategy.

As your value chain migrates to China, the nature and level of your value contribution can dilute. In the U.S., you may provide excellent service and technical support, close cooperation in product development and a long-term customer relationship. But when your customers move to China, they may need only some of the resources you provide. This situation may require that you move only selected competencies to China, not your full arsenal of weapons.

For example, many of our clients that do custom design work are used to beginning a project by discussing a concept with their customers' design departments and then developing a unique solution. However, in China, design resource requirements may be limited to the engineering department's need to "China-fy" any blueprints that come over from the West. Suppliers to these companies will have to maintain their connections to their customers' design centers in the U.S. while at the same time putting additional resources on the ground in China to support local applications development. These suppliers need to understand what support is needed and where it should be sourced.

In addition to resource needs straddling two continents, the decision power of the customer can be in a state of transition. As scale increases, local production processes mature and engineering resources strengthen, the specification and purchasing power will shift eastward. This transition can create tension within your customer as, for instance, the North American team argues for adoption of their technical standards and existing qualified suppliers, while the China team pushes for faster localization and lower costs, potentially using new suppliers that have local operations. You need to play both sides delicately while accurately gauging the pace of the power shift. This is the power loop, illustrated in Figure 2.6.

This power loop is ever changing, causing the deployment of resources to support customer needs to also change and sometimes become redundant. Companies must stay on top of these dynamics.

As you follow your customer base to China, you may find that they need less technical support and greater emphasis on lower costs. If your China customers don't need the high-tech value-add you offer at home, you may need to move backward in the product cycle, in a sense dumbing down your offer in order to be competitive (see Figure 2.7).

FIGURE 2.6: THE POWER LOOP

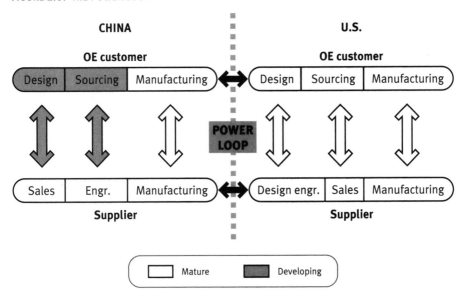

For example, one of our clients, a supplier of electronic components for the medical industry, found that the majority of demand in China was for its commodity and "make-to-print" product. Our client's real value proposition was for custom product, something not yet being demanded in China. But in order to be in position to exploit the eventual transition to higher value-add product, it needed to jump into the cycle and participate in the relatively immature, and less attractive, market. To do this meant changing its value proposition from high-tech manufacturer to trader and being able to leverage contacts and expertise to source product from all over the world to supply its customers.

This situation is common among second- and third-tier suppliers across various industries. Making this transition from highly relationship- and technology-oriented designer and manufacturer to trader is a difficult cultural and functional leap for many companies, but it is a necessary first step to position themselves for future China opportunities. Their customers' China needs are adolescent in development (immature, rapidly and sometimes chaotically changing and frustrating to deal with). In this context, our medical component client needed to be a broader caregiver than it was in the U.S.

FIGURE 2.7: EVOLUTION OF TECHNICAL SELLING IN CHINA

	Segment 1: Commodity	Segment 2: Make-to-print	Segment 3: Engineer-to-print	Segment 4: Custom
Customer requirements	• Standard products • High volume • Select on the basis of price and delivery	• OEMs provide blueprint, supplier responds to an RFQ • Still price sensitive • Often the entry point for working with OEMs in China	• Basic blueprint requiring local engineering resources to "China-fy" the design • Moderate price sensitivity	• Work with OEM product development and design • Significant U.S.-China communications (i.e. need to fully staff the power loop)
Supplier capabilities	• High volume at a low price • Little or no technical differentiation	• Light assembly • Multi-sourcing of finished product not made in own factory • Trading and distribution functions	• Manufacturing engineering • More high tech processing required	• Design engineering • Advanced technical support

Relative share of China market   Supplier's primary focus in U.S. market

However, China's less mature market can also provide opportunity for those willing to do things differently. A combination of an immature market and traditional Chinese business culture often comes together to form unique value chains not found in home markets. Where U.S. and European value chains in a given industry may present a profile of strong independent distributors or even buying groups with significant market power (as in the auto aftermarket in Europe or industrial bearings in the U.S.), China may present a picture of fragmented, unorganized distributors that are much more dependent on their suppliers for marketing support, applications training and even logistics. This type of differing distribution structure provides unique opportunities for a company willing to shape the value chain by participating downstream at some level of distribution or retailing—thereby preventing the eventual power shift away from suppliers, as witnessed in the West.

China's embryonic market can often open the door for going up or downstream in the value proposition. In the West, there are often customer barriers to forward integration (you would alienate your customers by participating at their level), but in China, these customers may not yet exist or are too weak to worry about. A case in point is a client of ours, an international supplier of fiberfill for sleep products. It discovered that converters and end product manufacturers downstream were not receptive to upgrading their product quality by using higher technology fiberfill. In fact, the end products of pillows and mattresses were generally too low quality in China to justify such an upgrade. By going downstream itself and developing the final, higher-quality end products, the company was able to change the market structure and pull its fiberfill through the value chain.

When considering your path to market in China, it is wise to keep the following in mind:

- Even if the value chain looks similar to that in the West, the inner workings may be different and the power of participants along the chain may not be the same.
- It is important to monitor the dynamics in the value chain and the shifts in decision and influence power. Localize the necessary competencies to stay in tune with these changes.
- Have an open mind as to where you will participate, exploiting undeveloped distribution structures and weaker players as well as opportunities to add value to your offering.
- Consider your value chain in a global context, understanding the evolving role of China and the implications to your participation and resource deployment.

Sun Tzu said, "In battle, there are not more than two methods of attack—the direct and the indirect; yet these two in combination give rise to an endless series of maneuvers." Your value chain in China can also present many dimensions requiring different tactics to address. Exploiting these dynamics can be a critical variable in your success. Careful investigation and creative thinking are key elements to achieve this goal (I will explore ways you can exploit China's value chain in chapter four).

BEING COST COMPETITIVE

The phrase, "China is becoming the workshop of the world" has been bandied about a great deal recently as the country seems to be sucking manufacturing activity from the West. Will Rogers said, "If the other fellow sells cheaper than you, it is called dumping.

'Course, if you sell cheaper than him, that's mass production." Though many Western executives protest that Chinese firms have unfair competitive advantages due to government subsidies, selling below cost (dumping) and an undervalued currency, etc., the simple fact is that many Chinese producers indeed can make good-quality product—comparable to that made in the West—at substantially lower cost with fair profit. This ability is not just in low-tech, commodity goods. Chinese producers continue to creep higher up the value-add chain as they improve both their technologies and processes.

Many of these same Western executives have looked at establishing their own production facilities in China to capture similar low costs, but their financial proformas still don't seem to close the cost gap sufficiently with their Chinese competitors. Generally, Chinese producers have significant advantage in fixed or general overhead costs, despite potentially having higher variable or manufacturing costs compared to international players, depending on the industry. On almost every fixed-cost item, a Chinese producer will have an advantage due to lower people costs, lower depreciation due to substantially less plant and facility investment, subsidies on land use rights and other factors—not to mention their willingness to take less profit. Western firms often complain of an uneven playing field due to government subsidies, tax breaks and various financial shenanigans. While in many cases these complaints are not without merit, they do not tell the whole story.

Western firms have struggled to replicate these "China costs" via their own local facility. Their goal is to match these lower costs as much as possible without compromising process, quality, environment, safety or ethics. Finding an acceptable balance here is very important and may challenge a company to question and even re-evaluate long-standing operational and management principles. We have found that Western customers of these companies (whether based in China or not), as a result of severe cost down pressure, may start to compromise on product specification and performance in order to realize cost gains from Chinese producers. For example, major automotive companies have established manufacturing operations across China and are now trying to lower costs aggressively as competition heats up dramatically. To do this, they are taking a hard look at local Chinese suppliers that may be lacking in technology, application experience and business practices. But the prospect of reducing costs 30% to 50% is encouraging an attitude of, "Let's see if we can work with these guys." The local producers are eager to comply and have done well in many cases to close the quality gap with foreign suppliers. The big win for them, and the huge threat to the foreign supplier, is the prospect not only of supplying these auto companies in China, but offshore as well once they have been qualified locally. A company needs to be able to accurately read this tendency in its customer base.

Our firm looked at the case of a global leader in elastomers that was being threatened by a rapidly growing Chinese enterprise. This company, in a matter of five years, grew from an annoying second-tier competitor nipping away at the periphery of our client's markets in the West to a 900-pound gorilla threatening to reshape the global market's structure. Despite our client's advantage in variable costs, which could be transferred to China to some degree, the gap in fixed costs more than compensated for this difference (see Figure 2.8).

FIGURE 2.8: CHINA VS. U.S. MANUFACTURING COST COMPARISON INDEX

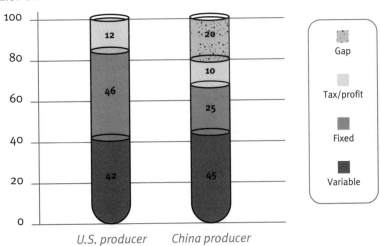

(FOR ILLUSTRATION PURPOSES, BASED ON A RECENT COMPARISON OF A 70,000-TON CHEMICAL PLANT)

As our client unfortunately did, many Western firms evaluate a China facility investment using a developed-country paradigm, missing fertile opportunities for cost reduction. We have witnessed Western firms that have sent their engineering team (often with a fresh, unstamped passport) to China to investigate setting up a local facility, only to return with a site factor of 0.9 to their U.S. plant (in other words, a plant in China would be 90% of the cost of a comparable facility in the West). However, the reality is that a China facility investment can be as little as 50% to 60% that of a comparable facility in a "developed" country, and produce good-quality product. Of course, the type of facility influences how low the ratio can go. In environmentally cleaner industries such as pharmaceuticals and light manufacturing, one can typically fare better than in a business such as corrosive chemical production (I discuss this challenge further in chapter five in the site factor debate).

Opportunities for cost reduction are missed in a number of key areas. Western firms often overestimate equipment costs, primarily due to their reliance on imported equipment. China has made significant advances in production and process equipment manufacturing in the last five years, to the point where equipment specified to similar international standards can be acquired or built in China, often at 50% to 60% of imported equipment costs. Many of the local equipment suppliers are wholly-owned foreign enterprises (WOFEs) or joint ventures of international equipment companies. Equipment such as pressure vessels, piping, furnaces and HVAC are all available locally. High-end control systems typically are still imported but even many of these are being localized now.

Significant cost reduction can be made in land and facility costs as well. Obtaining competitive land use rights is often a key negotiating variable in setting up in a locale. Good deals can be made with local government hungry for foreign investment and jobs. A word of caution here: Companies considering this option must be careful about grandiose claims made by local officials or suppliers. Often these promises are empty in the end—they don't deliver on the pledged low-cost facility, competitive utility rates, extended tax benefits or other subsidies. You still get what you pay for, so deal with reputable players and manage the process carefully.

Reductions can be gained in ongoing operating costs as well, notably in the manufacturing process itself. Of course, a foreign firm will want to retain the integrity of its manufacturing processes and will often replicate them in total in China. However, given the low labor costs, wisely using "manual intervention" at various points in the process can be very effective. For example, taking out simple automation tasks at either end of the line can reduce costs without impacting the integrity of the core process.

Companies need to search aggressively and creatively for ways to modify their processes to take advantage of low labor rates in China. We have seen many successful cases, even in more automated processes like compressor production, where the use of manual labor has been effectively deployed and is achieving throughput levels that have astounded Western engineers. The talent pool of skilled and semi-skilled workers is vast in China. With training, well-defined processes and diligent management, they can be very productive.

The aggressiveness with which a company addresses closing this cost gap should be directly related to the urgency on their business to do so—such as the level of threat they face if they do not close the gap. A key result of the China Readiness Assessment is to help measure this relationship. For some companies, not closing the cost gap threatens their very existence. Even when data suggest this condition, we have seen some management remain in a state of denial and do nothing. Why? Because the consequences, such as shutting down a plant in the West or even exiting a business segment altogether, are so significant. This denial is often masked by unrealistic future assumptions on pricing levels, existing customer loyalty and the inability of Chinese producers to move up the quality curve.

When the stakes are high in this regard, we like to propose the approach taken in the popular movie "Apollo 13" starring Tom Hanks—the need was to build a square filter for a round hole with only the materials on board the spacecraft. Our challenge to management is find a way to get to the lowest site factor possible (whatever the necessary target is to be cost competitive). It is senior management's job to determine whether the conditions of hitting this target are acceptable to the company. To reach the cost targets, management may face compromising core values, especially in safety, environment, health and social welfare. Our position is to face these issues head on and not sweep them under the table and hope that fate will change market conditions. The net result may be the need to make a tough decision among some very hard choices. The tragedy happens when external conditions make the choice for you due to management procrastination.

DEALING WITH CORRUPTION

The hippie philosopher Ashleigh Brilliant is quoted as saying, "I want either less corruption, or more chances to participate in it." One cannot talk about doing business in China without considering the problem of corruption, which has received much attention in the last few years, especially in the wake of WTO.

The root of corruption in China goes deep as officials working in both the public and private sectors blur the line between the two worlds. In the early 1990s, the shadow of government surveillance was not subtle. We installed a scrambler on our company's fax machine when we first set up in China. Not long after our operation began, the Public Security Bureau, or local police, knocked on our door asking if we would be so kind as to remove the scrambler because they could not read our faxes! Certainly, the environment has improved from those days but graft, nepotism and self-interest are still widespread and tangible risks exist regarding patent, trademark and product piracy.

Intellectual property laws have gotten stronger, though court interpretation and rulings have been inconsistent. In general, the legal structure is vague and leads to a wide degree of interpretation by the courts, often not in favor of an enterprise without deep local roots. As a result, a foreign company's recourse is unpredictable. Some estimate that 90% of software used in China today is pirated. Indeed, Chinese staff members often look at Western management quizzically when they propose actually paying for the software being used. To some, the idea of paying when it is readily available free is nonsensical.

A key hurdle in China's progress in the area of corruption is that its legal system is still one of rule by man vs. rule by law. The WTO is improving the current situation but progress will remain slow. The International Anti-Corruption Conference in 2002 estimated that counterfeiting is a US$16 billion business in China—it is a business, and an economic phenomenon, that will not soon go away. Foreign companies must have proper governance to stem the possibility of corruption at all levels of the organization. Proper IP protection measures are critical to succeed in China (I suggest some tactics in this regard in chapter five).

The risks of IP infringement can sometimes outweigh perceived market benefits and change a company's approach to doing business in China dramatically, especially if you need to transfer a key technology or process. Can your company's core technology be safeguarded, even in a wholly owned operation? If your company empowers a local China partner, is there any assurance that this partner won't someday set up shop next door? Many companies are struggling today to defend their brand, technology or process from local pirating. Even after a midnight raid, one can often find the target counterfeiter back in business the next day.

Western firms must also deal with many gray-area commercial tactics. Often under the guise of commissions, under-the-table deals are common across many industries. In fact, these practices are often not considered illegal or even unethical in the eyes of local firms, just a different (and normal) way of doing business. There is a popular Chinese saying: "The water needs to be a little polluted to attract the fish." Western firms who wish to stay "clean" are certainly disadvantaged. These issues will confront a company's principles head on. Management will be forced to (1) play the game, (2) opt out of the game or (3) try to circumvent the game. In this last area, Western companies often try to stay one level back in the value chain and create a layer of insulation between them and any illicit transactions. For many companies, a primary contribution of a distributor or agent is to serve this purpose. However, many firms often balk at even this structure, concerned that the shadow of corruption may be cast over their operation.

Business ethics and practices often make partner relationships very challenging, from basic trust in your partner's integrity to agreeing on acceptable practices. We have seen countless situations where the foreign firm's Chinese partner has taken liberties with the resources of the local business, from setting up parallel side businesses using company technology, brand and manufacturing capacity to exploiting company resources to purchase a local apartment for their family. After investigative efforts, Western firms have discovered illicit activities by even longstanding, allegedly trustworthy partners. In attempting to sever these relationships, many companies have been caught off guard by China's laws regarding legal person status and minority equity stakes. According to Chinese statute, unanimous consent is required by the board of directors to approve five major actions: (1) increasing or decreasing capital, (2) amending the articles of association, (3) transferring registered capital, (4) merging with another firm or (5) dissolving the joint venture. The result for some Western firms was to be held hostage to the local minority partner's demands to get paid off to go away.

Not only can there be an uneven playing field with local Chinese firms, the pitch can also have an uneven slope between firms from different foreign countries as they operate under varying legal restrictions as well as what are considered acceptable commercial practices.

Western management must accurately measure the nature and degree of corruption in its marketplace (not so easy to do in many cases) as well as the pace of improvement resulting from better legislation and enforcement. Your company's ethics, guidelines and policies with regard to corruption and illicit business behavior must be clearly artic-ulated to the troops. One case of a U.S. building material supplier demonstrates the vulnerability to technology leakage. The company's management discovered that a local competitor was using almost a replica of their manufacturing process. They followed the trail and discovered one of their assembly line engineers had been selling the process knowledge, and for very little money relative to its worth. This type of leakage is hard to stop completely but constant vigilance, distributing knowledge and power among multiple managers, and black boxing as much as possible can curtail the flow.

FINDING AND RETAINING HUMAN RESOURCES

Despite its 1.3 billion people, finding and keeping qualified personnel is widely cited as a major challenge for Western firms operating in China. As you go up the skill and expe-rience pyramid, the challenge intensifies.

FIGURE 2.9: HIERARCHY OF CHINA'S LABOR MARKET

General / Senior management
Few available – often need to go to Hong Kong or Taiwan for senior Chinese management experience, or bring in expensive Western expats.

Mid-level management
Huge void—demand exceeds supply for Western business experienced managers or department heads

Skilled factory worker
Large pool of engineering educated workers—continual flow from SOEs that are shutting down. Costs are going up, however, and training is needed as there is a shortage of skilled operators.

Low/Unskilled factory worker
Large pool, mostly migrant workforce. Starting to get tight supply in some south coast areas (e.g. Guangzhou, Shenzhen) because of poor labor protection.

While there is generally ample supply of unskilled and semi-skilled labor, as well as engineering degreed workers, there is a dearth of professional talent in functional areas such as accounting, human resources, operations and finance and those with leadership and people skills. This tight supply has led to overcompensation and a significant amount of poaching. Foreign companies will need to use other incentives beyond just compensation to both attract and retain qualified staff. These intangibles can include special training, opportunity for overseas travel and placement, performance bonuses and even pride in the organization. The simple fact, however, is that China is just not churning out enough MBAs to satisfy China-based foreign firms, which employ 10% of the urban workforce, but also local companies. From 1991 through 2003, China produced only 20,000 MBA graduates, against a demand of 300,000.

Despite a better situation at the factory level, the characteristics of the labor environment can be challenging. China's labor market is emerging from a paternalistic, socialist pattern. Wages, though very low, often are accompanied by relatively significant cash allowances, a difficult system for Western firms to handle given strict accounting guidelines and governance procedures. While labor law is drawn up at the national level, local governments are free to interpret and implement it with much flexibility. Laws, regulations and circulars are often complicated and inconsistent, some are out of date and many are not even enforced. Western-type unions do not exist as centers of labor power but the shadow of the Communist Party is clearly visible. Welfare costs, including housing, health care, unemployment and pensions are very high—often 50% to 70% of total compensation costs.

Many foreign-invested Hong Kong and Taiwanese enterprises have been very adept at exploiting the significant pool of migrant workers, estimated at 15 million to 20 million a year. These companies make a trek inland, or capture the flow as rural folk emigrate from the countryside, and round up an ample supply of very low-cost and hungry workers who, with basic training, a hard bed to lie on and a daily bowl of rice, supply an excellent base of factory assembly and construction workers. While this flow has been recently ebbing a bit and rising in cost, based on a supply of some 700 million people in the countryside, the stream will remain steady for years to come.

For Western firms needing more skilled factory workers, especially on the more costly east coast, the supply is not so ample. While able to do basic assembly and simple tasks, there is not enough training and experience for more skilled areas such as welding, tooling and die work, CNC machine operators, electronics testing and the like. As a result, effective training programs are very important. Unfortunately, there is no guarantee that, once trained, you won't lose the staff to a nearby operation willing to pay a little bit more out of its own desperate need.

Balancing the number of expatriate staff is becoming a critical need for foreign companies wishing to be competitive. Gone are the days of shipping in huge numbers of expatriate managers at total annual costs of US$300,000 and up. Experienced foreign operations are wisely localizing as many management functions as they can prudently. But the lack of available experienced local talent makes localization especially challenging. Indeed, a number of Western firms are even struggling to find qualified expatriate staff. This condition has resulted in relatively inexperienced junior managers having far too much responsibility. A case in point is a Fortune 100 firm that had more than 60 expats stationed in China. Each staff member had an average housing cost of US$8,000 per month. The HR manager in charge of this group was a junior staffer who had limited financial responsibility in the past, but was now responsible for overseeing US$6 million of annual leasing expense.

This human resource deficit will strain your organization's management in the West as you delegate more time and trips to the China initiative—typically more than you planned for, sometimes with very high opportunity costs to your base business. Smaller firms have attempted to fill this gap with an unqualified, ethnic Chinese staff member based in the U.S. This person may be on their assembly line, and by virtue of his language skill and ability to name more than five Chinese cities, he is appointed their "China guy." This person probably hadn't been to China since a trip to visit his grandmother when he was three years old. There can often be an unwanted bonus to this situation as he will likely have an uncle in a remote province who can get them "connected" in China and be their local partner. At this point, the company is well on the road to disaster (I will look closely at these issues in chapter six).

DOING EFFECTIVE RELATIONSHIP MANAGEMENT

Much has been said about the Chinese practice of *guanxi*. The term conjures up shady deals in smoke-filled rooms sipping *Maotai*, the infamous Chinese rice liquor. *Guanxi* implies relationships that help one get special treatment by entering through a closed door or lowering the cost of entry. The word makes Western firms very nervous as they endeavor to stay clean in a messy business environment. In reality, *guanxi* is much more than mere connections. As I noted previously, *guanxi* literally means "relationship." It is conventional wisdom that Asian cultures, especially China, are more relationship-based in business than are many Western cultures. What sets the Chinese relationships apart from those in the West is the social context; China is still very much a rule-of-man society with an immature market economy. Foreign companies wishing to set up a local facility or explore acquisition or alliance opportunities need to understand, cultivate and utilize these relationships. In China, there is a saying: "If you have a relationship, you have a road." Chinese government and business structures often lack transparency, making it difficult to clearly understand the situation or the players involved.

This is especially true when assessing an alliance or business partnership. Many bad relationships stem in part from ignorance about one's partner. It is no easy task to be fully familiar with potential partners, stakeholder interests or true financial performance given the opaque nature of the business environment in China. Before one establishes an alliance, a clear understanding of the company's structure, owners and influencers is needed. Often, lack of accurate documentation, the inaccessibility of information in the public domain and questionable accounting practices (and two or three sets of books) make it difficult to understand a local company's operations.

In the due diligence process, companies need to go beyond financial statements and the bravado of stakeholders to assess the real story behind the scenes and to better measure off-balance sheet risks. This knowledge is critical to qualify an alliance opportunity as well as outline the best way to manage the ongoing relationship. And it will certainly minimize the surprises experienced by many Western firms that made deals in the 1990s ("You mean I have another 100 employees on the books?").

Recently, we were involved in a deal in which a U.S. company was looking to acquire a local firm in the process of being privatized from its local government ownership. On the surface, the company's profile looked fairly straightforward, but in reality, its structure was a web of direct and indirect ties that had profound implications to the deal. Our company used a relationship mapping process, which we have developed over the last four years, as a method to uncover relationships and connections within and around a company to understand power, influence and hidden liabilities. A simplified relationship map of the target company, A, is presented in Figure 2.10.

FIGURE 2.10: A SAMPLE RELATIONSHIP MAP OF A CHINESE COMPANY

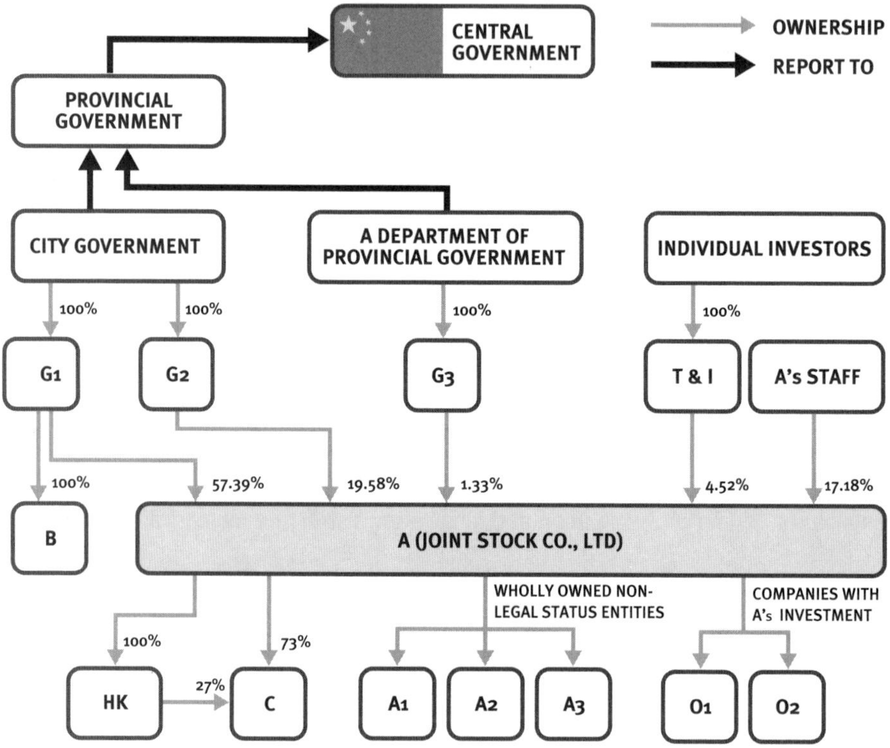

Through a relationship mapping process, we were able to better describe the target company and the key players involved in the deal. The details of the relationship web were critical to understand. Highlights are presented below to give you a sense of the complexity (and probably a slight headache!).

- G1 and G2 are the corporate arms of the city government and, between them, are the majority owners of A, the target company.

- In a bid to restructure A for an IPO in the early years (which failed), G1 created a separate corporate group or "waste basket," B, to hold A's poor and non-performing assets (historical baggage) to make A look attractive. B is owned by G1 and still managed by the team of A.

- Under the urgency of "ownership transformation" or privatization, G1 and G2 would like to sell off their stakes in A but G1 and G2, representing government interests, want to defuse social tension by protecting individual shareholders' interests.
- G3, initially intended to add "fancy" in the stock market because of its links with the provincial science and technology department, wishes to cash out on its 1.33% share in A because of dashed hopes to exit through an IPO.
- T&I is a shell company to represent individual investors holding a portion of A's shares, which can only be subscribed by legal entities. Now those individual investors, along with A's staff shareholders, worried about the poor operating results of A and with no immediate opportunities through the stock market, are desperate to seek liquidity.
- HK is an offshore subsidiary, 100% owned by A. A has used Hong Kong to "round trip" money to launch C, a joint venture, to take advantage of preferential treatments (tax, etc.) accorded to "foreign" invested companies.
- C is a major supplier to A. "Transfer pricing" helps A to optimize profit structure and tax obligations.
- A1, A2 and A3 are A's divisions contracted out in terms of operational management. A1 is A's core business and cash cow. A2 and A3 are suppliers to A1.

Admittedly, the above description conjures up one of Harry Belafonte's Jamaican lyrics, "It's clear as mud, but it covers de ground." However, these revelations were critical to the acquiring company in order to qualify the deal's attractiveness as well as develop a game plan to negotiate the transaction. The mapping process revealed that the real power and decision maker for the deal was the chairman of A, backed by a power camp in the city government, not A's majority owners, G1 and G2. Having identified the real power as well as an understanding of the objectives and concerns of the powers and influencers, our client devised a package of deals that took care of all concerned: the insiders' interests in the "ownership transformation" through a little bit of cash, ensuring stable employment and tax revenue for the local government authorities, the chairman's objective of exiting the business with proper compensation, and the younger generation of management's hopes for a bright future and improved career opportunities with a multinational.

Western companies often do not take a rigorous approach to understand, cultivate and utilize relationships in China and hence make key mistakes and miss attractive opportunities. "It is not what you know, it is who you know" is very true in China. Western companies often do not know how to manage this network. It is complex and dynamic and is often very time consuming for local senior management. It is not unusual to see 30% to 40% of a managing director's time taken up by this process. These relationships require face-to-face contact and can be very personal.

This process is not only an external one but encompasses internal management as well. China staff often operate in silos—hesitant to share knowledge and work as a team, and they all want to deal directly with the *Laoban*, or boss. It is important to note that China has almost an entire generation of single-child families, as a result of the government limit per family. The social and relational implications of this family structure in terms of work relationships will no doubt be studied for years to come.

Given its unfamiliarity to most Western managers, effectively managing relationships in China can be a unique and daunting challenge (this issue will be further explored in chapter six).

THE CHINA CHALLENGE

These conditions represent some of the major challenges that most companies will face. Their relative importance will vary depending on your company's situation as well as the resources you have available. Understanding your company's DNA and how these challenges will stress your organization is critical. To succeed, companies will often face totally new challenges outside of their comfort zone, as in dealing with corruption, relationship management or local alliances.

These hurdles will make strategy development more difficult and the due diligence process more complex. Facing these challenges will strain a company's resources, stretch its business principles and culture and potentially even risk the company's core competencies. China, indeed, offers many challenges to offset its apparent allure. For many, however, dealing with China is no longer an option. Its growing international competitiveness mandates a response, at least a defensive one. For a number of firms, their response may change the very nature of their company. While management is naturally reluctant to make these changes, their company's very existence may be at stake. Recognizing and facing these challenges head on is the best way to mitigate risk.

I will close with more wisdom from Sun Tzu. "We are not fit to lead an army on the march unless we are familiar with the face of the country—its mountains and forests, its pitfalls and precipices, its marshes and swamps."

Indeed, preparation is key. Now that I have put these daunting challenges before you, I will set about the task of describing a process you can employ to effectively address them. The China Readiness Assessment is an excellent first step to look deeply into your company's preparedness to pursue what will be a long, often difficult, but ultimately rewarding journey of expanding your business in China.

CHAPTER SUMMARY

This chapter made the case that China poses intimidating and sometimes unique challenges to a Western firm looking to expand its operations in China. These challenges, coupled with the generally poor track record of foreign firms investing in China over the last decade, make it imperative that your firm is well prepared before launching an initiative. I likened this preparation process to a general making plans to go into battle, drawing on the wisdom of one of China's most renowned generals, Sun Tzu. I reviewed seven major challenges warranting specific attention and preparation.

China's frenetic pace of development creates a moving target, which is difficult to accurately hit for Western firms and the first challenge is **addressing the rapid pace of change** in China. Swift economic growth, changes in infrastructure, evolving legal and business practices, a changing consumer and significant flux in the competitive landscape all contribute to a high level of uncertainty. This dynamism calls for flexibility in your game plan, and a nimbleness in your decision-making process. Successful companies will consistently monitor the market and act decisively on emerging opportunities or threats.

This changing landscape enhances the second challenge of **defining your addressable market**–the market space where you can profitably compete. Though a large and growing economy with more than 1.3 billion consumers, China presents a wide spectrum in market attractiveness. Purchasing power is concentrated and economic activity is centered along China's eastern seaboard. Even within this more limited territory, customer requirements and price points are stratifying to multiple levels, making it critical that you focus your efforts where your value proposition has merit and your costs are competitive.

Reaching your target market presents both challenges and opportunities as China's value chain and distribution structures are in early stages of development, leading to the third challenge of **understanding your value chain**. Further, as Western manufacturers continue to shift parts of their supply chains to China, understanding how to best reach your customers will become more complex. As your value chain matures, you will need to carefully plan what resources you need and where they should be placed to address your customers' changing requirements and decision-making process. Because of China's less-developed state, there may be opportunities for your company to participate upstream or downstream of your typical value chain position. I recommend that you keep an open mind about your approach to market, considering alternative ways to capitalize on undeveloped distribution structures and weaker players, as well as adding value to your offering.

Being cost competitive in China, the fourth challenge, is a significant struggle for Western firms. Chinese producers will often have cost advantages due to their structure, business practices, and sometimes unfair support from local government. While closing this cost gap can be very difficult, by being creative in approach, Western companies can meaningfully narrow the advantage of local China firms. Again, to be successful here may require that you do things differently than in your home market, learning to "China-fy" parts of your manufacturing and business processes. For some companies, the necessary steps to narrow the cost gap will challenge their core company values and principles. Your aggressiveness to take these steps should directly relate to the urgency on your business to do so in order to stay healthy or even to survive.

The fifth challenge is **dealing with corruption,** a widespread problem that will not soon go away, despite China's entry into the WTO and the introduction of more laws. Corruption, counterfeiting and pirating support very profitable enterprises for local "entrepreneurs" who are not easily dissuaded even after their operations are raided by police. Western firms should be justifiably concerned about transferring their core technologies or processes to China, and need to ask themselves some key questions:

- Can your company's core technology be safeguarded?
- Is there any assurance your China partner won't set up shop next door, or siphon product out the back?
- Can you afford the economic impact of counterfeits entering your market?

- What is the true cost of having your IP stolen?
- Will your stolen IP be exported back to your home market to compete against you?

If you transfer key assets to China, you need to diligently build defenses around them.

Despite China's 1.3 billion people, **finding and retaining qualified staff** is one of the most often mentioned problems by Western managers in China and is the sixth challenge. The higher you climb the skills and experience pyramid, the more difficult the challenge. Although there is an ample supply of unskilled and semi-skilled labor, and a good pool of engineers, a glaring shortage exists of professional talent in accounting, HR, operations, finance and other areas requiring leadership and people skills. This tight supply has led to disproportionate compensation and frequent poaching. Foreign firms must be creative to attract and retain good staff. Taking shortcuts by hiring the first Chinese face that comes along is a prescription for failure. An effective China organization will have successfully integrated east and west business practices, people skills and culture.

Anyone with even a little experience in China has come across the term *guanxi*. This often-misinterpreted concept is not about shady deals transacted in back rooms; rather, *guanxi* means relationship and is a fundamental part of life in China. **Managing relationships**, the seventh and final challenge, is a complex, dynamic and time-consuming task, oftentimes unfamiliar to Western managers. Opaque structures and connections between organizations and individuals make it difficult to assess prospective partners and fueled many failed ventures in the last decade. Foreign companies wishing to set up and operate a business in China or explore a local alliance need to understand, cultivate and fully utilize relationships at multiple levels–from customers and suppliers to all levels of government. Relationship building requires face-to-face time by senior Western executives, often comprising up to 30% to 40% of their time.

These seven challenges are indeed imposing. The balance of this book will describe the process as well as provide advice on how to effectively address them, and prepare your company to succeed in China.

Chapter 3

An Overview of the China Readiness Assessment

 By three methods we may learn wisdom: first, by reflection, which is noblest; second, by imitation, which is easiest; and third, by experience, which is the bitterest.

Confucius

In the late 1980s and early 1990s, hotel bars in China's major cities were filled with Western executives unwinding after yet another stressful day of trying to establish a foothold. Impromptu groups would form and, drinks in hand, the executives would commiserate about their trials and tribulations in establishing their operations. My colleagues and I were participants in and observers of these discussions, which helped seed the concept of the China Readiness Assessment. Our goal, in the spirit of Confucius, was to take these "bitter experiences" and "learn wisdom" by creating a framework for management to better plan their China initiatives. The architecture of the China Readiness Assessment process was inspired and designed by the assimilated views of more than 100 companies that have invested in China over the past 15 years. These views have been synthesized and set against the backdrop of China's market landscape to create a picture of the company that is well prepared and "ready" to pursue business in China.

A helpful analogy can be drawn between the China Readiness Assessment and premarital counseling. My wife is an experienced premarital counselor and has developed programs to guide other counselors in their work with engaged couples. While I don't mean to imply that doing business in China is as difficult as marriage (in case you are unduly alarmed by the analogy), I do see some parallels in the premarital counseling process that can help you to better grasp the overall concept and intent of the China Readiness Assessment.

The essence of premarital counseling is to draw from the many and varied experiences of married couples to create an early warning system of challenges to come for soon-to-be wed couples. By assimilating these experiences, a couple can identify the likely areas that will challenge them as they make their way through marital bliss. By understanding, at least to some degree, the nature and scope of these challenges, a couple will be more emotionally and mentally prepared for what is likely to come. Of course, the challenges will manifest themselves differently with each couple.

In some cases, the premarital process reveals particular areas of likely struggle based on the couple's background and profile. This realization allows the couple to better prepare for these eventualities by, say, reading a book on the topic, getting further counseling or simply by engaging in deeper and more honest discussion together. In rare cases, the process can even result in the couple delaying or calling off the wedding, realizing that their motivation for marriage is not strong enough to give them the will to wrestle through the struggles that are expected—they are just not prepared or even suited to tie the knot.

At a minimum, the process will help the couple stay on track when the inevitable challenges come. By anticipating the difficulties and preparing to deal with their consequences, the couple will navigate through them with less pain. I think it is safe to say that most married readers would acknowledge that they would have been better prepared to deal with challenges such as ghoulish in-laws or free-spending spouses had they been forewarned.

So, too, with doing business in China. The purpose of the China Readiness Assessment is to flag the issues that challenge most foreign companies, some more deeply than others, and to better prepare your company to address them more effectively and with less pain. Like marriage, circumstances and personalities create innumerable variations in scenarios. My aim is to identify and characterize the more common challenges of doing business in China the way a premarital counselor helps a couple identify challenges such as finances, everyday conflicts, in-laws, children and the like. In China, these challenges take the form of transferring a manufacturing process, protecting intellectual property, dealing with corruption, taking unexpected financial risks, etc. Your specific circumstances and company profile will be unique in terms of what challenges will be most stressful for you. The China Readiness Assessment will help you discover where you are most vulnerable or least prepared and what areas of your organization are likely to be especially stressed.

BEING READY FOR CHINA

The most difficult words to define are often those used in everyday life: "Readiness" is one of those words. We ask our kids, "Are you ready to go?" By this we mean, "Have you done everything you need to do so I won't have to ask you later why you didn't go to the bathroom before we left?" Or, in the case of my wife, "Are you really ready to leave or am I waiting at the door another 10 minutes!?" Readiness means satisfying a set of requirements before undertaking an activity. It also implies that there is "something" we are prepared for, and that "something" greatly affects how we prepare ourselves and the conditions or state of our readiness. Being ready for a sunny day is much easier than being ready for an incoming hurricane—we don't have to board up our windows and buy emergency food supplies for a sunny day. So we are not simply ready, in and of itself; rather, we are ready for something. For our purposes, China is that "something." For most companies, being ready for China is more similar to being ready for a hurricane than for a sunny day. A China initiative will blow through your company with great force—and you have to make sure everything is tied down first.

The first chapters of this book were designed to give you a better idea of what to be prepared for in China. We are now ready to explore the implications these challenges will have on your company so that we can tailor a preparation or response plan. I define China Readiness as **a state of adequate organizational preparedness to respond effectively to a clearly defined motivation to expand into China**. In this sense, readiness means not only that your organization is well prepared to handle the challenges China will throw at you, but also indicates that your motivation to do business in China has a high level of urgency and must be addressed.

There are two main dimensions that interact with each other to determine readiness: a company's Motivation to pursue a China expansion, set against its Organizational Preparedness to do so (Figure 3.1). A company's state of China Readiness provides a starting point to identify specific steps a company can take to plan and execute a China strategy more effectively.

Figure 3.1: The China Readiness dimensions

I will provide an overview of these two dimensions and discuss some factors contributing to each and, ultimately, their interplay that will result in a company's China Readiness profile. Subsequent chapters will discuss each of these dimensions in much more detail.

MOTIVATION

Many of us over the course of our lives have been challenged to get into good physical shape. Our motivation to implement any exercise program, however, often varies in intensity and commitment. Some of us, with only the dubious strength of a New Year's resolution (probably made under the fog of a post New Year's eve hangover), will go out and buy an expensive treadmill or elliptical machine. Unfortunately, our enthusiasm often wanes as the prospect of actually *using* the equipment looms over us like a dark cloud. The more ambitious of us get a few workouts under our belts before the effort becomes too much. In the end, the equipment gathers dust in the corner of the basement.

This lack of resolve was common among early investors in China. One of the most significant lessons learned has been the importance of company management clearly understanding *why* they want to expand their business into China. This point may sound obvious—but many early entrants to China made an investment with minimal strategic substantiation, driven by their shareholders' expectations to grab a share of China's "gold," a period of near-euphoria. Once the foreign investment trend began in earnest in the 1990s, a lemming effect took hold. Companies felt a strong pull to be in China (like the pull you feel to exercise after seeing your friend Bill jog by your house each morning and then seeing your own beer gut). Most companies simply assumed they would make money. However, few probed very deeply into how this would happen. Some executives are still being prompted to venture into China based on alarming articles in *The Wall Street Journal* or a segment on CNN. After the move is made and the challenges begin to mount, the validity of their initial motivation seems to escape them. As a client of ours, an executive at a global chemical company, reflected, "If a company enters this market simply because others are coming, they are likely to lose their shirt" (and then that beer gut would really be revealed!).

Many early entrants, if they could do it over again, have said that they would more clearly lay out the reasons *why* they were going to China, and probably enter in a different way, if at all; said one Fortune 50 executive with early China operations, "We didn't know what to do, but we thought we had to get there." Working through the Motivation dimension of the China Readiness Assessment helps a company clearly identify its reasons for pursuing a China investment as well as the need to do so at that point in time.

There are several reasons that might motivate a company to expand into China. The potential impact of these motivations on a company's future health will determine the level of urgency to pursue a China initiative. In some cases, one motivation is sufficiently important to cause a high level of urgency—as in the need to follow a key customer to China. In other cases, there will be a mix of motivations that collectively result in a high level of urgency, such as attractive new market potential and the need to establish low-cost production. The level of urgency in motivation to pursue a China initiative will directly affect the amount of risk that the company can reasonably take to pursue it. If getting in better physical shape is needed to save my life, I will not hesitate to buy whatever equipment I need, hire a personal trainer or take 10 hours a week out of my busy schedule to work out.

Key factors of the Motivation dimension that support a company's China entry or expansion include:

- **Attractive market:** There is an identified market opportunity for the company's products/services in China.

- **Customer pull:** A key customer wants the company to locate more resources in China to serve its needs better. The company may need to comply in order to retain that customer's business.
- **Competitive threat:** Global competitors have a position in China that could give them an advantage in cost or proximity to the company's key customer base and/or local Chinese competitors are penetrating the company's home market.
- **Operational efficiencies:** The company can improve proximity to customers and suppliers, lower production costs, speed delivery, etc., thereby lowering manufacturing and/or supply chain costs.
- **Stakeholder push:** There is tangible pressure by the company ownership (board, CEO, stockholders, Wall Street) to become active in China.

Figure 3.2 shows how each of these motivational indicators is assessed and plotted. Notice on the left-hand side of the graph the labels from "monitor" at the bottom up to "high urgency" at the top. Ranking the urgency of these motivations will assist you in properly assessing each one. For example, you may be hearing from a board member that "the company should not expand to China because it is too risky"; if you only listened to that motivation, you might not hear your key customers saying, "We need you to support us locally in China or else you cannot supply us anywhere."

FIGURE 3.2: A SAMPLE COMPOSITE MOTIVATION SCALE

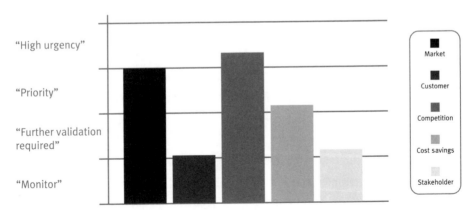

Therefore, the Motivation dimension is a combination of the urgencies, or strengths, of the above factors, typically including several at one time. The China-Ready Company knows clearly why it is expanding into China and considers its strategy and appetite for risk with this motivation firmly at the center. It is important not just to say, for example, that you are going to China to follow your main customer, but that you understand the urgency to do so, the upsides if you do and the downsides if you don't. If there is competitive threat, it is crucial to understand how best to defend yourself and what would happen if you do not respond. These qualifications are often missing in the planning process. I will dive deeper into each of these motivations in the next chapter to demonstrate the importance of doing a detailed assessment.

ORGANIZATIONAL PREPAREDNESS

The other area that a China-Ready Company must evaluate with brutal honesty is its readiness to initiate and support such an expansion move—what I call Organizational Preparedness, the second dimension of the China Readiness Assessment.

Let us return to our exercise analogy. If I am highly motivated to get into good physical shape, but have been a couch potato for 20 years, I can't immediately sign up for a marathon. If I have a trick knee or bad back, I need to make some special preparations or allowances in designing my exercise program. Certainly, I need to get the advice of my doctor and start slow. I may need equipment like a knee brace or heating pad. In essence, I need to temper my motivation against the realities of my body's level of preparedness to embark on such a program. Otherwise, I could cause further injury to myself or even precipitate the heart attack I am trying to prevent!

Again and again, early entrants to China have said they wish they would have known the impact their entry had on their organization. "We were very naive when we first came to China," one executive said. "We thought we could simply set up a China initiative as another project and assign a few people to pursue it—we did not know how it would completely challenge our organization."

Few companies accurately estimated the organizational costs to effectively play in China, from personnel and systems to culture and financials. When a company extends its operation to another, very foreign environment with different rules of the game, it can be sure that any existing flaws in it's organization will be amplified. Investing in China with a weakness in your company profile is a bit like beginning an exercise regime with damaged cartilage in your knee. If you limit yourself to a walk, everything will probably be all right. But your knee is a ticking time bomb that will suddenly give out and cause severe pain when you begin to pick up speed or make a quick turn. So, too, in expanding into China without adequate preparation. Your business in China will not be a leisurely walk in the park—it will be more like a series of wind sprints and obstacle courses, much of it uphill, so your organization must be in tip-top shape. We have seen situations where companies with significant existing shortcomings have gone to China anyway in the hopes that the move would improve things. But China is no cure for what ails your organization, just as a marathon is no cure for a bum knee.

A company's resources and competencies in three distinct areas—*operational, managerial* and *financial*—define its Organizational Preparedness. Together, they indicate how ready a company is to explore and then support a China expansion initiative. An ideally prepared company will have satisfactory or strong readiness in all three areas. In most cases, a company will have deficiencies in at least one or two factors within each dimension. The China Readiness Assessment identifies and highlights these areas as potential risks to the company's successful implementation of a China initiative. These potentially vulnerable areas then need to be evaluated by management to determine their level of importance and their latent risk, and how they can be addressed before launching the initiative. Understand that these risks can also significantly alter the way your company goes to China, as we will see in a series of case examples in subsequent chapters.

The three dimensions of organizational preparedness are outlined below:

- *Operational Preparedness*: The company is able to transfer or replicate part or all of its business operations in China under some viable structure.
- *Managerial Preparedness*: There is sufficient depth and experience in the organization to support a China initiative without creating holes in management's attention to the core business.
- *Financial Preparedness*: The company's financial condition is stable and there are sufficient resources to risk a China growth initiative.

Each of these dimensions has four indicators that represent key attributes defining the state of a company's readiness in that dimension. These indicators will be characterized in detail in subsequent chapters.

These dimensions and their key indicators are plotted on a readiness scale in Figure 3.3. In subsequent chapters, I will provide some ways for you to plot your company on this scale. However, the most important methodology to developing an accurate profile of your company is through objective and honest discussion among your company's management team.

FIGURE 3.3: SAMPLE ORGANIZATIONAL READINESS PROFILE

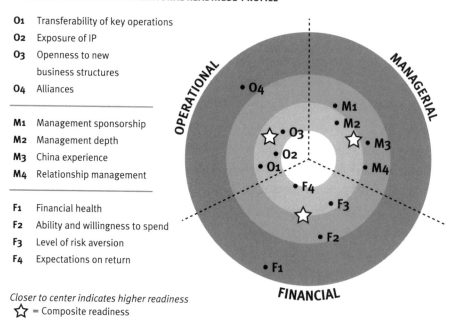

O1 Transferability of key operations
O2 Exposure of IP
O3 Openness to new business structures
O4 Alliances

M1 Management sponsorship
M2 Management depth
M3 China experience
M4 Relationship management

F1 Financial health
F2 Ability and willingness to spend
F3 Level of risk aversion
F4 Expectations on return

Closer to center indicates higher readiness
☆ = Composite readiness

The closer an indicator is positioned to the bull's-eye of the profile, the higher the company's state of preparedness. Indicators approaching the outer rim are "red flags" that need to be specifically addressed by management to determine their relevance and importance to a China initiative as well as how they can be moved closer to center.

For instance, if the indicator on transferability of manufacturing processes is positioned near the outer rim, this means it will be very difficult and potentially risky to effect this transfer to China. If it is necessary to make such a transfer to set up a local manufacturing facility, then management will need to carefully assess the intensity of their motivation to go to China against the risks of this move. If the motivation is strong enough, then the company has no choice but to find a way to transfer its process economically and effectively while protecting its intellectual property. This insight could dramatically affect the way in which a company enters the Chinese market, for example, investing in a wholly owned operation vs. a joint venture; "black boxing" its technology in a creative way, or localizing only part of its process and keeping its core technology offshore.

In another case, an indicator such as "China experience" may be on the outer rim. This positioning may be obvious to management if the company has no previous history in China. However, recognition that this variable contributes to a company's readiness can spur management to more aggressively seek out resources to address this gap. For instance, most companies have a circle of service providers, customers, suppliers or other contacts that could contribute to improving this indicator. A law firm or accountancy may have resources in China. A key supplier or customer—perhaps the one that is asking you to go to China in the first place—may have an existing operation there. We have seen (and helped) companies leverage these outside resources in many creative ways, such as partnering with a customer or supplier, or even a competitor, to go to China. Many companies don't fully exploit these resources to fill gaps in China expertise, experience or *guanxi*. I will explore these points in more detail when I describe each dimension in subsequent chapters.

YOUR READINESS POSITIONING

These two dimensions, Motivation and Organizational Preparedness, are then set against each other to determine your overall state of readiness for a China investment. It is the juxtaposition of these two major dimensions that exposes your true readiness. Generally, companies fall into one of four quadrants in terms of their overall readiness to do business in China, as illustrated in Figure 3.4. A company's China Readiness Assessment score on the specific dimensions and indicators previously described determines the quadrant into which it falls. Again, I will review later how you can develop these scores.

A Type A positioning, of course, is the best scenario: Your strong motivation to expand into China is matched by a relatively high state of organizational preparedness. In this case, your risk-reward outlook is very positive, and you should "go for it" aggressively. At the opposite end of the spectrum is the Type D position, a combination of low motivation and multiple areas where your organizational preparedness is suspect, likely requiring significant resource investment to address. This situation clearly indicates that you should put any China initiative on hold at least until a compelling motivation is identified.

FIGURE 3.4: CHINA READINESS POSITIONS

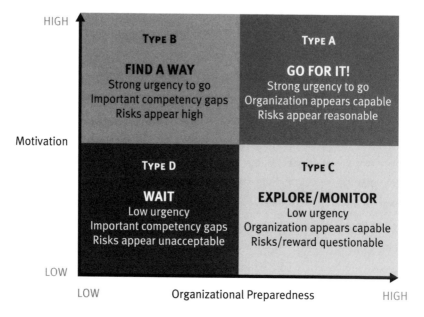

The other two quadrants suggest a more ambiguous situation. If your motivation is relatively low but your organization is very well prepared to take advantage of opportunities in China, you can afford to be more aggressive in exploring business potential. In this case, your China Readiness is a latent asset looking for a situation to exploit. As a result, it makes sense to proactively explore opportunities in China, or at least monitor them closely (Type C). The most problematic—and often most frequent—positioning of a company's China Readiness is the combination of a strong motivation to go to China with an organization that is relatively unprepared to do so (Type B). Companies facing a near-term, growing threat from China due to customer migration or aggressive competition frequently find themselves in this quadrant. Because of the high urgency in motivation, management needs to "find a way" to get better prepared because the threat or lost opportunity of not going outweighs the risks of investing in China.

In subsequent chapters I will provide numerous case examples for each dimension and their specific indicators that give real-life perspective. Further, I will provide suggestions on how you can better understand your state of readiness in each indicator and offer some tactics to improve your level of preparedness. In the last chapter, I will describe a case study of the ABC Company to demonstrate a more complete view of this process, its results and how a company can respond to its readiness positioning.

CHAPTER SUMMARY

The initial chapters described the key phases in China's economic development and the early experiences of foreign investors. Next, we explored a number of key challenges that will confront Western companies as they expand into China. This chapter outlined the concept and key metrics of the China Readiness Assessment, a process and framework by which Western firms can more effectively prepare to address these difficult challenges.

The China Readiness Assessment has two main dimensions which, when set against each other, describe the state of readiness of a company to develop and pursue a China initiative. The first dimension is your **Motivation** to expand into China. While seemingly a straightforward issue on the surface, we found that many foreign companies only casually evaluated the drivers urging them to invest. A kind of China euphoria dulled the normally acute business sense of many Western executives, as they followed their peers to what promised to be the "land of milk and honey." Many firms actually found a raging battle they were ill prepared to fight.

Today, the motivations of Western firms to go to China have become more complex, often involving both opportunity for new business and the need to defend existing business as their customers shift production to China and local China-based competitors emerge. The China Readiness Assessment provides a process to dig deeper into these motivations to discern their true character and level of intensity. I identified five major drivers that can characterize a company's motivation to expand into China, namely:

- Attractive market
- Customer pull
- Competitive threat
- Operational efficiencies
- Stakeholder push

An objective and probing view of these drivers will determine your overall motivation level, which can then be set against what it will take to get your company prepared to successfully design and implement a China strategy.

With your motivation clearly understood and positioned, you can then begin to measure your level of **Organizational Preparedness**, the second dimension in the China Readiness Assessment. Early entrants to China did not realize the impact such an investment would have on their organizations, nor did they understand the key competencies they would need in order to succeed. I likened the China Readiness Assessment to premarital counseling because it prepares you to operate more effectively in China by exposing beforehand the challenges and risks your management team is likely to face. By assimilating the many experiences and lessons learned of those going before you, the long road ahead will be better illuminated. In knowing what's ahead, you can shore up weak areas and fill in competency gaps—even plan an alternative path to get to your end goal, one more suited to your specific capabilities and resources.

I grouped these organizational factors into three main areas, each comprising four specific indicators.
- *Operational Preparedness*
- *Managerial Preparedness*
- *Financial Preparedness*

When the results of your assessment of motivation and organizational preparedness are brought together in an overall readiness profile, your company can be strategically positioned in one of four quadrants. This positioning can range from two extremes–from highly motivated and well prepared to weakly motivated and poorly prepared. The next chapters will dive deeper into each of these dimensions and their supporting indicators, demonstrating how they affect your organization's readiness for China.

Chapter 4
Understanding Your Motivation to Expand into China

> " *Illusions commend themselves to us because they save us pain and allow us to enjoy pleasure instead. We must therefore accept it without complaint when they sometimes collide with a bit of reality against which they are dashed to pieces.* "
>
> *Sigmund Freud*

When our team takes clients through the China Readiness Assessment, the exercise on Motivation is often the most difficult, despite seeming on the surface to be the most obvious. There are two aspects of the Motivation dimension that are often poorly developed and underline the danger in launching an initiative into China without a more careful consideration of the underlying reasons behind your doing so.

First, the *rationale* for your Motivation is often not clearly understood. For instance, we will hear, "Our customers are telling us that we have to be in China," certainly a common phrase these days. Okay, but why? Do these customers want lower costs? Better logistics? Closer technical development and support? What do they need specifically in these areas? Often, your customers don't really care if you are in China; telling you that you need to be there is simply shorthand for their wanting some assumed benefit of your being there to support them.

Second, the *intensity* of the Motivation to invest in China is typically not measured carefully. How urgent is the Motivation? What are the possible consequences if you don't go? What are the opportunity costs if you do go? This measure of intensity is critical to balance against the costs and risks of expanding into China (this will be explored in the other dimension of the China Readiness Assessment, Operational Preparedness). Depending on where this balance lies, you will determine whether you go as well as the form of your investment approach. Many companies have underestimated the risks or overestimated the Motivation in their investment planning.

The intuitive understanding that you need to go to China based on customer comments, rumors about competition or even the inundation of news on China may get you to the planning table, but only a rigorous review of the driving factors behind that intuition opens the checkbook. For some companies, investing in China should be a last resort, only made when all other options have been considered carefully and ruled out. Companies that invest more on fancy or hype, without a compelling reason to do so, are straying onto thin ice. As a recent humorist said, "Eagles may soar in clouds, but weasels never get sucked into jet engines."[1] Companies we talk to often have trouble getting their arms around their motivations for a China expansion. Management can easily get muddled between opportunities and threats, especially with alarm bells being sounded by the media that they'd better do something. In their urgency to respond, management does not adequately explore the detail and ramifications of their motivations.

There are five fundamental categories, outlined in Figure 4.1, under which all possible push/pull forces fall. There is profound simplicity in this categorization—but the devil is in the details of what, how and why these forces are impinging upon you. Too frequently, companies view these drivers from 35,000 feet and as discrete motivations instead of taking a ground-level, encompassing view. After peeling away the obvious aspects of the motivations, management will soon get to powerful subtleties that can impact the nature and urgency of these drivers, as well as how to respond to them.

FIGURE 4.1: PRIMARY CHINA MOTIVATORS

Attractive market	There is identified market opportunity for your products/services in China. This potential is incremental business for you.
Customer pull	Key customers want you to locate more resources in China to serve their needs better. You may need to comply to retain business with them in the West.
Competitive threat	Global competitors have a position in China that could give them an advantage in cost or proximity to your customer base, and/or local Chinese competitors are beginning to penetrate your home market.
Operational efficiencies / cost savings	Moving to China will improve your manufacturing and/or supply chain costs due to proximity to customers/suppliers, lower labor rates, etc.
Stakeholder push	There is tangible pressure by company ownership (board, CEO, stockholders, Wall Street) to become active in China.

[1] Attributed to both Jason Hutchison and John Benfield.

After looking at each of these motivations in more detail as well as some experiences of companies working through them, we will then be able to develop a composite view of this first key dimension of the China Readiness Profile.

ATTRACTIVE MARKET

Many companies have been attracted to China because of its massive potential, driven by a population of more than 1.3 billion people coupled with strong economic growth. Consumer products companies such as P&G, Nestle and Unilever were among the first to rush to the market. In fact, *new market potential* was the main driver for many companies entering China during the gold rush years of the 1990s. But low prices, overcapacity and unruly market behavior quickly dispelled hopes of decent margins. "We forecasted volume accurately but overstated market value by about 30%," lamented one executive who led his company's China investment in the mid-1990s.

The cost of exploiting the perceived potential became very high for many companies as well. Because China markets were often considered more opportunistic vs. its core domestic market, a company's stamina to push forward waned rapidly as the challenges mounted. What appeared to be low-hanging fruit was either a bit out of reach or was simply rotten. Knowing the true nature of your opportunity and where you can make money are foundational to any successful China strategy. As one seasoned China executive said to us, "There was too much instinct, not enough analysis."

Indeed, China may offer attractive new market growth for your company, but you need to measure the importance of capturing this potential against what you are willing and able to do to get it. When discussing new market opportunities, we often tell our clients, "It's either Sheboygan or Shanghai." If you can find new market opportunities in your own backyard (i.e. the idyllic Midwestern town of Sheboygan, Wisconsin), then by all means go after them first. If your growth outlook in markets closer to home is more robust, then China's market may be more opportunistic and the risks you take to go after it should equal the level of urgency.

However, if your company's growth outlook in your home markets or those within closer reach is not sufficient to satisfy your stakeholders, then Shanghai may indeed have more potential than Sheboygan. In the end, the equation, as illustrated in Figure

4.2, is straightforward. As you move up and to the right you can (and may need to) take more risks in terms of financial investment, venture arrangements and exposing your intellectual property.

FIGURE 4.2: CHARACTER OF GROWTH APPETITE

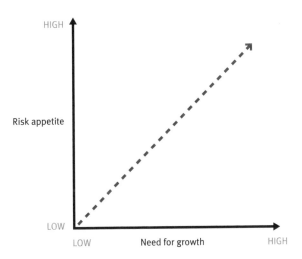

The reality is that most companies do not have a good idea of their current and future opportunities in China and the difficulties in accessing those opportunities in a profitable way—this often requires sophisticated market segmentation and accurate prognostication. You do not need a consulting firm to tell you that China is a large and growing market. But you may need help to understand in what segments of the market you should play. As you expand your addressable market, and move from high-price and high-quality niches to more mass-market segments, your value proposition and key success factors will undoubtedly change, as illustrated in Figure 4.3.

We have observed that one's addressable market often can be segmented into four areas, as illustrated in Figure 4.4, and see countless examples of this segmentation playing out in the marketplace, whether in consumer products, high-technology equipment or basic industrial goods. The challenge for many companies is determining to what extent and in what form they can play in the different segments of the market pie.

FIGURE 4.3: SPECTRUM OF ADDRESSABLE MARKET OPPORTUNITY

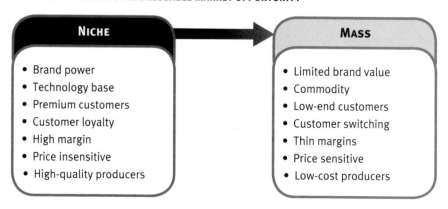

A recent client of ours in capital equipment was looking to expand its then very limited position in China. It had been trying to penetrate the market via a local sales agent for several years but had only a few warm leads to show for its efforts. The company decided to take a deeper look at the market, what customers needed in equipment specifications and what competitors were offering. This analysis revealed the four-piece pie depicted in Figure 4.4. In that case, the priority segment was only a small sliver, served by imports to a select few customers. Our client had been going after this very segment but without success. Continuing its present approach to the market, no matter how much energy was applied, would probably not improve penetration much and certainly would not expand this small piece of the pie. To penetrate the much larger potential opportunity slice of the market would require some fundamental changes, notably in price point. Further, local Chinese competition was already encroaching on this segment, having made significant gains in technology and product quality. To attempt to beat them *mano a mano* was akin to taking on Muhammed Ali in his prime. Management decided to approach the leading local supplier to form an alliance, bringing its best-in-class technology to the local firm's low cost structure and in-depth channel coverage. The deal is in process—the company is now looking forward to slugging it out in a much larger market space.

As difficult as it may be in its own right, understanding your current addressable market pie is not enough, however. Equally important is your ability to forecast what it will look like five years from now. Customer requirements are changing rapidly in China, often driven by the impact of foreign invested companies offering better quality and technology. The competitive landscape is similarly dynamic with new competitors entering from inside and outside China. Objective market research and detailed competitive analysis are imperative to accurately map your potential, especially in a complex and highly dynamic marketplace where competition is fierce.

FIGURE 4.4: ADDRESSABLE MARKET PIE FOR CAPITAL EQUIPMENT COMPANY

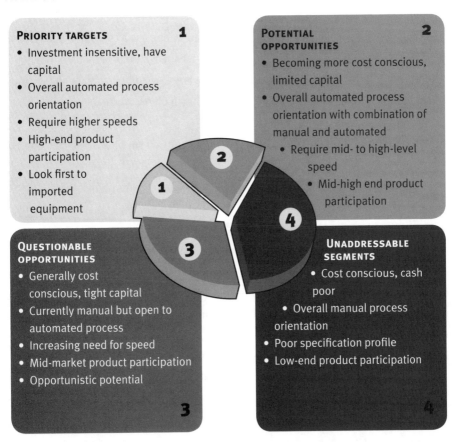

PRIORITY TARGETS 1
- Investment insensitive, have capital
- Overall automated process orientation
- Require higher speeds
- High-end product participation
- Look first to imported equipment

POTENTIAL OPPORTUNITIES 2
- Becoming more cost conscious, limited capital
- Overall automated process orientation with combination of manual and automated
  - Require mid- to high-level speed
    - Mid-high end product participation

QUESTIONABLE OPPORTUNITIES 3
- Generally cost conscious, tight capital
- Currently manual but open to automated process
- Increasing need for speed
- Mid-market product participation
- Opportunistic potential

UNADDRESSABLE SEGMENTS 4
- Cost conscious, cash poor
  - Overall manual process orientation
- Poor specification profile
- Low-end product participation

CUSTOMER PULL

If the theme of Act One in the Chinese Opera on foreign investment is new market opportunity, Act Two's is *customer pull*. As Western firms in such industries as automotive, electronics, chemicals, telecommunications, etc., expand operations in China, they are encouraging their key supplier bases to follow suit (often the same way the government encourages you to pay your taxes ... there is very little room for a response other than "yes," while at the same time we look for loopholes). Many companies are being forced to take on potentially big risks with little tangible support or guarantees. We find the main impetus for small and mid-sized companies to enter China is often customer pull. Many of their Fortune 1000 customers set up in the 1990s and early 2000s and continue to expand today.

A common phrase has been heard in industry lately: "We are reducing our suppliers to a limited number who can serve us globally. If you want us as a customer, you need to be where we are." This is a compelling statement, especially if the customer is a major revenue contributor. Unfortunately, some of the large customers making these statements are not sure what they themselves are doing in China.

A good example of this type of situation is a client of ours, a supplier of telecom components for whom 70% of its business was with one multinational customer. The supplier's CEO received "the call" from this key customer late one afternoon, telling him that he needed to be able to supply the customer in China in a very short time, otherwise business would be severely reduced. It threw the company into a panic as employees scrambled to locate a global map and find out if key staff had passports. But when the supplier eventually came to China, it found its customer waffling on its own China strategy due to a negative turn in its business fortunes. Fortunately, the supplier was moving cautiously and checking out other business prospects. "Our major customer got us thinking about China," the CEO said later, "but they are not necessarily going to be the only reason to come here."

Suppliers motivated by their customers to take the leap to China have made the effort to better understand what is behind the pull. The task is not easy—sometimes your customer is just as confused and stressed about China as you. Generally, we find several important sub-drivers behind the customer pull Motivation, all of which should be proactively explored with your customers:

- **Lower costs:** Customers assume that if you are in China, your costs will be lower, which they often are. But be careful to avoid a cost-down spiral as you delightedly find that you can lower your costs 30% but your customer expects 40%! You must carefully explore what they mean by "cheaper".
- **Logistics:** Given the high logistics costs within China and the time required to

support your customers from offshore, just being closer to your customers' production may address their main need. If so, you might be able to satisfy this requirement by local warehousing or some simple last-step processing in China while retaining your core operation in the West. Many companies are going back to their bills of material and finding creative ways to break down their products and manufacturing process into discrete parts, with final assembly being done closer to the customer.

- **Technology/design:** Perhaps the most widespread advantage Western firms bring to China is a higher technical competence than is currently available there. But even though your customers may want your technology, you must balance their need for localization with your need to protect your intellectual property. If your core technology is at risk of being leaked to competitors, then moving into China ultimately undermines any benefit of being closer to your client.

- **Relationship:** Your longstanding relationship with—and knowledge of—your customer can be a compelling draw to have you in China, especially for more technical products. Don't underestimate your *guanxi*—you have worked hard for many years to develop close and mutually beneficial relationships with your customers. They know this and will want someone like you serving them in China. On the other hand, don't think your relationship will outweigh major cost reduction needs (one of our clients told us that a customer of his said, "We love you like a brother but you need to be with us in China or you are out of the family!"). We have seen many multinationals compromise on quality, service and relational comfort as they become seduced by China's low costs. The relationship asset can be a differentiator but is generally not enough on its own. All things being equal, your longstanding customers will want to work with you—it's the "all things being equal" part that's the stickler.

Successful companies responding to customer pull do their homework carefully. Your customers may be asking the same questions of their customers as you are of them, so you need to take a broader view of your value chain. For example, if you sell material to a supplier making automotive connectors in China, you need to understand the situation of the wire harness suppliers it sells the connectors to, which vehicle makers ultimately consume the wire harnesses and if the end product stays in the country or not (which can have a significant impact on your product's specifications). The fate of your customers' customers, and on down the line, will trickle back to you. While this condition is true in all markets, the high level of change and uncertainty in China's value chains makes planning more challenging.

Additionally, it is wise to explore opportunities to develop supplemental customers in China to spread the risk. This goes back to the first Motivation of finding attractive new market potential, and not simply relying on the prosperity and goodwill of your main customers. We advise our clients to actively explore potential both outside the core customers that are pulling them to China and the end-use markets in which they may participate. As an example, one of our clients in computer hardware was being drawn to China by one of its main U.S. customers. Instead of limiting its follow-up investigation to this company, it also explored opportunities in other industries it served that used similar technologies and product families including medical devices and power tools. The view was, "We may go to the dance with our main customer, but we'll open up our dance card to others when we get there." By expanding its addressable market scope, it essentially created another Motivation to be in China. The combination of customer pull and new market opportunity provided a more compelling case and also diluted the investment risk.

Our telecom supplier also deduced that what brings you to China may not keep you there. As proactive companies like our telecom and computer hardware clients gain a foothold with new customers in China, they get a bonus opportunity by using this new-found customer penetration as a lever to do business with the same companies back in their home markets. As we shall see in the next Motivation driver, companies that are first movers in China can disrupt the customer relationships of their competition that may not be as responsive to their customers' needs.

COMPETITIVE THREAT

As customer pull has more recently emerged as a Motivation to go to China, so too has another equally compelling factor, *competitive threat*. William Knudsen is quoted as saying, "In business, the competition will bite you if you keep running. If you stand still they will swallow you." Like it or not, many companies are witnessing the competitive landscape shift before their eyes as their international competitors move to China and local Chinese companies begin to compete globally. As a result, the threat of competition is motivating companies to enter China for defensive purposes. I discussed in the section on customer pull that if you do not follow your customers to China, someone else will. In this way, customer pull and competitive threat are intertwined and feed off each other.

We find that many companies generally can identify the threat from their well-known and highly visible international competitors. Where we see more vulnerability for Western firms is the threat from local China competitors—Western management seems to deny that a local Chinese player could rise to the level of a multinational company. One client was being threatened by a Chinese specialty chemical producer that had emerged to prominence and scale in the last few years. Management went through several years of agonizing analysis of whether they should set up a production capability in China to defend themselves, or even do a deal with the China producer directly to quell the threat. They had constructed a sophisticated financial demand and supply model to forecast the impact of price changes on the global market as well as their own revenue and margin realization. Each time the project team processed the data, the findings suggested that continued price erosion as a result of China capacity increases would significantly undermine the company's market in the medium, if not short, term. These findings seemed to support making an investment in China. However, each time the analysis was reviewed by U.S. business unit management, the global price assumptions would get bumped up, thereby casting serious doubts on the merits of a China investment—especially as the company had little available capital to invest. It finally became clear to the China project team that the game was rigged: U.S. management was not going to invest in China no matter what analysis was put on the table. Corporate management simply did not want to deal with the implications of shutting down facilities in the U.S. or Europe, so they finessed the game until everyone got tired of playing.

Many Western producers are confident that the quality gap between their own product and one from a Chinese firm is so wide that their preferred position with their customers is safe. Many today marvel at how quickly this gap is bridged when local Chinese producers offer "adequate" quality at 30-40% less cost.

The evolution of Chinese competitors is taking place as a result of a rather insidious cycle, one we like to call "Losing business to the Chinese in five easy steps" (see Figure 4.5). Here is how the cycle typically evolves:

FIGURE 4.5: LOSING BUSINESS TO THE CHINESE IN FIVE EASY STEPS

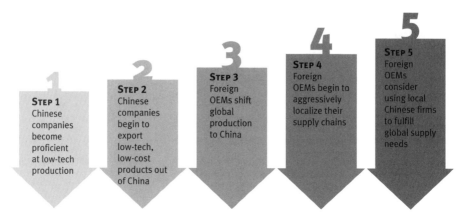

STEP 1 Chinese companies become proficient at low-tech production

STEP 2 Chinese companies begin to export low-tech, low-cost products out of China

STEP 3 Foreign OEMs shift global production to China

STEP 4 Foreign OEMs begin to aggressively localize their supply chains

STEP 5 Foreign OEMs consider using local Chinese firms to fulfill global supply needs

STEP ONE: EMERGENCE OF CHINESE COMPETITION

As a result of robust domestic growth in China over the last 10 years, many Chinese companies have grown rapidly in scale and capability. In addition to expanded capacities, these companies have improved their technical competence and product quality up to world standards. Highly labor-intensive industries in low-technology products — such as toys, household goods, textiles, etc. — were the first to prosper, exploiting China's very low labor rates and abundant workforce. More recently, we have witnessed the growth of Chinese companies in core industrial and consumer segments, many of which are relatively mature in the West such as some petrochemicals, building materials, primary metals, low-end automotive parts and the like. As the technologies needed are relatively old and available, the result has been the development of some strong and increasingly sizeable Chinese producers.

STEP TWO: EXPORTS BECOME ATTRACTIVE

As industries grow in China, there has been a tendency for over-investment in capacity, leading quickly to very competitive pricing in the local market. Given intensifying competition within China among low-cost and aggressive competitors, these firms have naturally looked outward. Export markets, particularly those in developed countries, not only offered new demand potential but much higher margins. These prospects, coupled with China's low-cost manufacturing base, were a very attractive equation.

Initially targeting developing countries in Asia, Africa and the Middle East where product standards were lower, China producers soon found access to the more developed markets of Europe, Japan and the U.S. Channels opened up as distributors and traders sought to match low-cost China suppliers with eager international customers. In this phase of the cycle, we have witnessed Chinese producers also migrating up the quality chain, expanding from low value-added, commodity products to moderate value-added, mid-technology products, even with their own "global brands," e.g. in appliances, electronics, computers, etc. These brands have expanded outside of China's borders and are beginning to make inroads in the West, surprising their U.S. and European competitors who never dreamed of facing a legitimate Chinese brand in their home markets.

STEP THREE: FOREIGN FIRMS SHIFT PRODUCTION

As noted earlier, with a continually growing Chinese domestic market and the appeal of a low-cost manufacturing environment, foreign manufacturers began to shift production to China. Hong Kong and Taiwanese firms were the initial investors in the early 1990s but were soon joined by major U.S., European and even Japanese manufacturers. This phase in the migration has had a cascading effect, attracting sequential layers of the supply chain to China through customer pull. The automotive industry is a recent example of this phenomenon. Major international vehicle makers have expanded their production capacity aggressively in China to meet growing domestic demand for vehicles. As quality parts were not yet locally available in the early stage of migration, these major vehicle makers have pulled their first-tier suppliers (such as Delphi, Visteon, Valeo, Dana, etc.) into China. Now, these major parts companies are returning the favor by pulling second- and even third-tier suppliers to support their production needs. This same phenomenon is occurring in many other industries such as electronics, appliances, medical devices and telecom.

The result of this third step has been the establishment of a base of foreign-invested enterprises in China, sometimes building incremental capacity to their facilities in the West or even making a complete shift in manufacturing from the West to China.

STEP FOUR: FOREIGN INVESTED FIRMS LOOK TO SOURCE LOCALLY IN CHINA

These transplanted OEMs then look to localize their supply chains more aggressively and source from China-based suppliers to further reduce costs. As a result of a slow response from their suppliers in the West to move resources to China, and due to the often significant cost gap between Western suppliers and local Chinese firms, these OEMs proactively evaluate local sourcing options. Their goal is not only to lower product costs but also to lower supply chain costs and improve responsiveness.

Many second- and third-tier suppliers have been surprised at the aggressiveness and flexibility of their OEM customers in this regard, as well as the strong performance of local Chinese competitors. These suppliers were confident that the gap in quality, technology and the inability of their Chinese competitors to meet environmental, safety and health standards would protect them; however, the gap has not been as wide or unassailable as they assumed. Much to the dismay of their U.S. suppliers, many OEMs have been willing to compromise performance requirements to gain cost advantage, thus lowering the bar for Chinese producers.

STEP FIVE: FOREIGN INVESTED FIRMS CONSIDER USING LOCAL SOURCES FOR GLOBAL SUPPLY

The last step in the process, which is in the early stages of development today, involves these OEMs using the now-qualified local Chinese sources to satisfy demand in other parts of the world. Given their competitive costs, once the Chinese suppliers have been let in the door, this last step is a relatively easy transition. The implications of this final sequence in the migration could be the most lethal for Western-based suppliers.

Many leading OEMs have set up sourcing operations in China with their sights set on supplying global customers—in some cases, they are even moving global sourcing management to China. These operations are being supported increasingly by local R&D capabilities established to work more effectively with local producers on new products for both the domestic and export markets.

This tactic of going through the back door to become a global supplier is not limited to Chinese companies. One of our clients, a U.S. supplier of software to smaller manufacturers, was a very early entrant into China, where it built up a significant customer list among locally based, larger foreign manufacturers—companies not traditionally the target market in the U.S. However, once our client effectively proved itself in China, these OEMs started purchasing and installing our client's systems in their European and U.S. operations, surprising much of our client's competition, which did not previously see it as a threat.

Don't be lulled into a false sense of confidence that you are somehow "safe" from the above cycle. As an old Arabian proverb goes, "Do not stand in a place of danger trusting in miracles."

LOWER COSTS

There has been a loud sucking sound in the last few years as China has evolved as the workshop of the world, pulling manufacturers into its gravity of low-cost and abundant labor. Some companies are looking at China purely from a supply chain or manufacturing cost point of view, either to serve Asia or other global markets. Many firms will find this Motivation commingled with others, such as setting up a local facility to compete in the China market (new market growth), or to better serve the logistical needs of multinational customers (customer pull).

Establishing a lower-cost base in China will entail some level of asset localization other than simply sourcing from a China-based supplier. Localizing which assets and when is a critical choice and typically involves a trade-off between achieving lower costs and exposing your financial and technical resources. Achieving the right balance can be a delicate exercise (chapter five dwells on this topic in more detail). A helpful approach is to look at your manufacturing assets in a hierarchical way, as illustrated in Figure 4.6. For some companies, localizing logistics assets such as a warehouse in China is enough, at least in the short term, to satisfy customer needs. But to achieve meaningful cost reductions, a company generally needs to do some level of assembly or manufacture in China, eventually moving to full-scale manufacture to optimize costs and maximize investment. Full-scale manufacture is pursued when the stakes are high, i.e. when compelling drivers exist to access new market demand or to lower costs to stay competitive. The downside, of course, is a high level of risk, from potentially both investment and exposure of IP.

Many firms take steps toward full-scale manufacture as a compelling case is confirmed for incremental cost reduction. This approach is especially effective when intellectual property risks are a major concern. Stratifying your overall production process to clearly determine where the break points are for each incremental localization investment is key. We have seen the concerns of many companies, initially overwhelmed by the prospect of setting up a facility in China, ameliorated once they could envision a more conservative, step-by-step approach. In this regard, some firms will initially do a joint venture to accelerate their learning curves and exploit the *guanxi* of their partners as they learn how to do business in China. Once established, they then go wholly owned on the larger investment when their core IP needs to be transferred.

FIGURE 4.6: TYPICAL ASSET LOCALIZATION HIERARCHY

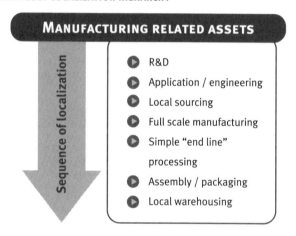

Along these lines, it is logical to move your low-end line or process to China first, retaining the higher-end and more custom manufacture in your home market. The Taiwanese have been expert in this transition, having shifted most of the bottom end of the more manual production processes to the mainland, while maintaining more custom, automated production lines in Taiwan. Typically, it is the low-end range of the product spectrum that is under more cost duress and is likely a better fit in the less sophisticated China market. In fact, many firms find themselves exhuming old products and technologies that have passed through the mature growth cycle in the West but are on the upward growth slope in China.

Localizing assets to lower costs involves a number of related factors such as initial investment needs, operating costs, availability of raw materials and equipment, appropriately skilled labor, location of customer demand and risk of IP exposure. In this step of the China Readiness Assessment, each of these elements needs to be carefully eval-uated to ensure they are covered. Some tactical suggestions:

- Accurately assess the cost and future dynamics of each element such as labor rates and availability, import duties, customer migration, etc. Don't cheat by producing simple spreadsheets; force yourself to capture all possible details.
- Move low-end, less value-added products first and look for opportunities to utilize "retired" technologies or processes, which have likely been depreciated.
- Consider transferring existing manufacturing lines or machinery where applicable—and subject to China tax law and import licenses—to optimize costs and minimize cash investment.
- Make sure you "China-fy" your facility to minimize costs (as discussed in chapter two).
- Explore different forms of ownership, using local resources and partners where they can be more competitive than you while at the same time protecting your IP.

SOURCING

Many companies, both large and small, are increasing their vendor sourcing activity in China as a means to lower costs. This action can be a prelude to making your own invest-ment in China manufacturing. Companies often work their way through a sequence of steps to increasingly lower cost and further control the supply source:

FIGURE 4.7 PROGRESSION IN SOURCING APPROACHES TO CHINA

Most companies started their China sourcing under what we call an "opportunistic" approach, typically through a third-party organization such as a Hong Kong broker or trader. Through this approach, they obtained some meaningful and relatively easy reduction in cost without any investment, or even trips to China, for that matter, because the trader took care of everything. However, many companies found out, often the hard way, that they had left too much money on the table by not understanding the real costs of their supply sources in China.

Many companies sourcing from China using an opportunistic approach must now take more control over the sourcing activity to maximize cost reduction and control the supply chain, as the level of sourcing volume has increased and taken on more importance to their firm. For instance, after a period of time working through a trader (and maybe a couple of trips to China), a company may find that, although this approach has provided some cost savings, it is still leaving money on the table. In response, companies have sought to do the work to explore sources themselves, in essence eliminating the trader—or at least minimizing that role. The last several years have witnessed airplanes full of Western executives going back and forth to China, making deals directly with local Chinese operations and substantially lowering their purchase costs.

More recently, as their customer base gets smarter and starts asking such questions as, "What value are you really bringing to the table?", companies are looking to go a step deeper into what we refer to as strategic sourcing. Large retailers such as Wal-Mart or Home Depot have set up their own sourcing operations in China—not to mention their own retail stores—to further squeeze out the middle man. Companies are now required to show a direct facing in China through their own factory or via a more intimate sourcing relationship with a local supplier. This third step in the cycle results in more aggressive strategies, such as setting up operations, the acquisition of local facilities, strategic sourcing relationships, etc. This last phase in the cycle, however, requires that companies put some resources in China, effectively raising the stakes to an uncomfortable level for some firms. The alternative is to risk leaving money in the supply chain instead of your pocket and potentially even losing competitiveness.

One of our clients in home improvement products was faced with this transition. For more than 10 years, it had sourced successfully from China, shifting production out of the U.S. as products commoditized. It began to concentrate more on new product development and a high level of customer service to key clients like Home Depot, Wal-Mart and Lowe's. The structure was comfortable and profitable and the company was very good at it. But as the customer base started to look for more direct sources to squeeze costs, even calling on our client's supply sources in China, management realized they needed to further localize their sourcing competencies. Their initial inclination was to invest what would have been significant dollars for a minority equity stake in their largest China supplier. Management believed that this investment would achieve direct source status in the eyes of their customers and would nullify the longer-term threat of this supplier circumventing them and going direct to their customer base. However, further analysis exposed the huge risks of this investment, both financial and managerial. At this point, management began to look more creatively at the situation, as well as their own long-term outlook on China. After a very revealing and interesting exploration of other options, they established a novel strategic sourcing relationship with another one of their key suppliers, successfully moving to that third sourcing box without investing meaningful dollars. (At this point I will leave you wondering more about the solution, picking it up again in the next chapter to illustrate another point.)

STAKEHOLDER PUSH

In the 1990s, *stakeholder push* was more of a pseudo-driver to enter China—less a matter of vision and more a matter of CEO hubris as they scurried to be in the early wave of those to tap China's huge potential. On the one hand, stakeholder push must be clearly understood, as it is a potentially dangerous Motivation—often based on shallow logic and support, as was frequently the case in the last decade. On the other hand, there are examples of forward-thinking stakeholders who can clearly see China's impact on their company, and the need for them to be there.

In the 1990s, companies such as Emerson Electric used stakeholder push shrewdly and boldly to entice and support its fragmented group of subsidiary companies to seriously look at China. In the mid-1990s, Emerson sent its vice chairman to Hong Kong to encourage, mentor and facilitate exploring China and the region as a whole. He became a beacon, of sorts, for subsidiary management as he guided their navigation through the treacherous waters of China. As a result, Emerson Electric established many operations in China successfully (not that it didn't have its fair share of bad investments, poor strategies and dreadful ventures).

Some companies today are dealing with the complexities of China wisely by using stakeholder support to provide financial help, find opportunities for synergies between divisions, lead the exploration team, rally support from "related" companies such as through board members and advisors, etc. As an example, we have seen parent companies with multiple divisions set up a corporate business development function in China. This operation becomes a local resource for subsidiary companies to make useful contacts, organize trips to China, handle human resources and deal with financial and legal requirements. In many ways, they are implementing stakeholder pull as much as push by planting an executive flag in China in the way Neil Armstrong of Apollo 11 did on the moon when he took "one small step for man, one giant leap for mankind."

In another positive case of stakeholder Motivation, a diversified manufacturer of industrial products and material processing had encouraged and even cajoled its subsidiary management to take a hard look at China. The CEO hired a corporate international director who pushed some of the reluctant subsidiaries to explore the market and then follow up with an implementation plan when opportunity was ascertained, which interestingly was the case for virtually all the half-dozen or so subsidiaries. One Oklahoma-based division with sales of only US$5 million was particularly reluctant to do anything, even though an opportunity was identified which could double its sales via a deal with the leading China-based distributor. Despite this unexpected find, subsidiary management's response was later rather than "Sooner" (I could not resist the pun). So corporate took up the slack and went to China and negotiated the deal, dragging the boys from Oklahoma like reluctant teenagers to church on Sunday morning—an effective case of stakeholder push.

Remember, however, although stakeholder excitement and support is a necessary condition for a China expansion, it is not a sufficient one on its own. In the end, stakeholder push (or pull) is not a reason to go; rather, it is a reason to look in order to determine if the other motivations have enough substance and urgency.

UNDERSTANDING YOUR COMPOSITE MOTIVATION

To understand fully your Motivation to go to China, you need to review carefully all of these potential driving factors while recognizing their interplay. These must be viewed, not just in today's market landscape, but with a forward view of changes in both China and your own company. Although I alluded at the beginning of this chapter to the profound simplicity in the five categories of motivations, don't be fooled into thinking that the work of identifying the details of your own motivations is either quick or simple. This task is very strategic and can even be a bit daunting due to the complexities of variables involved and the pace of change in China.

There are three disciplines to observe as you work through your Motivation analysis:

DIG DEEP AND LOOK FOR DIVERSE INPUTS

It is important that your management team digs deep to find the underlying drivers—the multiple pressures points pushing and pulling you to China. It is the subtleties and nuances that frequently hold the keys to your strategic thrust into China. Often, this is difficult to do if you are limiting yourself to management discussions around the boardroom table. Certainly, senior management's perspective is crucial—and their final approval and support is necessary to any successful China initiative—but it is generally not enough to develop a comprehensive and market-sensitive strategy. To help accomplish this depth, it is important to bring in a diversity of views in order to be thorough in your assessment.

Your China initiative will likely touch on many aspects of your business, so the team evaluating your motivations must mirror this breadth. Sales and marketing, procurement, manufacturing, engineering and even service support could be affected by your China strategy.

We conducted a seminar with a company whose customer service representative ended up being the catalyst in the China evaluation process. While the direct sales team had relevant perspective on what selective customers were pressing their company to do in China, these views were disparate and unclear. The customer service representative had a broad view of all of their customers and brought a more cohesive and unbiased picture to the table; she was able to see how China touched the organization all across their customer base. This view became the foundation on which their Motivation assessment was built.

In the case of our home improvement products company, its China initiative was clearly driven by purchasing. However, part way into the process of exploring its China strategy, The CEO realized that there were additional potential benefits of the newly conceived sourcing structure. Because the company would now have a local partner instead of an arm's length vendor relationship, it could use the partner's low-cost resources for application engineering work in China for the U.S. market. It further realized that its partner's management team also had good ideas for new product development using its own unique skills in plastics processing. And lastly, with a local China operation, our client could begin to cultivate more efficiently the emerging home improvement market in China for its products made in the U.S. With these realizations, the CEO began to bring in other management staff from marketing and engineering to the China related discussions.

Additionally, digging deep requires looking outside the four walls of your company. You may already be engaged in discussions with some customers about their needs in China, but how about those customers who are not talking about it? Their silence might only reflect the fact that they just have not gotten around to discussing it with you (or are discussing it with someone else!). Initiating the topic of China shows enterprise and could even uncover some as-yet-unknown issues with your customers. We have found a number of instances where suppliers actually led their key customers to China after opening their eyes to the possibilities that it presented. Your suppliers are also a great source of insight into your motivations to expand into China and will be particularly interested in how your strategy will impact them (remember, just as you are looking to your customers for motivations, they will be looking to you for the same). Talk with your major suppliers now about your thoughts on China. We have seen very creative supplier-customer partnerships come together to pursue a China strategy to the benefit of both parties.

Finally, there is the broader business community, most of whom are wrestling with the same challenges you are facing. My colleagues and I often speak at seminars for trade and business organizations where there are a wide variety of industries represented. During our talks, we encourage all participants to speak with as many of those around them as they possibly can before the day is out. Ask them what their motivations are for being interested in China and why—what subtleties they have uncovered, what pain they have already gone through and what advice they would give.

LOOK FOR INTERPLAY BETWEEN MOTIVATORS
If your Motivation chart has only one motivator on it, you probably aren't thinking hard enough. An interplay of motivations can mean a wealth of opportunity—and threat—when these motivations play off each other. For instance, if you are feeling pressure from customers about China, then there is likely competition out there about to knock on their door, if it is not already happening. One of our clients said, "My customers

love us because they need our products so badly ... but if that is the case, then they have to be looking at other supply options as well!"

In the same way, a strong customer pull to go to China may indicate that an attractive market is developing there. Talking with your customers about their competitive threats in China may reveal opportunities for you to pursue as well. Certainly, identifying the interplay between current customer needs and future market requirements will provide you with a more realistic and mature picture of the market.

The competitor Motivation is related to every other Motivation. If you are feeling pressure to lower costs, from customers or the market in general, then your competitors are likely feeling the same stress. If you are considering incremental China market opportunities, identify your competitors' key customers and pursue them with a China strategy in mind; you could even catch one of your international competitors asleep at the wheel and preempt them with one of their customers that is migrating to China.

While going to China may lower costs and position you more favorably with current customers and against competition, it may also open up other application segments where historically you have not been able to compete. During a strategy session for a client of ours providing custom electronics solutions to global OEMs, we wondered, "If we could get price X for this product line, what bids could we go after that we have been ignoring because we are priced out of the game?" The vice president of sales became highly motivated to expand his market segments. Assume that there is a link between all of your possible motivations—the job of your China team is to find those links, describe them in detail and identify how they will impact your composite Motivation to invest in China.

DRIVE FOR CONSENSUS

Both executives and shareholders must reach consensus on why they will pursue a China investment and what level of risk is appropriate to support it. This conviction allows the company to plan resource allocation effectively, establishes realistic expectations for the benefits and risks of such a venture, and better ensures that there will be support down the line when the going gets tough, which it likely will.

In one executive management workshop where we were unpacking their Motivation, three divergent directions quickly developed. One executive thought serving the current needs of customers was the most important driver, another thought pursuing the newly emerging China market was the main driver, and the third thought cost savings should be the primary motivator. The group nearly came to blows at one point from their unwillingness to compromise. After multiple rounds, consensus began to emerge as the underlying factors of each Motivation were clarified and validated. They were able to agree at the end—with full eye contact and mutual confidence—that certain customers were indeed motivating them to go to China, but that cost savings could help them serve other customers and significantly expand their market scope while at the same time making them more defensible down the road. This agreement was crucial for them to be able to take the right next step and in a unified manner. I will discuss these points when I review stakeholder support in more detail in chapter six on Managerial Preparedness.

This consensus also provides a solid anchor to your China initiative when disruption occurs in the China market or at home—which it invariably will. A client of ours sent a team on their first trip to China to see for themselves the opportunities and threats that our research work had uncovered for them. They spent a whirlwind week visiting customers, prospects, industrial zones and potential partners. By the end, they were overwhelmed. The CEO, in particular, was obviously agitated, having been challenged on a number of fronts during the past week and seeing just how steep the mountain was in front of him. As we were all chatting over dinner just before they left China, suddenly the CEO blurted out, "Well, this is all well and good ... but why are we really doing this?" There was a stunned silence around the table—we had been working on why for the past five months and had reached an agreement on it before they came to China, or at least so we thought. The vice president of operations, in a very patient voice, spoke up, "Mark, we all know why ... " and proceeded to very clearly articulate their key motivations. There was a pregnant pause after his speech and we all looked toward the CEO. With a sheepish grin on his face, the CEO nodded his head and said, "Oh yeah, that's right. Okay, then. Let's do it!" This type of hesitation and uncertainty will creep in at unexpected intervals over the course of pursuing your China initiative so you will need that touchstone of agreement as a constant reminder to your management team on exactly why you are pursuing a China initiative.

To facilitate the processing of your Motivation drivers, we have developed a basic four-level scale summarized in Figure 4.8. After detailed review, each Motivation is placed into one of these four levels. A high level of urgency, as the phrase implies, indicates the need for a deliberate and concerted response. At this level, not taking action outweighs the risk of action, in either significant threat to your organization or major lost opportunity. You will be prepared to invest to make sure your organization is ready to expand to China, either to achieve new gains or to defend your turf. In some cases, where customers are rapidly moving their production to China and local Chinese competitors are emerging to greet them at the border, you may need to re-invent your business model to survive. Today, many small to mid-sized companies' very existence is being threatened in this way. Even larger companies, which were reputable manufacturers of textiles, tools, electronics, fasteners, toys, etc., are no longer making anything (except money). They have reshaped themselves into brand marketers, service companies or even traders.

FIGURE 4.8: MOTIVATION URGENCY SCALE

Urgency level	Need for response	Risk appetite
High urgency	Imperative: Failure to respond results in serious downsides to your organization	High
Priority	High: Suggests a more measured response with reasonable cushion against failure	Moderate
Needs validation	Questionable: Need to provide more tangible validation before action is taken	Low
Monitor	Opportunistic: Look for low-hanging fruit only	Very low

As you go down the urgency scale, your risk-reward equation changes. More caution is required as you qualify and quantify what it will cost your organization to address these motivations. When your Motivation falls below the priority level, you must be able to demonstrate your ability to implement a China initiative with very limited risks.

An example of a completed Motivation scale is presented in Figure 4.9. This scale can be developed through an intuitive process or more mathematically through a set of defined and weighted questions.

FIGURE 4.9: YOUR COMPOSITE MOTIVATION SCALE

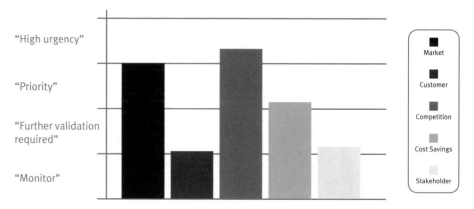

The lack of intensity and clarity of the Motivation behind many companies going to China in the last 10 years resulted in early withdrawals and disappointed shareholders. This collective pain should provide valuable wisdom for future investors. As W.C. Fields said, "Beginner's luck, gentlemen . . . although I have devoted some time to the game."

CHAPTER SUMMARY

This chapter described the first dimension of the China Readiness Assessment and one of the axes that will determine your company's overall readiness level. While a company's Motivation to expand into China is, on the surface, a fairly obvious issue, I discussed how many companies fail to dig deep enough into the specific nature and intensity of their Motivation. Experience has told us that this deeper understanding is necessary to accurately assess your investment risk while at the same time determining an optimum strategy and structure. I outlined the five main drivers behind a company's Motivation and emphasized their frequent interrelationship. Generally, a company will be motivated by a combination of the following drivers, each showing a unique character and intensity.

1. Attractive market
2. Customer pull
3. Competitive threat
4. Operational efficiencies/cost savings
5. Stakeholder push

The opportunity to tap attractive *new market potential* dominated Western company interest in China throughout much of the 1990s. With the doors thrown open to a market with more than 1 billion people and an economy let loose to expand, foreign firms tripped over each other to get to China. In their rush to enter the market, companies did not do adequate analysis and due diligence on their market opportunities, and ultimately paid a dear price for this deficiency. China still presents significant growth opportunity for Western firms but there is an even greater need today for deep and objective analysis of that potential before making an investment. The dynamics and complexities of China can make it a difficult task to clearly define your addressable market where you can make money.

Changes in the competitive environment have accelerated as local firms are increasingly going head on with Western companies in the same market space. New market opportunity remains a compelling motivator to go to China if it can be fully substantiated. This new potential needs to be considered in light of other corporate opportunities and your overall appetite for growth. A clear and comparative understanding of these opportunities will enable you to accurately weigh the costs and risks of pursuing a China expansion.

A more recent driver to expand into China is *customer pull*. This Motivation has created a dilemma for many companies that are not inclined or prepared to make an investment in China but must respond to defend their customer share positions. Often these customers are unsure of their own China strategies. Also, their requirements in China may not be enough to support your operation. However, not responding to their needs can risk your relationship. I discussed the importance of probing the reasons behind your customers' requests for you to be in China. A better understanding of the sub-drivers behind the pull will clarify the specific support you need to provide and may suggest some alternative, less onerous ways you can provide it without full-scale investment in a facility.

Proactive companies use this initial customer pull as a catalyst to look at broader opportunities in China, both with other existing customers that may soon want them in China or even for their competitors' main clients. Additionally, these firms look at broader application segments beyond those served by the customer(s) pulling them to China, but within the scope of their core offering. This expanded demand potential can spread the risk of your investment, and make the difference between a meager financial return and a very profitable business.

This customer pull has accelerated the possibility of *competitive threat* coming out of China. As Western companies expand into China to tap new market opportunity or in response to customer pull, they now have expanded capabilities and likely a lower cost base that will present a new threat to you, both in China and offshore. While the emergence of this new competitive dynamic is often on the radar of Western management, the surfacing of strong local competitors can be on the periphery or even off the screen—sometimes leading to Western companies being blindsided by new players in their market. I described an insidious cycle facetiously termed "Losing business to the Chinese in five easy steps." In this cycle, we can see how local Chinese companies are emerging as formidable competitors, both in China and on the global market landscape. Western compa-nies often put too much confidence in the strength of longstanding customer relationships in the West to protect them from competition in China. The seduc-tion of significant cost savings has disrupted the strongest of these relationships. No matter how great your relationships are with your customers, the Godfather Principle holds true: "It's not personal, it's business."

China has been coined the workshop of the world recently as Western compa-nies continue to migrate their manufacturing and supply chain resources to the mainland in order to achieve *lower costs*. China's large pool of low-cost labor is undergirding a strong wave of manufacturing investment to serve both the domestic China market and as an export platform. As companies have more aggressively moved manufacturing to China the risks in these investments is becoming more apparent. As a result, companies are creatively looking at their manufacturing process and ways to transfer it to China in a more conservative, step-wise fashion—what I referred to as the asset localization hierarchy. Even companies that traditionally have only sourced from third parties in China are now being forced to localize more of their sourcing functions to stay competitive and present a more direct face to their customers.

The last Motivation, *stakeholder push*, is more of an intangible driver to expand to China, essentially a force to encourage or even compel a company's manage-ment to fully explore the other four motivators. Like karma, there is good and bad stakeholder push. Especially in the last decade, but still occurring today, stakeholder push was abused. But stakeholder push can also be a very posi-tive and even necessary driver to both support proactive investigation of China and help empower the company to better implement it. To be a valid Motivation, stakeholder push needs to be carefully and appropriately applied as a support to the exploration and follow up process, and to enable more effective implementa-tion through efficient use of all relevant company resources.

I recommended a comprehensive and honest process in your review of these five motivations, which...

- Digs deep to identify the underlying drivers behind each Motivation by bringing in the right team of management early in the process.
- Identifies the interplay between the motivators and the resultant implications to your overall Motivation.
- Achieves consensus among the management team that will provide stability and consistency as you work through the China exploration plan.

In the end, a **Composite Motivation** profile can be developed which fully characterizes the nature and urgency of the combined drivers behind a China expansion. This profile defines the first axis in our readiness matrix and prepares you to look at the state of your Organizational Preparedness to move forward.

Chapter 5

Operational Preparedness: Transferring your Key Competencies to China

 The wise adapt themselves to circumstances, as water molds itself to the pitcher.

Chinese proverb

With your motivation to go to China now clearly understood in terms of both the main driving factors and their relative intensity, you are ready to begin looking at your Organizational Preparedness to respond. As outlined in chapter three, your organizational readiness to pursue a China initiative is measured against three major factors:

- *Operational Preparedness*: The company is able to transfer or replicate some or all of its business operations to China under some viable structure.
- *Managerial Preparedness*: There is sufficient breadth and depth in the organization to support a China initiative without creating key holes in management's attention to the core business.
- *Financial Preparedness*: The company's core business is financially stable and possesses the necessary resources and flexibility to pursue a China expansion.

The main purpose in measuring the level of preparedness in these areas is to identify the factors that will be critical to support implementation of your China initiative as defined by the outcome of your evaluation of the Motivation dimension. A well-prepared company will be strong in all three areas. However, most firms will have some deficiencies or gaps between the resources and experience they possess and what is needed to succeed. The lesson learned by companies investing in China in the past (and, unfortunately, still today) is that lack of clarity on these gaps will ultimately undermine your performance in executing a strategy, in some cases even lethally. Just as with the Motivation dimension, consensus on what these gaps are as well as the actions to address them will focus your development efforts and improve the probabilities of long-term success. I will provide numerous examples in the following three chapters of companies falling short in this regard but also a few that did things right. The readiness exercise will help you take inventory of what will be important to your strategy given your unique company profile and business situation.

As a means to accentuate the character of these organizational measurements as well as their respective indicators, I will draw different analogies with something uniquely Chinese. Hopefully, these analogies will help you remember the key aspects of each dimension as well as add an interesting flavor to their description.

According to the CEO of a client company that went through the China Readiness Assessment, you have to be able to "do what you do well" in China to have any chance of success. Operational Preparedness implies that the company can transfer or replicate some of "what they do well" to China under a viable structure and with a reasonable level of long-term defensibility. We use four related indicators to flush out Operational Preparedness and better qualify your capabilities and experience base to address key challenges in establishing an operation in China:

- Transfer of key operations
- Protecting intellectual property
- Business structure
- Alliances

These indicators are part of a critical due diligence process, which I will discuss in chapter seven, but it is worth introducing at this point. Not all these operational issues will be pertinent to your company—their relevance will depend on your business profile, size, resources and the nature of your Motivation to expand in China. But the transfer of some operational competencies is fundamental to doing business in China, whether it's manufacturing, brand, technology, services or even trading functions. They all require some shift of resources and capabilities to a local setting in order to participate meaningfully in the market. In fact, being prepared to establish your base of operations in China, whatever function it performs, no matter its size or structure, is the key element of the entire readiness process.

FIGURE 5.1: OPERATIONAL PREPAREDNESS FACTORS

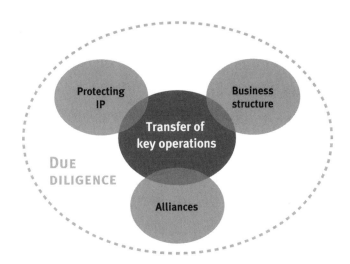

The metaphor I will use to illustrate the relationship of these four operational prepared-ness indicators is what, in Chinese history, is called the Four Treasures of the Chinese Studio: *wen fang si bao*, or paper, brush, ink block and ink stone (Figure 5.2). The Chinese language is, first and foremost, a written one. Chinese characters are not phonetic as are the words in written English; you typically cannot know the pronun-ciation of a character by looking at it—it must be memorized. In fact, the hundreds, and maybe thousands, of spoken dialects in China all use the same written form, each region pronouncing the characters differently.

FIGURE 5.2: THE FOUR TREASURES OF THE CHINESE STUDIO

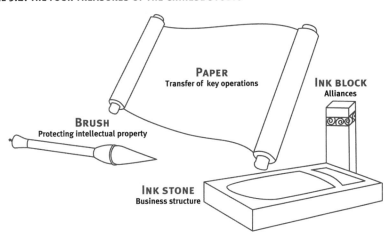

As such, the written word in the form of calligraphy—an art form in itself—was a way to record human events and communicate culture to a broader society. Government officials and scholars spent lifetimes perfecting their calligraphy and learning to properly use and value the Four Treasures. Each of the items in the Chinese studio had its own history and importance, yet each was inextricably linked with the others: All four were necessary to create written Chinese.

The following pages align each of the operational preparedness indicators with one of the Four Treasures: *the transfer of key operations* is the paper, the medium upon which everything is written; *protecting intellectual property* is the brush, the tool through which the intent of the writer is expressed in often unique ways; and *business structure* and *alliances* form a unique partnership with the ink block and the ink stone, working together to produce the ink. Although I discuss each one individually, like the Four Treasures of the Chinese Studio, one must keep in mind their relationships.

TRANSFER OF KEY OPERATIONS

It is common knowledge that paper was invented in China, sometime around 100 B.C., scholars believe. Previously, writing was done on stone, animal bones or long strips of bamboo (which forced the up-and-down orientation of early Chinese writing, some of which survives today). However, it was discovered that hemp fibers soaked in water, mashed with a wooden mallet and then suspended to dry on a screen in a wooden frame, would produce a flat, smooth, light and absorbent surface upon which to write. Future developments would improve the paper's durability and resistance to pests and environmental conditions. From China, the art of papermaking spread throughout the rest of Asia and the Middle East and, after about a thousand years, to Europe and the rest of the world.

As I reviewed in chapter four, a China initiative will require that you localize some operational assets to that country, either transferring some capability or replicating it to some degree. As you worked through your Motivation analysis, it should have become clear what processes and competencies are needed in China (recall the asset localization hierarchy). As paper provides the medium on which to communicate written language, so too the transfer of key operations to China forms the essence of your business and the foundation of your China strategy. This asset transfer, whether comprising manufacturing operations, brand, technological process, marketing resources, sourcing competencies, etc., is the root of your success in China—not strategic plans or capital, which are supportive. As with high-quality paper, this transfer requires stability, flexibility and the right ingredients to effectively "do what you do well" in your home market in a complex and dynamic environment. Let's explore each of these features further.

PROCESS STABILITY AND DOCUMENTATION

The risks associated with the transfer of your key operations to China are directly related to how complex and proprietary the business functions are that you will localize (see Figure 5.3). Where you fall on this matrix will indicate the depth and breadth of challenges you will likely address—the higher up and to the right you are positioned, the more stability you will require to effectively and securely manage the transfer of your competencies to China.

FIGURE 5.3: OPERATIONAL TRANSFER RISK MATRIX

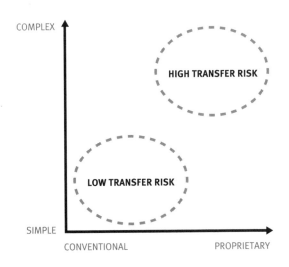

Chinese papermaking evolved into a process that produced an amazingly stable and resilient product. While they did not comprehend that process at the molecular level, ancient papermakers knew the proper additives to include that ensured the paper could withstand pest infestation, mold, moisture and a host of other environmental hazards. Paper scrolls could be rolled and unrolled many hundreds of times and transported many thousands of miles, the paper none the worse for wear. In fact, good paper got better as it got older. In the same way, the stability of your processes needs to be well established in your home market, using tried and proven systems and results. If you are still working the kinks out of your processes while transplanting them—if your paper has some "bugs" in it back home—well, good luck transferring them to China.

Improvements in paper over the generations in China were steady because of the many tomes written on the art and science of papermaking and the apprenticeship process instilled in papermaking guilds. So too, another key feature of stability in the transfer of your processes is the consistency achieved by having well-documented methods that can be effectively taught to others, thus minimizing loss in the transfer. The ability to make high-quality or even best-in-class product is achievable in China but needs solid process behind it.

Chinese companies make a lot of junk and suppliers often take many shortcuts to reduce costs. In many ways, this garage-shop approach is ingrained in the manufacturing culture and needs to be disciplined out, as it were. In 2004, the CEO of General Motors China told us that the Buick sedan produced locally was the best made within GM, having the lowest parts-per-million defect rate of any Buick platform of its facilities worldwide. To be sure, this comments favorably on China's labor capability but is more a statement on the importance of having well-defined and quality processes—as well as training, training, training.

Companies that perform best in China typically have inculcated how things should be done from the very beginning. An example is a leading U.S. building materials supplier that set up a facility in China in the mid-1990s. The company was well known for being very conservative, even to a fault, on any new investment. When it came to China it was especially cautious. In the operation's early adolescence, some 50 expatriates were cycling in and out of the country to support an operation of only $10 million in revenue. They took their well-documented and proven processes and painstakingly transferred them to China. "People from day one learned to do things the right way," said the local general manager. "They still use the same process today. They don't know any other way."

Operational preparedness is typically a bigger challenge for small to mid-sized companies. These firms are often very do-it-yourself oriented in their manufacturing approach, with procedures even handed down from generation to generation, often without adequate documentation. They do what they do very well, but it often takes a unique or customized approach. "We've done this for years and no one does it better," said the president of a precision stamping supplier in the U.S. But get their manufacturing people to clearly explain the magic to a Chinese worker fresh from the interior countryside and problems quickly arise.

If you have set up manufacturing facilities in other countries before, especially in another emerging market, then you are ahead of the game. If you have not, it is worthwhile to review your process and the documentation behind it to ensure that they are robust, clear and transferable. Taking the time to set this foundation will pay big dividends later on with fewer transfer errors and process hiccups.

FLEXIBILITY

The advantages of paper over earlier technologies, such as stone or bamboo, were many, but the most important was the flexibility of the paper—the ability to cut it to size by length and width, roll it up in a scroll, hang it on a wall or bind it into a book. As a written culture, China had, at a very early age, already amassed uncountable volumes of writing. The flexibility of paper made large-quantity production, storage and retrieval possible. So too, having process flexibility is often one of the most important factors for Western firms to cost-effectively transfer their operational capability to China. Paper's flexibility allowed many more uses than stone, so early scholars used the new medium in different ways to meet the requirements of the documents produced. In the same way, a company's flexibility allows it to stretch its operations in order to operate more elastically in a very foreign environment.

Process flexibility touches several important areas:
- How adaptable are your manufacturing processes? Can they be broken up into job shop, batch flow, continuous flow or JIT (just-in-time) capabilities?
- Can your processes be made more manual in certain places to exploit low labor costs? Many Western companies have just completed cycles of automation, forcing labor out of their costs. But in China, it may be more cost effective— and much simpler—to put those manual processes back in to take advantage of lower local labor costs.

- Can the material flow and layout be readily modified to suit a different work environment or setup, especially if you will wish to change the process to better protect your intellectual property?
- Are your operations scalable given the potential lower volume requirements in China—likely the case in the initial years when market development and your customers' needs may still be embryonic?
- Are your operational standards appropriate to China, where a mix of regulations exists? In many industry sectors, China is actively developing its own standards (often a cosmetic change to U.S., European or Japanese approaches). I have seen clients become paralyzed by even the basic need to be metric. If your standards are not well accepted or compatible, you need to carefully measure the time and cost to get them there.

Making changes in your well-established processes can also be dangerous as you might compromise their effectiveness. The most conservative approach is to replicate them if possible, but that option is not always available or feasible from a cost or implementation standpoint. Make adjustments cautiously and only when tangible results can be achieved.

Let's take a look at an example of this need for flexibility. One of our clients, a U.S. metals processor, was being encouraged to come to China to support the growing automotive operation of Delphi, a leading producer of auto parts. The processor was the dominant supplier of its specific product niche to Delphi in North America and was clearly a technology and process leader in its industry. After investigating the market in China, including demand size, growth vector, customer profiles and competition, it determined that it could supply Delphi's annual needs in about four manufacturing days from the existing U.S. operation—so establishing a local facility seemed absurd. Still, the company was being urged by Delphi to localize operations for logistical and, ultimately, cost reasons. Further, one of our client's global competitors was already operating in China to serve its growing Japanese customer base, having followed its own customers with no questions asked about volumes (in classic Japanese style). In the end, our client had to find a way through either expanding its market or lowering investment costs to at least protect its key customer relationship, no matter how unreasonable the proposition appeared on the surface.

Supportability

The original inventors of paper initially searched exhaustively for commonly available resources with which to make the new medium. Material such as animal skins, large leaves and the like were tried, but finally the fibers of the hemp plant, many varieties of which existed in abundance, were used. A precursor to paper was writing on silk, an expensive material that was time-consuming to produce. While maintaining the flexibility, toughness and portability of paper, silk required more expensive and relatively less available raw materials. Paper, on the other hand, suffered no such resource constraints and had all the other good qualities besides.

Having the right resources available in China to support your processes is a third factor affecting their transferability—encompassing such things as skilled labor, quality raw materials, equipment availability and the proper tooling. For companies with special technical needs, finding the right resources locally can be a challenge, especially where very skilled labor is required. Often, intensive training is needed. Our building products company invested heavily here, even sending all mid-level and senior Chinese operators to the U.S. for several weeks of training at its facility. Being able to access the right labor skills and experience can also be challenging, especially with the recent high growth in the manufacturing sector in China. The use of poorly educated and untrained migrant workers, fresh from the farm, is common today as an abundant, on-hand pool of cheap labor. This condition will look very different across China's geographic landscape, given China's regional diversity, so your worker capability needs may drive the location of your operation.

The right raw materials may not be available and thus would have to be imported at higher cost and longer lead times (assuming you do not rely on steady supplies of hemp fiber!). Even if your raw materials may be available in China, their quality may be suspect. Our Delphi material supplier needed quality brass alloy for its product. While there were several large mills active in China, selling brass at very competitive prices, the quality was just not up to snuff. The company did direct research on this issue in its feasibility assessment, including testing the brass at its facility, and concluded that it needed to import brass for the foreseeable future. This had a significant impact on operational costs and supply chain requirements.

Don't be fooled either by the plethora of local manufacturers with ISO certification, thinking that they have solid process behind their operations. While there are legitimate ISO certifications in China, there are many bogus ones as well. My favorite noodle shop near our Shanghai office proudly advertises that it is "ISO 9000 Certified"—the ultimate impact of this certification on the quality of the food has yet to be determined, in my opinion. Make sure the certification has teeth and is not merely window dressing.

Two additional issues can impact your asset transfer and warrant specific commentary— issues that will affect most companies looking to make a direct investment in China.

THE SITE FACTOR DEBATE

If you are a manufacturer, you will no doubt become exposed to one of the bloodiest corporate games I have encountered in China: the site factor debate. This conflict occurs when the pressure to lower costs collides with established facility and manufacturing guidelines, the rules and regulations that tell your company what facilities are appropriate and what they should cost. The cost pressures are sometimes so great as to cause normally sensible and well-mannered executives to froth at the mouth. Typically, the debate pits business unit or commercial management against design engineering and manufacturing management. The nature of the conflict is about achieving the lowest cost but still retaining sound and quality operational assets and procedures. The primary conflict is in balancing the two issues of what are acceptable compromises vs., in the words of the famous limbo song, "how low can you go?"

Simply stated, site factor is the comparative cost of setting up a facility in China vs. an established norm, let's say Gulf Coast USA. The latter site factor cost is set at an index basis of 1.0. The goal is to be as competitive as possible by getting the site factor as low as possible when setting up a facility in China. The conflict can best be portrayed as a spectrum as shown in Figure 5.4.

I introduced in chapter two the "wet behind the ears" engineer who takes his first trip to China and, religiously applying U.S. standards, policies, processes and even equipment brands, comes back with an almost even 1-to-1 site factor—in effect, a plan to build a garden of Eden in a swamp. At the other end of the spectrum are hearsay and anecdotal claims, typically voiced by local Chinese or even other Asian management team members or advisors who say that savings of 60% or more are possible

—but without the proof to back it up. It is important to quickly draw the demarcation line for these two extremes and focus on the real battle in the middle. Unfortunately, even among responsible Western companies I see the temptation to play in the far left because of the severe cost pressures they are facing.

FIGURE 5.4: THE SITE FACTOR SPECTRUM[1]

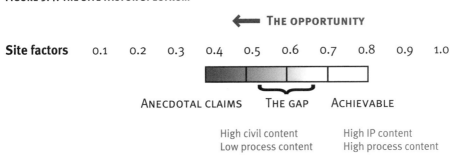

With proactive but still prudent initiatives, a China site factor can generally reach the 0.7 level by addressing such issues as localizing equipment sourcing, modifying the process to be more manual, realizing lower construction costs and aggressively negotiating on land use rights. (Recognize, though, as noted in chapter two, that your manufacturing process type—heavy or light industry, high tech or low tech—will further define the demarcation points on your site factor spectrum.) Many of the leading engineering and construction companies, using acceptable international design and build practices, will attest to your ability to reach the 0.7 level. Ordinarily, setting aside the occasional naïve engineering and design analysis done by a neophyte to China, achieving this level of reduction will not overly challenge a company's core values and operating principles. The real challenge, and source of stress for management, is pushing down deeper into cost reduction, moving further left on the spectrum. Going into this level of cost reduction, by definition, will introduce some uncomfortable elements to the process, such as:

- Working with new, local and unproven—yet lower-cost—equipment manufacturers
- Partnering with local organizations or individuals
- Compromising on safety standards in construction and operational phases
- Acquiring local, low-cost assets of questionable quality

[1] Thanks goes to Peter Ellefson of DuPont for his thoughts on this topic.

These elements can lead to tangible compromises such as more production break-downs, higher maintenance costs, less operational safety, etc. If you will be setting up a local facility, whether organically or via a venture or acquisition, you will be challenged by this site factor debate. If you're not, you are either very lucky or you are missing tangible opportunities to lower your costs. To arrive at an optimum site factor, I recommend that you take the following key steps:

1. Validate at what site factor level you need to be in order to compete, not only in today's market landscape, but in the future market environment. This will set the target you need to reach.

2. Bring in the right departmental staff early in the process—generally at the beginning. Too often, the design and engineering team is brought in with full force only after the commercial deal is done. Their role then becomes to fix the problems instead of optimizing the approach.

3. Implement an objective and aggressive due diligence process utilizing experienced third parties when appropriate (remember the six Ds). Another useful axiom to keep in mind is when you hear "*mei wenti*" (Chinese for "no problem"), it usually means "*da wenti*" ("big problem").

4. Achieve consensus on the rules of the game, including where are you willing to compromise. Getting top management involved here is critical as a major safety or quality problem down the road could severely hurt the company's reputation.

There are countless examples of shoddy work and failed promises in China, so you have to be very suspicious about what is claimed. Many facilities have had to be rebuilt and foreign design and construction companies called in on an emergency basis to fix the problems at a much higher cost in the end. Nevertheless, the need to be competitive is a daunting and unrelenting challenge for Western companies in China. You will need to work very hard to find the right balance between low cost and quality operation to suit your firm's needs. Making full use of China's resources is necessary while being vigilant on the process as well as the players involved.

TRANSFERRING SOFT ASSETS

For some companies, the assets they will need to transfer are primarily soft or intangible in nature, such as brand, marketing and merchandizing skills, technologies, selling model, etc. This is especially true for consumer product companies—even though they may manufacture or source product in China—as well as service providers, but it also can be a key element for manufacturing firms that need to change market practices and promote technology adoption. Typically, these soft assets are housed in people, reputation or well-established merchandising or brand development approaches. Just like hard manufacturing assets, these competencies need to be effectively localized in China by transplanting the process skills, techniques and programs that work for you in other markets. The issues you will face are essentially the same as in the manufacturing environment, including intellectual property risks.

Let's review several examples of soft asset transfer in different types of industries. One such case is a leading international health care product supplier that had strong positions in many countries and an internationally recognized brand portfolio (for throat care, eye care, pain relief, etc.) The company's intention in China, at least for the foreseeable future, was to build its brand and market channels, supplying product from its other Asian facility. It had no near-term plan to manufacture anything locally. The core competencies it needed to transfer were brand power and a delivery system to market. The company's brands were known in China but needed much cultivation. To accomplish this, it needed to China-fy its experience and skills in brand development and merchandizing while setting up an effective sales and distribution capability to reach the modern retail trade channel (vs. the traditional, low-end wholesaler channel) as well as the hospital sector. The actual assets to be transferred were a small group of key people from the U.K. who could implement the market development. This core group needed to be supported by a strong local team with experience in the market and access to the right channels.

A key goal in the transfer of soft assets is often to change how the local China market works and how consumers think, essentially encouraging the market to more quickly evolve into your market space in terms of quality, price, process or technology orientation. To succeed means you need to change or convert typically engrained habits, relationships or cost-benefit perspectives. As an example, we see this condition in many construction sectors in China where specification and purchasing processes are very entrenched, and often fed by gray market tactics. To effect change, you need to influence multiple points in the value chain.

FIGURE 5.5: INFLUENCING THE VALUE CHAIN—CHINA CONSTRUCTION MARKET CASE

	Local and national government	Architects, design institutes	Contractors and installers	Owners and developers
Role in specification process	• Sets codes / regulates market • Influences construction practices	• Strong influence on construction techniques and materials • May recommend or "spec in" supplier	• Often selects supplier or makes deal • Could change spec	• Establishes budget • Varying degree of specification influence on project
Client goals	• Lobby to adopt your approach • Educate on international practices	• Educate on its process/ approach • May need to pay a "fee" • Exert *guanxi*	• Educate on its process/ approach • Provide commercial incentive	• Sell image of quality, reliability • Influence process selection and players involved

In a recent case along these lines, I observed a Canadian company that invested in a venture in China in concrete reinforcement products. These products were used to strengthen concrete in a variety of applications from residential and commercial buildings to road and other infrastructure applications. They transferred the necessary manufacturing process and some key equipment, but stopped short in terms of the softer skills of market development. No Canadian employee was involved in the operation. The result was a struggling and marketing-deficient operation that had a limited effect in persuading the market to use its reinforcement technology vs. the very engrained, conventional approach used in China at the time. The sales team did not have the muscle or know-how to change very deep-rooted market behavior at key points in the value chain (as illustrated in Figure 5.5). They needed to touch on all players to implement change. An interesting reflection of this lack of soft skill transfer became evident when I visited their facility and observed that the Canadian flag was flying upside down.

Consumer products companies have a similar need to explore carefully their value chains to discern key influence points that positively impact the market. Establishing brand awareness and brand power requires skills and investment similar to any other market. But it's necessary to understand the nature and location of the specific barriers to the adoption of your product or solution in order to know where to invest marketing dollars to generate the best payback. For instance, a client of ours was a world leader in a type of lens for eyewear. The China market demand for this lens was still in an embryonic stage. There were some similar products in the market—although most were of poor quality—as well as some of its own. The value proposition for our client's offering was not well understood and the key players in the sales process were poorly equipped and trained to market the product.

FIGURE 5.6: IDENTIFYING MARKET BARRIERS IN THE VALUE CHAIN—CHINA OPTICAL INDUSTRY CASE

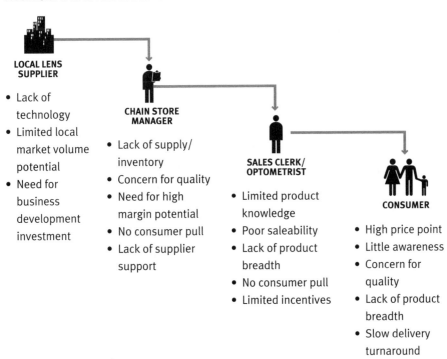

LOCAL LENS SUPPLIER

• Lack of technology
• Limited local market volume potential
• Need for business development investment

CHAIN STORE MANAGER

• Lack of supply/ inventory
• Concern for quality
• Need for high margin potential
• No consumer pull
• Lack of supplier support

SALES CLERK/ OPTOMETRIST

• Limited product knowledge
• Poor saleability
• Lack of product breadth
• No consumer pull
• Limited incentives

CONSUMER

• High price point
• Little awareness
• Concern for quality
• Lack of product breadth
• Slow delivery turnaround

Our client's key challenge was to change market perception in a cost-effective way while educating all levels of the value chain about the benefits of its eyewear. In exploring how best to do this, it needed a deep understanding of market barriers at each level of the value chain (as illustrated in Figure 5.6). This knowledge directly fed its strategy in terms of where and how to invest in marketing, and what promotional assets were needed to transfer to China. It enabled the company to maximize its promotional spend by focusing on the most important points to influence change. It identified the specific programs in its business development arsenal that best applied to China's state of evolution and transferred these competencies in the early stages of market development. Many firms, as this optical supplier did, find it effective to also transfer their existing relationship with an advertising or public relations firm in the West to China, assuming this company has resources there. In this way, they can more efficiently transfer programs, culture and company DNA via a firm that already knows them and their industry well.

INTELLECTUAL PROPERTY EXPOSURE

The second Treasure of the Chinese Studio is the brush, a very special writing implement made in a singular manner. In fact, the comparison of the brush to a company's intellectual property (IP) is very appropriate, as many ancient brush makers had their own unique techniques and closely guarded the secrets of their materials and processes—their own IP, if you will. The best calligraphers had their favorite brushes: large ones with sable or wolf hair for major pieces and smaller ones finely tipped with rabbit hair for delicate work. The IP of the brush was a signature of the artist's work.

Like a good brush, a company's IP determines the uniqueness of its business and value proposition as well as its differentiation from competition. Lose the brush and you have no calligraphy; lose the IP and you have no business. Therefore, IP protection must be an integral part of planning the transfer of your key assets to China—if you lose your IP in the transfer, you might as well have not come in the first place.

For our purposes, intellectual property covers a broad array of elements hard and soft, tangible and intangible. These IP assets are not just limited to those that are legally protected, such as patents, trademarks, copyrights, etc. It is important to look beyond these legal areas to include any assets you possess that have some tangible value in the marketplace and give you power with customers—in other words, if you forfeited these assets to a competitor, then you would lose your advantage in the marketplace and all the benefits that go with it, like making decent margins. It is also important to factor in the global consequences of this IP loss should it get re-exported back to your home markets. Not only could you risk your China investment, but you could also damage your core business in established markets. This latter risk may far outweigh the downsides identified on the China end.

The readiness process to determine your level of exposure in IP involves four basic steps:
1. Identify what IP assets need to be transferred
2. Determine the nature and level of risk on these assets
3. Find ways to strengthen the walls of protection around your IP
4. Measure the net risk-reward of the IP transfer to China on a global basis

Let's take a look at each of these steps in more detail.

IDENTIFY WHAT IP ASSETS NEED TO BE TRANSFERRED
There are many elements of IP that could need protection depending on your business profile. Your first step is to inventory this list to determine their relevance and importance to your China strategy. This checklist provides a starting point to an in-depth internal discussion among your management team and the ingredients to your IP risk assessment. One of our clients is a technology solutions provider offering a broad range of embedded software, development tools, hardware and consulting services for engine control and management (EMS). These solutions enable engine makers to comply with emissions standards, increase fuel efficiency and improve overall performance.

Our client had developed proprietary software over the past seven years through organic development and acquisition. As it explored opportunities in China, it found a deep thirst for its technology and solutions capabilities as local engine makers were scrambling to meet increasingly stringent Chinese environmental regulations. Market demand was evident and, due to the technology gap with China and the limited options available to local engine producers, our client was being sought out for its solutions. Its China business proposition was predicated on its providing this core technology as part of the customer offer. Other assets that were considered to hold both IP and market value to the company were either irrelevant to its China opportunity or more supportive to its system solution. Exposure in these areas would have marginal direct consequences—but protecting its core technology was imperative.

Figure 5.7 shows the headlines of its IP inventory exercise. Your inventory may contain different elements but the approach will be the same.

FIGURE 5.7: IP INVENTORY CHECKLIST—EMS SOLUTIONS PROVIDER EXAMPLE

Asset*	Description	Relevance to China strategy
Brand	Not an issue	None
Formulation	Not an issue	None
Process	Solutions capabilities and tools around basic technologies provides high value	Supportive to delivering technology
Technology	Core of company's business success, essence of their competitive differentiation	Essential to put in play to gain business
Experience, trade secrets	Breadth of experience in applying technology can short-cut development process	Supportive to delivering technology
Reputation	Relative newcomer but growing awareness/expertise in it's technology space	Failure in China would have limited backlash
Customer relationships	Strong position among industry leaders, provides high credibility	Not directly relevant to China opportunity
Territorial rights	Had global rights to technology offering	None

*THERE CAN BE SOME OVERLAP OF THESE ASSETS. MOST COMPETENCIES CAN BE GROUPED UNDER ONE OF THESE CATEGORIES.

DETERMINE THE NATURE AND LEVEL OF RISK ON ASSETS

Once you have completed this inventory and identified those IP elements that will most matter to your China initiative, you are ready to assess your ability to build proper defenses around them. These defenses will be based on each IP risk element relative to the importance of the IP asset to your company's business. Calculating this equation, of course, is the hard part. Relying on the continuing strengthening of Chinese IP law is a slippery slope indeed and will not provide much assurance in today's environment. There is a saying among old China hands: "In China, there is no such thing as law, just good advice." While this is a slight exaggeration, it accurately reflects the frustration you will face dealing with China's legal and business systems. More recently, and thanks to WTO, China has showed progress in strengthening many laws, notably intellectual property rights, but as I pointed out in chapter two, court interpretation and rulings have been inconsistent due to the following factors:

- Rulings are based on individual judges, not historical precedent, leading to a wide range of legal interpretations.
- China's legal system is still based on rule by man rather than rule by law. Patronage and power are often more important than who is right.
- IP theft has been shown to be a very profitable business in China—the risk-reward ratio is very attractive for would-be offenders.

We use a basic IP risk matrix to highlight the assets that are most vulnerable and need protection (see Figure 5.8). For our EMS solutions provider, its core software technology was, in effect, the company's crown jewels. To lose it to competition would severely compromise its future business prospects and company valuation. As a result, its technology asset—specifically, the software code—was positioned very high on the Y axis of the IP risk matrix. Additionally, the transfer of technology to China, while necessary to its success, would require some level of disclosure or technology sharing so that the customer could tailor the solution to its engine design as well as create interfaces with other electronic systems in and around the engine. Our client's customer relationships, by necessity, had to be quite intimate. Indeed, a fluid and transparent customer relationship was a hallmark of its past success. To enter into such a relationship with a local Chinese customer safeguarded only with a legal contract is naïve at best, and suicidal at worst.

Fortunately, our client was able to build a solid wall of defense to protect its technology in the transfer by layering software codes, which provided an insulated foundation on which other application software could be built. As a result, its defensibility was considered reasonably sound (on the mid- to far right of the X axis) so it could proceed with caution. The company was not immune from risk, but the strong physical defense, wrapped in appropriate legal documentation, resulted in a favorable risk-reward scenario. Exposing some of its valuable supporting processes, such as software tools and experience, while damaging, would not lead to a fatal wound and was considered acceptable risk by management in light of the potential rewards, as long as the core technology was safe.

FIGURE 5.8: PLOTTING YOUR IP RISK

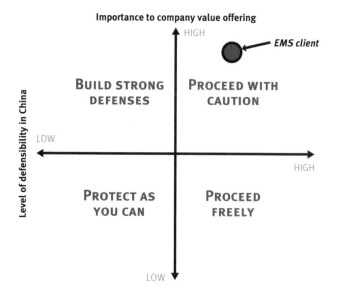

STRENGTHEN THE WALLS OF PROTECTION AROUND YOUR IP

Our EMS solutions provider built a strong technical wall around its core IP asset without too much trouble. For many, this task will not be so easy and will require a multi-pronged effort. Listed below are common sense, as well as innovative, tactics to consider to fortify your protective walls:

- Register all patents and trademarks in China. While enforcement is spotty, you don't have a prayer without registration. It is surprising how many companies miss this.

- Have relevant parties sign strong nondisclosure and non-compete agreements. Though not necessarily an effective protection, they do create some level of insulation. They also signal to the China party that this is a serious relationship and much more than a handshake agreement.

- "Black box" your processes. As our EMS solutions provider did, put your crown jewels in a vault. Another client curtained off the section of its manufacturing process where its secret recipe was applied and posted a 24-hour guard. Only select employees were allowed access to this area.

- Play the "shell game" by fragmenting your manufacturing or development process and only bringing the solution together in a protected environment. This approach will help establish multiple firewalls within your facility and in the design process.

- When a key or innovative technology is transferred, send along a guardian with the technology. An expert from the home office accompanies the technology transfer and, like a good chaperon, keeps close track of its whereabouts.
- Establish a relationship with law enforcement departments, especially at the local level. Having them as allies—or, at least, not as obstructers or worse yet, participants in the infringement—will strengthen your ability to mount a defense if needed.
- Use trusted international design and construction firms to provide manufacturing process security with local design institutes (which will also be involved in the process, as mandated by Chinese law).
- Build firewalls around process equipment vendors by not using local staff for installation.
- Develop clear internal guidelines for behavior such as a clean desk policy, no public posting of formulations, restricted keypad access, visible ID badges at all times, etc.
- Conduct a careful screening of key personnel who will touch the IP asset in some form. It is possible to run background checks on key employees in China these days—HR investigative firms in China are doing a booming business.
- Promote vigilant governance. Don't merely institute policies and procedures but proactively audit and enforce them. Many multinationals have good policy manuals collecting dust on the shelf.

The form of your China business structure will also affect the thickness of your protective walls. Alliances, joint ventures and even intimate customer or distributor relationships will create cracks through which your IP can leak. I will talk more about alliances and their impact on these issues later in the chapter.

MEASURE YOUR RISK-REWARD

Lastly, with your IP risks more clearly marked out as well as potential strategies and tactics to protect them, you can make a judgment on the risk-reward of your China initiative. Our EMS solutions provider came to a definitive evaluation because it had a tangible solution to lower its IP risk. If it were unable to black box its software code, it is unlikely it would have ventured to China, despite the tantalizing opportunity and stakeholder pressure to do so. At minimum, it certainly would have affected the way the company went to China and even the customers with whom it chose to work.

For many, the results of the risk-reward assessment will fall precariously on a fence—or, considering the severity of the issue, a sword. In these cases, it is important that you have evaluated objectively and robustly all upsides and downsides, as well as the tactics to improve your fortifications. Here again, we see the importance of fully evaluating the intensity of your Motivation dimension to go to China. Without a clear view of the reward side of the equation, assessing the risk side will have empty meaning. Some companies will have no choice but to take a chance with their IP because the risk of not responding is even greater. These are profound decision points for management so the analysis must be rigorous and objective.

For many who find themselves on the fence, some level of compromise is likely necessary, such as scaling back your investment, limiting your scope of operation (and IP transfer), being selective about which customers to work with (like our EMS friends), restricting your use of alliances though attractive prospects may exist, etc.

Because technology or know-how is so often the key factor to the success of a Western firm's business proposition in China, IP risk is one of the most frequent and difficult challenges being addressed today. There is no substitute for a very careful and rigorous assessment of all sides of this issue.

BUSINESS STRUCTURE

The last two indicators of a company's operational readiness—business structure and alliances—are related to each other and tightly intertwined with the transfer of your core competencies, including the protection of your IP. However, both have enough distinction to warrant individual commentary. In our Four Treasures analogy, the ink block represents business structures and the ink stone alliances. Like paper, the development of ink happened over time and with much trial and error. The best ink was made of the soot that resulted after burning vegetable matter or pine wood, mixed with glue made from animal horns or hides. For better storage and preservation, the ink was dried in a cake and was reconstituted by putting a small amount of water on a stone and rubbing the ink block to form a thick, black liquid.

One telltale factor regarding China investments common in both brilliant successes and abject failures is the choice of operational structure in which to transfer business functions to China. As ink is the visible representation of the calligrapher's art, your business structure in China is the visible representation of your strategy. A poor quality ink will not interact well with the paper and will fade over time; a poor quality structure in China will have much the same results, rendering ineffective the operational assets you so painstakingly transferred. In fact, we have found that companies willing to build and work in different and potentially radically new business structures often fared better than those taking the conventional or familiar route.

FIGURE 5.9: UTILIZED FDI INTO CHINA BY FORM

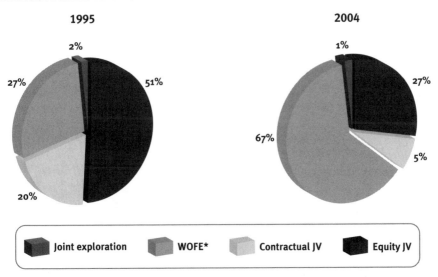

SOURCE: MOFCOM FDI STATISTICS   *WHOLLY OWNED FOREIGN ENTERPRISE

As in the 1990s and before, there are still sectors and business situations in China that will limit your options, such as those in industries where the Chinese government requires that you have a local partner, though these instances will continue to decline. In most cases, establishing a local partnership will be a matter of choice, not mandate. While for many companies the choice of business structure may be obvious on the surface, you will do well to step back and carefully examine all options to optimize opportunity and minimize risk. Simply replicating your current and familiar Western structure in China may not be ideal. As China's markets become more complex, competition intensifies and cost pressures mount, you will need to find new ways to conduct business to stay ahead of the pack. I encourage you to be open to new and even novel structures as you consider how best to transfer your assets to China. This section will provide some considerations for your management team and hopefully will also stimulate some creative thinking and discussion.

Since the gold rush years of the 1990s, when a 50-50 joint venture was the popular—and generally necessary—structural option to set up in China, there has been a significant shift to wholly owned operations (Figure 5.9). The force of this pendulum swing has been strong due to the frequent horror stories of partnerships in the 1990s. Many executives are still aimlessly wandering the halls back at corporate, mumbling under their breath about their bad venture experiences in China. Their pain is understandable but it should not get in the way of objective and openminded thinking in today's more developed and flexible environment.

FIGURE 5.10: FOREIGN INVESTMENT FORMS IN CHINA

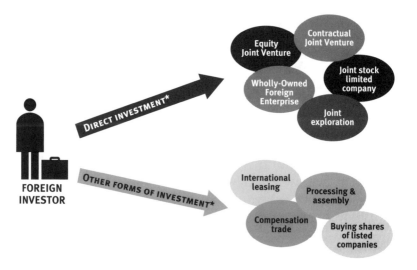

* THE SCOPE IS DEFINED BY THE CHINESE GOVERNMENT

There are more available forms of investment to consider vs. a joint venture or going it alone. Figure 5.10 highlights the main direct and indirect investment approaches. The many pros and cons of each must be considered in light of your strategic objectives and the relative importance of the driving factors behind your investment (see Figure 5.11).

Among these, control is often at the top of the list. Of course, it is almost always good to have control but the price may be steep in terms of higher investment level, time needed to get up and running, lack of local *guanxi*, inability to access certain markets, etc. Generally, it is very important to control key functions such as general management, quality, technology and finances. Conversely, sales and logistics tend to be less important to control directly and can even be more effective if not controlled. Many companies today are also considering not fully controlling (i.e. owning) manufacturing where their cost model is not as competitive as a local Chinese firm. As long as they can get quality product and protect their IP, contract manufacturing is a very viable approach. Certainly, there might be legal issues that limit your options (for instance, you may be in a restricted industry such as oil and gas production or vehicle assembly and may be required to have a partner), but legal restrictions are rare today. Investment size can be a restriction due to the availability and cost of capital, limits on your balance sheet, wary stakeholders, etc. Bringing another player into the mix can effectively dilute your investment ante, spread risk and facilitate implementation. Flexibility, especially in a dynamic market like China, can also be an important benefit to retain. Ransoming longer-term flexibility to gain short-term benefit through a partner or distributor arrangement is a common mistake. Often, the value of the partner's contribution rapidly depreciates and you end up saddled with dead weight. Market access, which could be limited by legal restrictions or commercial hurdles, can be facilitated through your structure, notably by working with a local entity that has access to the necessary channels and *guanxi*. Speed to market, an important benefit if you are responding to a competitor already present in the region, can motivate you to ally with a partner. For example, utilizing a partner with sales and distribution channels in place may greatly speed your time to market. And, as I have already discussed, IP protection can figure significantly in your structural approach, frequently raising red flags about alliances and pushing you to pursue a wholly owned structure even if there are some other negative aspects to it.

To see an interesting example of choosing an appropriate business structure, let's go back to our home improvement products company from chapter four, which had been sourcing successfully from China for more than ten years but was now feeling pressure from key customers such as Home Depot and Lowes to direct source from China to further squeeze costs. Its initial inclination was to invest in a local factory via an equity stake in its largest supplier. Deeper analysis of this option shed a significant amount of doubt on the deal's economic and operational viability. At this point, management began to look more creatively at their options. As they carefully and objectively reviewed the key driving factors compelling them to do something more in China (revisiting their Motivation dimension) they not only came up with new alternatives but tied their China plan more closely to their global strategic direction. All options and tactics considered were measured against their impact on, and contribution to, this strategic intent. They were able to focus their energy and resources on the value their company brought to the table, which was not in manufacturing. The real reason for the proposed equity investment in the supplier was to better control the key supply source while presenting a direct facing to their main customers. It was not about having a stake in a manufacturing facility.

FIGURE 5.11: KEY DRIVING FACTORS IN CHOOSING AN INVESTMENT FORM

The price for these benefits was far too high in the minority equity investment scenario and, in the end, management felt that the target partner could never be controlled anyway—so they looked for a better approach. After stepping back and taking a detailed and objective look at the market and supplier situations, they uncovered some fascinating dynamics. They discovered that their three key suppliers were, in effect, a cartel, all owned by the same Taiwanese family, specifically an elder sister, and two brothers. The company's revised objective became to manipulate this cartel to better control its supply structure through careful management of its sourcing portfolio, not through direct investment. Management realized it was less disruptive, given the rules of the cartel, to continue working with all three suppliers rather than only one, but to focus certain product line and manufacturing competencies on individual suppliers. By further probing the stakeholders at these companies, they found a strong compatibility with one of them—interestingly, not their original target. In order to achieve the direct facing for their customers, they established a rather novel strategic sourcing relationship with this supplier—which had, ironically, declined interest in an equity injection by our client a year before. The lesson here was that our client had initially been too narrow in thinking about the structure of its approach to China, not focusing on what it was trying to achieve. This parochial attitude turned off its supplier, which had sensitive issues relating to company ownership not unlike many Chinese family-owned companies. Once this ownership condition was removed, the door was open to achieve a win-win arrangement.

As a component of this strategic sourcing partnership, the China-based supplier dedicated a facility to produce only our client's products, which enabled the direct facing to customers who could freely visit the facility and see signage with our client's name. Further, the supplier initiated joint product development and even exploration of the local China market for our client's products made in the West. The main stakeholder of this company was the elder sister who had strong, almost matriarchal influence and a stabilizing effect on the two brothers. This structure took some delicate supplier management (we'll look at this issue more closely in chapter six) but in the end achieved 90% of the client's objectives without any direct investment. It also positioned the client relationally with the supplier that best fit its company DNA and opened the door for future equity investment if market or internal company dynamics should change.

As you move away from conventional or familiar structures, your abilities and experience to negotiate and execute the arrangement could be severely stretched. You need to reflect on your capabilities and the outside resources needed to support your efforts. To address this new structure effectively in China, our home improvement client needed to change its management approach from vendor-based to partner-oriented, not an easy task when its purchasing management was well schooled in traditional supplier management—i.e., pummeling its suppliers to get better prices and service. The company needed to be prepared to change some very ingrained practices and ways of viewing its business.

Although today anyone can purchase pre-made ink for calligraphy, the true artists make their own ink and then only enough for use on a particular project. Each project is unique, so the consistency and amount of ink needs to be customized. So, too, should your business structure follow your China strategy. Avoid the pre-made structures that look easy or are even shoved down your throat and choose instead to do a little extra work to make your structure fit your particular needs.

ALLIANCES

The last Treasure in our Studio, the ink stone, is considered by many experts to be the most important of the four but often the least understood. It is fitting to asso- ciate this treasure with China alliances, equally crucial to your success in China and yet quite often misunderstood. Thomas Jefferson said, "Peace, commerce and honest friendship with all nations—entangling alliances with none." Apparently, Mr. Jefferson had not done any business in China! No matter what your structure in China, you will face the need to work with partners on some level. For many multinational compa- nies burned in the 1990s by poor joint ventures, there is often a residue of manage- ment back at corporate (even on the board) so traumatized by their China experience that any proposal smacking of a partnership sent upstairs is quickly kicked back down. While the lessons of past partnership problems should be heeded, it is impossible to avoid some level of partnering in China, even in a wholly owned business structure.

Let us return to our ink stone. Quarried of special stone and carved into works of art in their own right, the quality of the ink stone and the shape of the surface, which was concave to serve as a well, were crucial to making good ink. Too rough a stone and the ink block would be wasted; too smooth and there would be no grip on it. Make the stone too shallow and the ink would dry up quickly. So, too, alliances along your China value chain "make good ink" by enabling an effective business structure.

Fundamentally, alliances allow you to do or obtain something in a more efficacious manner than by your own means. The flipside is that you have to give up something to get these benefits, such as control, flexibility, increased IP risk, management time, even profits. The form in which companies partner in China has diversified significantly since the 1990s and can take on a variety of structural types. Some of these alliance partners may make strange bedfellows to you, such as local government officials, the

Public Security Bureau (what the police are called in China), your customer or supplier, a distributor or even another competitor.

Today, a variety of means are used to structure an alliance or cooperation. A quick review of these options is below:

- **Joint ownership relationships** such as equity joint venture (EJV), contract joint venture (CJV), joint stock company, etc.
- **Contractual agreements** for sales, distribution, manufacturing, joint development, licensing, etc.
- **Cooperative relationships** on an informal but proactive basis, e.g. raw material supply agreements, sourcing relationships, joint marketing and promotion, sharing of facilities, etc.

FIGURE 5.12: VENTURE VS. WHOLLY OWNED STRUCTURE

JV (Equity JV, Contractual JV)	WOFE
PROS	**PROS**
• Partner resources facilitate entry and speed to the market • May benefit from connections (*guanxi*) • Access to a restricted sector • Spread risk/limit investment level	• Complete control of operation • Greater protection of IP • Flexibility of operations • Simpler establishment procedures and easier termination
CONS	**CONS**
• Local partner's statutory veto power over some major issues even as a minority shareholder • Alliance negotiation process could be lengthy and incomplete • Tendency for interests of parties to diverge • Possible leakage of technical know-how • May need to take over some "unwanted" assets including redundant labor (sometimes these are hidden)	• Takes time and effort to get local staff in place • Takes time to build necessary connections (*guanxi*) • Off limits to some "restricted" sectors and IPO opportunity in the near future under current policy • Subject to less cooperation by local authorities in some cases

In order to better identify where and with whom an alliance could support your China strategy, our consultants use an Asset Ownership Profile as a starting point (Figure 5.13). Often, a company's initial tendency is to want to own everything—certainly the modus operandi for many firms after the joint venture debacle of the last decade. However, after careful analysis of the assets you intend to localize and your need to own them vs. partnering or subcontracting for them—a different solution often materializes. If you don't bring particular value to an asset, whether or not you own and operate this asset in your home market, then why invest to own it in China?

Companies have often found that they may even burden the local operation by ownership. This can be true in more conventional manufacturing. It is easy to suffocate a local operation by applying international cost structures and approaches. If you do not need to own it to bring value to the production process or to achieve operational control, then contracting out for production may be a better way.

Our home improvement company discovered this fact and it freed them from making a significant cash investment in a facility to which they provided little added value. This has typically been the case with distribution assets. The cost to replicate an effective distribution structure in China, vs. what local counterparts can do, is high for many Western firms. These local firms work on thin margins and very lean overheads, often just eking out a living. Focusing your energies on marketing and pulling sales through is frequently a better use of resources than building a logistics capability.

FIGURE 5.13: SAMPLE ASSET CONTROL PROFILE

Asset or competence	Need to own it?	Need local partner?	Can outsource?
Production	No	May be most efficient	Consider
Brand	Absolutely	Supplemental brands	No
Distribution/ logistics	No	Consider	Preferred
Sales force	No	If effective	Unlikely
Market knowledge	Ultimately	Could be very helpful	No
Customer/channel access	Major barriers exist	Probably	Unlikely
Guanxi	Need some help	Helpful in short term	Maybe through relationships
Technology	Absolutely	IP concern	Not feasible

As you consider alliances, assess your experience with the intricacies of developing partner relationships. Are you open to various types of relationships at multiple points in the value chain? Do you have direct experience elsewhere in forming a strategic partnership with another organization where the lessons can be applied to China? Some of the more successful firms in China have been creative in their approach, even to the point of venturing with competition where the business case was compelling. Joint ventures with competition, local government, customers, suppliers or contract manufacturers, etc., are all creative ways to potentially maximize penetration and minimize risk.

Let's consider a creative approach in this regard. PPG, a leader in the fiberglass market, exploited its established relationship with Nanya in Taiwan to set up a supplier-customer venture in China to produce fiberglass. The facility was established in Kunshan, west of Shanghai, as part of Nanya's larger facility to produce printed circuit boards (PCB), which consumed the fiberglass. Production went right from the end of the fiberglass line into the next phase of PCB production. Nanya became a captive customer that accounted for a significant portion of the fiberglass plant's production. PPG's leverage with the local Chinese government was significantly enhanced because it came in as part of a much larger facility investment—plus it could tap into Nanya's deep China connections and *guanxi*. This foothold then allowed PPG to explore additional market opportunities with a stable base load of business. PPG did a couple of things right: First, it looked outside of China at relationships that could be imported to support the China initiative. Second, it used a creative structural approach in the joint venture that yielded a strong partner and captive customer. This approach facilitated its China strategy while diluting the risk. This concept of working with a partner upstream or downstream of your business can be very effective in improving your risk-reward equation.

In another case, a small division of a mid-sized U.S. industrial conglomerate making electrical products and materials was looking to grow its business in China from a zero base. Its main competitor was another U.S. firm with a dominant global market position that included China, where the key applications for these products were just entering a high-growth phase. To build a position from scratch was too impractical and risky for this small firm. In its effort to look for other ways into the market, it approached the leading distributor of its global competitor, showing a bit of hubris in the process. The company, to its delight, discovered that this distributor was increasingly discontent with its relationship with the market leader, believing that eventually it would be cut out and the principal would go direct. As a result, the distributor was very open to a relationship and even proposed a more strategic manufacturing cooperation that had the potential to escalate our client's position in the China market. Our client did not settle for the traditional find-a-distributor route or, worse yet, give up in light of the seemingly daunting task of building a business in China with few available resources. Knowing well their limitations and that they needed help to catch up with the big guy on the block, management was proactive and openminded enough to ask, "What if...?" Their boldness enabled them to uncover a rather fortuitous alliance opportunity and to capitalize on it.

A company should have a good and honest self-appraisal in this area, especially smaller firms with less organizational depth. Said one executive of a mid-sized U.S. firm, "We became successful in the U.S. because we learned how to work with other companies; our success in China was just a matter of finding the right company with whom we could just be ourselves." The creative tension provided by working proactively with partners all along your value chain will return much more than the investment of time, effort and friction required. I will talk more about how to manage these relationships in the next chapter.

CHAPTER SUMMARY

This chapter introduced the first of the three key elements that will characterize your Organizational Preparedness for China. **Operational Preparedness** is measured by your ability to transfer what you do well in your home territory to China in an efficient way, under a viable structure while exploiting local relationships in and around your value chain. This transfer has to be done in a protected way so that you do not unduly expose your company's core competencies or IP in the process. I considered four key indicators of operational preparedness and likened them to the main elements of the Four Treasures of the Chinese Studio: paper, the brush, the ink block and ink stone. Like the Four Treasures, each of the indicators of operational preparedness is important in its own right as well as inextricably linked to the others. The right combination of these indicators is necessary to successfully establish an operation in China.

The first major indicator I reviewed is the ability to **transfer or replicate what you do well in your home market** to China—the paper in our Four Treasures metaphor. This transfer is the foundation of your operational preparedness and its successful completion will directly determine the success of your China initiative. In reviewing this transfer, we considered several important factors that need careful attention.

- The stability of your process—its robustness, maturity and clear documentation
- The flexibility of your process to adapt to China's environment to fully exploit low-cost resources while producing high-quality goods
- The supportability of your process whereby the right mix of resources are available locally, such as skilled labor, raw materials, equipment, etc.

If you are transferring manufacturing resources, you will likely become involved in the site factor debate, a complicated evaluation you will likely need to do to find the right balance between low cost and viable operation. Finding a workable yet acceptable compromise in this debate is significantly challenging Western companies of all sizes and types.

Companies that transfer soft assets such as brand, marketing competence and services will be similarly challenged to transplant their abilities effectively. For non-manufacturing firms, transfer of these more intangible assets comprises the essence of their China business initiative and will elicit similar challenges in achieving the right balance of cost efficiency, operational effectiveness and protection of their IP.

IP exposure is the second indicator to measure in assessing operational preparedness—the brush in our calligraphy analogy. I emphasized both the importance and complexity of evaluating the risk to your IP as well as the tactics to protect it. A four-step process was recommended to bring rigor and order to your analysis:

1. Based on a detailed articulation of your motivation to go to China, identify precisely what assets need to be localized and in what order.
2. Determine the nature and level of risk on these assets.
3. Find ways to strengthen the walls of protection around your IP.
4. Measure the net risk-reward of the transfer to China on a global basis.

The last two indicators of your operational preparedness are closely linked together, as are the ink block and the ink stone in our Four Treasures metaphor. The ink block correlates to **business structure**, the legal and visible representation of your China operation. I noted the significant shift from a strong joint venture orientation in the last decade to an equally strong bias to wholly or at least majority owned structures today. China's shift to a market economy over the last five to ten years has provided much more flexibility and choice in business structure, so that most foreign companies will have a free reign in determining the type of operation they want. I reviewed the variety of structures now available to most Western firms and highlighted the key investment driving factors you need to evaluate to determine which structure is most appropriate to your strategy, resource availability and risk aversion. I encouraged you to be open-minded about your options—not simply taking the most familiar or comfortable route. China's dynamic and relatively immature market landscape provides opportunities for unique structural approaches.

The last indicator, and Treasure in our Studio, measures your familiarity and ability to work with **alliances** both in and outside of your business value chain. As I have related in several instances, good relationships are essential to doing business in China, and touch on all levels of the organization. Working with partners, even on an informal basis, will be necessary no matter what business structure you have.

Chapter 6

Management Preparedness: Supporting your China Operation

 The secret is to work less as individuals and more as a team. As a coach, I play not my eleven best, but my best eleven.

Knute Rockne

In chapter five, I established the first of the three organizational readiness dimensions by carefully examining a company's ability to transfer the necessary operational capabilities to China in a viable structure and with proper protection of intellectual property. Fully understanding the implications of transferring these capabilities to China will prepare you to think effectively through important aspects of the "people side" of making it happen.

In the China Readiness Assessment, Managerial Preparedness to execute a China strategy means strong stakeholder support to empower enough of the right people, at the right cost and with the right approach, to set up and manage a China operation. One of our clients calls it the "four rights": the right people at the right time at the right location with the right skills.

Your company's Managerial Preparedness is characterized by four key indicators:
- **Management sponsorship**: Your senior management is solidly behind the exploration of China and will actively support the initiative, even in tough times.
- **Management depth**: There is sufficient depth in the organization to sustain a China expansion without compromising the ability to run the core business back home.
- **China experience**: The company has direct or indirect China experience and resources to facilitate the execution of the planned initiative.
- **Relationship management**: The company has experience building relationships across multiple layers of its value chain as well as with government, institutes

and regulatory bodies, all inevitably strong participants in any Chinese business environment.

FIGURE 6.1: LINGXIAO PAGODA OF TIANNING MONASTERY

Steeple = Relationship Management

Sheathing & Eaves = China Experience

Main Body = Management Depth

Base / Pillar = Management Sponsorship

To help illustrate the nature and relationship of these indicators, I will use the design and structure of a classic Chinese wooden pagoda, linking these four management preparedness indicators to four crucial elements of a pagoda (for you experts in traditional Asian architecture, I ask for latitude in drawing this analogy). To establish this association, we need to understand a bit about a pagoda's construction. Typically, wooden pagodas were built using a central pillar or base support from which the tiered roof is hung, thus creating downward pressure on the pillar and providing the pagoda increased structural stability. Sometimes this pillar will go down into an underground palace of sorts, a place to store and preserve valuable relics. This pillar relates to management sponsorship. The main body of the pagoda varies greatly depending on style of architecture. It can comprise multiple levels, rooms within each level, balconies to enable visitors to walk its circumference, spiral staircases, etc. This main body correlates to management depth. Key also to a pagoda's design is its ornamentation, as expressed by the sheathing and eaves that are its presentation to the outside world, giving it beauty, meaning and uniqueness. This feature will tie to your China experience.   Lastly, we will consider the pagoda's steeple, which is important both functionally and aesthetically. These can vary greatly in size, complexity and style and will be related to your relationship management ability.

MANAGEMENT SPONSORSHIP

In discussions with executives who established China operations in the 1990s, we discovered a deep reservoir of painful issues and memories (for which many no doubt required follow-up therapy); however, the one issue that elicited the most angst was headquarter management's lack of ongoing support for the China initiative. As we have seen, a major reason undermining Western corporations' staying power was the lack of a well-defined and substantiated motivation to be in China in the first place. This shortcoming was often the result of stakeholder frenzy, as many of the Fortune 500 clamored to capture a share of China's alleged gold. In their rush to get to China, management did not measure the true cost and stress on their organization. "We had no idea what we were getting into. We just figured we had to be here," lamented one senior executive in the building tools sector. A lack of management sponsorship can manifest itself in various forms, which offer telltale warning signs of a company's future prospects in China.

A common occurrence is that top management has not specifically signed off on the China investment. Getting approval for this type of investment sounds rather obvious, but you'd be surprised how often China initiatives are launched with only tacit approval or acknowledgement by the powers that be. "Top management" can mean different things depending on your company's structure. In some cases it is the board; sometimes the CEO, business unit manager or—in the case of privately held firms—owners. China's pervasiveness in the media and in the business community at large can easily rouse top management's initial enthusiasm about China—but you need to make sure they know what they are committing to (assuming, of course, that you know what you are committing to). Several questions posed to stakeholders can be illuminating in this regard:

- Do you realize that if we do this China initiative, I need half our engineering department for the next six months?
- Are you okay with red ink over the next three years?

- Will you commit to coming to China in the next six months?
- Do you realize our intellectual property will be at risk in this deal?
- Can you sign off on $250,000 of exploratory funds to determine if and how we should invest in China?
- If our U.S. business turns south this year, would you regret doing our China initiative now? Or, worse, would you abandon it?
- Do you realize that doing this initiative means we can't do Project XYZ this year?

These few examples provide a flavor of the issues involved. Sound and well-founded management sponsorship is the center pillar of our pagoda. Though it generally is invisible to the beholder, it holds the weight of the entire structure. In the case of our nine-story Lingxiao pagoda, the pillar is of particular importance and can hold a high degree of downward stress—a phrase that could have special meaning as you set up in China. Like the parable of the builders, one who built his house on sand, and the other on solid rock, when the storm came—and China storms will come—the house built on sand, beautiful as it was, crumbled, while the house built on rock stood firm. Without this center support structure and foundation, the China operation will surely wobble as time progresses. I am tempted to extend our pagoda metaphor a bit here, correlating the underground palace or vault where the Chinese would store ancient and valuable Buddhist relics to the place where those unfortunate senior executives went after they returned from a failed China venture.

One of our longstanding clients, a leading U.S. consumer products company, demonstrates one of the most schizophrenic stakeholder attitudes toward China I have ever encountered. Starting in the mid-1990s, the company did an almost biennial strategic review of a potential investment in China. To a person, the executive team in both Asia and the U.S. knew they had to be there, but they just could not pull the trigger. A big part of the problem was that the CEO position was a revolving door over this period and the company was under constant financial duress. Nevertheless, like clockwork every other spring, there would be a flurry of excitement at corporate: Missives would be sent to China, research conducted and capital request forms completed. Everyone would nod approval and local Asian management would gear up for launch. Then ... silence. The poor Asian business head (who outlasted all the CEOs, by the way) looked like a bride who'd been left at the altar multiple times. In the most recent cycle, it was obvious that the spring had gone out of the Asian team's legs, like a basketball team down by 30 points with two minutes to go in the game.

In retrospect, it was fortunate that management never did make the investment based on such a tentative commitment. Clearly, the first sign of dark clouds on the horizon would have triggered retrenchment. What the local business head did correctly throughout the process was tell the truth about the real costs and risks of the proposed investment; he did not try to soft-pedal it in order to get acceptance from a tepid and disorganized senior management. His Asian experience and management integrity injected enough cold reality into the deal to prevent management from prematurely supporting a program that they likely would have compromised in the very near future. Top management's intuition was correct that China was an important future market for them—but they simply were not ready to pursue it. Prematurely doing so would have been a serious mistake, resulting in a classic case of good motivation being trumped by poor management preparedness.

In another example, a client did not have such experienced management in place to provide this stopgap. In this case, corporate management pressured the divisional head to get to China. Their interest was well founded, as China offered significant opportunity in the mid- to long term. Unfortunately, the opportunity collided with the realities of the business unit's current circumstances—a small company only several years old with a very young and stretched management team. They were faced with a series of domestic opportunities and challenges and the need to get in the black as soon as possible. Despite this, the business unit head made an exploratory trip to China, as he was instructed, and started patching together a rather complicated joint venture with a leading Chinese auto group. While he caught the China fever in the process, he was constantly looking over his shoulder at his domestic business. Because his budget was tight and his management team thin, he could not sustain development of the venture. In this strained position, new acquisitions in his domestic group and increasing corporate pressure to make his quarterly numbers caused attention to the China venture to dissipate rapidly. In typical fashion, e-mails went unanswered, the project work plan was pushed back, and the Chinese venture partner's frustration grew. Eventually, the deal died quietly. While not much money was invested, the damage to the company's reputation in China could make it difficult for them to return in the future. Certainly, it closed the door on a relationship with this powerful auto group.

While attractive opportunities were evident, the company's Organizational Preparedness was not. To pull off the China initiative, corporate needed to back off near-term domestic targets and provide more direct resources to the division instead of starving them. But the realities of the business situation sucked the air out of the commitment, leaving the business unit head with little choice but to retreat from the China deal. A realistic and honest assessment of the company's management preparedness at the outset would have saved time, money, aggravation and a compromised future in China.

Another important element of stakeholder support is having a China champion at the head office, someone with passion and belief in the project but also with enough power in the company's management hierarchy to secure resources to support it, maintain appropriate attention from the home office, and defend the China-based team when stakeholders begin to waffle on the deal. I mentioned a good example of this type of champion in chapter four in the case of Emerson Electric, which dedicated its vice chairman to mentor the Asia-China program. Another good case is Roche Pharmaceutical in the 1990s as it expanded rapidly in China. Its local general manager often commented to us that the support of the vice chairman enabled him to fight a number of battles with home office staff who, even when well intentioned, knew too little about China and did not trust the local team enough to give them needed support. The head of a global leader in construction equipment unequivocally put stakeholder support as the first key organizational success factor: "Absolute corporate support from the home office is needed. One needs assurances from the home office that the plug will not be pulled prematurely."

So, before you start to pursue a China program aggressively, make sure your management support pillar is in place. A simple yet effective process to measure this is to complete the checklist in Figure 6.2. You should probe these points relentlessly with the appropriate powers that be to confirm that you have the right support behind you. Don't settle for casual acquiescence—get documentation and a commitment to the necessary resources. Stakeholders' unwillingness to open the checkbook is a harbinger of bad things to come.

FIGURE 6.2: MANAGEMENT SPONSORSHIP CHECKLIST

Sponsorship indicator	In place
Top management can articulate in detail the company's major motivations to pursue a China expansion strategy.	
Top management has formally signed off on the China initiative.	
Opportunity costs have been fully reviewed and accepted.	
"What if" scenarios have been developed with their implications on the China initiative.	
A corporate champion has been identified and has agreed to sponsor the China initiative.	
Top management (at the very least the corporate sponsor) has made (or has definite plans to make) a trip to China to see, first hand, what the company is up against.	
People and financial resources have been committed to the China program and will be sustained.	

MANAGEMENT DEPTH

Now that we have put in place a solid support pillar and base for our organizational pagoda, we can turn our attention to the materials needed to build the main body, which will serve as the usable and functional elements of the structure. These materials comprise the key management team who will implement the planning and strategy execution, and even go on to manage the China operation (with some likely changes and additions over time). As the architect of a pagoda considers how many floors and rooms to have, the type of balconies and even how the staircases will connect the floors, so you also must design a well-structured and balanced management team. This effort will often require costly materials and a good amount of time to construct. In building the team, you will no doubt borrow materials from your home organization as well as bring in some from the outside.

I attended La Lumiere High School—a small prep school in Indiana. Despite having only a little more than 100 boys in grades 9 through 12, we were nevertheless a local force in several sports. Our football team often upset much larger schools, notably at their homecoming. But we had one major problem: no depth. With only 12 to 13 skilled players for 11 positions (not considering the need for both offensive and defensive squads), if someone went down with an injury, we were in trouble.

Holes in your organization's depth chart can be a significant liability in even a well-designed strategy. Often, you will need to dedicate some of your best players, across several business functions, to the China initiative, having them frequently travel to or live in China for a period of months or even years. Because these staff members were assumedly busy and productive before the China initiative came along, there will be some opportunity costs in reallocating their attention to China that need to be fully understood. We have observed several typical mistakes made as a result of having limited available management talent to allocate to the China program.

One common mistake is to assign the wrong people to the job. Doing what you do well in your home market is probably not so easy or you wouldn't have much of a defensible competitive positioning. Transplanting human resource capabilities thousands of miles away creates an even greater challenge. Assigning the most convenient or available staff to the China project, vs. the most qualified, is a prescription for failure. Nevertheless, sending the B team into the game is a frequent fallback for companies that do not have the necessary in-house resources or the inclination to go outside to find them.

A client that manufactured telecommunications components was going to make its first trip to China following a market opportunity and competitive intelligence program we completed for them. At the last minute, and despite our recommendations that he not do so, the CEO backed out of the trip and sent two mid-level managers. As we predicted, these managers had neither the strategic vision to understand—nor the corporate political clout to communicate—the implications of China to their company, and the project stalled. Eight months later, when we were able to get the project back on track and the CEO to China, he confessed to us in the middle of the trip: "You were right, I should have come here myself eight months ago. …We wasted a lot of time, didn't we?"

Another mistake is to hire a "China guy" prematurely, a local Chinese or expatriate with China background, and rely solely on their experience and connections to lead the exploration and implementation of your plan. This experience, without industry expertise, familiarity with your company and relationships with your corporate team, can be inadequate for the task. China knowledge will certainly be helpful to your management preparedness, as I will describe later in this chapter, but too much emphasis can be placed on the China experience factor in lieu of the necessary functional skills or company knowledge to effectively transplant your competencies.

Still others may make the mistake of initially putting the A team on the job but then too quickly pulling them off and delegating responsibility to a newer and less experienced local team, an all-too-common error. Needing your key staff back in the core business in addition to their relatively high cost to the China project can be compelling motivations, but you must consider carefully the impact it will have on your emerging and potentially fragile China operation.

The task of staffing your China management team is a little bit like the job of a general manager of a professional basketball team. You are trying to field the best 12 athletes you can while working with your existing roster, potential future draft picks and limited funds, not to mention a salary cap. Some teams are endowed with a winning tradition, being in a lucrative market like New York and with plenty of money and endorsement opportunity to attract the best talent in the league. These are like major multinational companies. Their main challenge is often having a good coach to help the highly skilled players work together as a team rather than individual stars, and to deal with their strong egos. SMEs, on the other hand, tend to be more like teams in second-tier cities like Charlotte. They are typically newer franchises with less money and drawing power. They may need to rely more on teamwork rather than a host of marquee players such as the Los Angeles Lakers put together in 2003. For companies looking to build their China organization, they too need to look within and outside the company to assemble a winning team while at the same time being cognizant of their available resources. I suggest you review your needs in two steps:

1. Identify what critical management functions need to be filled from your home operations to effectively transfer the core competencies to establish the operation successfully.
2. Determine where you are going to obtain additional talent to supplement these key staff and fill the remaining slots.

Let's explore both of these points in more detail.

WHAT KEY MANAGEMENT FUNCTIONS DO YOU NEED TO FILL WITH TALENT FROM YOUR HOME OFFICE TO SUPPORT THE CHINA INITIATIVE?

An important aspect of building your China organization is transferring your company culture or DNA effectively to the China operation, notably the unique set of attributes that differentiate your company and make you successful. This transfer can be a bit tricky, as you are not trying to establish a clone of your home organization but a derivative of it. The most effective China organizations are a mix of east and west. They are able to do well in China what they do well in their home market, yet they have been effectively localized (referencing the now common term of "glocalization," globalization plus localization).

The key question that companies, particularly SMEs, need to ask themselves is: "How many people from my home office do I need ensconced in China to transfer my company's DNA and to maintain it effectively?" Allocate people to critical areas that will accomplish the transfer of your core competencies, as discussed in chapter five, to ensure that the operation runs smoothly. Often, the right people are those with experience from your home operations; however, it is important to achieve the proper balance so that you don't under support the initiative or overkill the organization with expatriates (crucially important for SMEs with typically fewer resources to spend). Review each key management function in terms of its criticalness to the China initiative, both in the start-up mode and to support ongoing operations.

One client of ours, a leading food ingredient company that rapidly expanded in China during the mid- to late 1990s, determined that three key positions needed to be filled by experienced company managers from the home office: general manager, technical development, and sales and marketing. These three staff formed the nucleus of the China team, which was then expanded through local China and Asia regional hires. The company believed that these three positions reflected its core competencies and what it needed to effectively "seed" the China organization. They also had a strong center pillar in place with the direct support and enthusiasm of the chairman. These staff members were able to leverage local resources, notably in distribution and manufacturing, to support the company's aggressive growth plan. Today, after nearly ten years on the ground, the company has localized two of these three positions. As another client stated to us, "Don't sell the wine before its time."

FIGURE 6.3: IDENTIFYING KEY FUNCTIONS TO TRANSFER TO YOUR CHINA ORGANIZATION

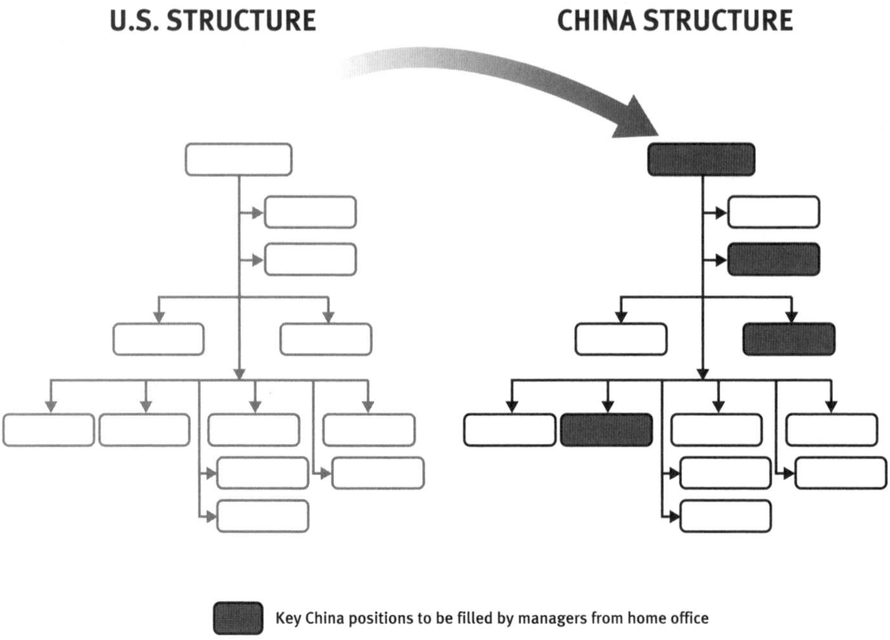

U.S. STRUCTURE   CHINA STRUCTURE

■ Key China positions to be filled by managers from home office

Another major global player, Caterpillar, believed that its ability to level the market's playing field was a key factor to its early success in China. As a result, it set up a strong lobbying capability in Beijing in tandem with its established Washington, D.C., group. One of the main aims of this activity was to push China towards WTO membership. The company assigned the head of its D.C. lobbying group to Beijing to personally direct this activity, his functional position being a critically needed competency in their early China market development.

The judicious use of expatriate management is an important factor to consider in a China expansion program. Even if you have the right people available in your home office to allocate to the project, the economics of transferring them may not be viable. The local China head of a leading design and construct firm stated well the dilemma of many companies when assessing their management preparedness: "You must have the right people who can make things happen. But you can't have too many expatriates because they are too expensive." Expatriates are still very costly in China (Shanghai and Beijing annually fill some of the top slots on lists of the most expensive places to live abroad) and, given the local talent available, might not always be necessary—which leads us to the second question.

WHERE CAN I GET THE RIGHT PEOPLE TO SUPPLEMENT MY IN-HOUSE MANAGEMENT TEAM?
Once you have identified key positions to be filled with management from your home office, another difficult challenge emerges: where to get the people to fill all the other positions (or, if you have determined that you cannot afford to fill any of the positions with expatriates, where you can find an entire team). The good news is that the pool of available resources for staffing a China organization is getting bigger. In general, there are five main sources to explore for talent to supplement your internal resources.

Ethnic Chinese: Historically, Western companies have first drawn on ethnic Chinese management talent from other Asian countries, most notably Hong Kong, Singapore and Taiwan. In some cases, these managers have worked out very well. In other cases, Western management often too readily assumed that if an executive was ethnically Chinese that they knew China. In fact, many of these managers hired in the mid-1990s didn't know China any better than Western management did, and sometimes didn't even speak the language (for example, they were from Hong Kong and spoke Cantonese, not Mandarin). While competent Chinese managers do exist from countries outside China, their experience and capabilities need to be carefully vetted.

Non-Chinese Asian managers: Non-Chinese Asian managers can be a viable choice, notably those from other emerging markets such as India and Indonesia. These managers bring like-market experience and often a very seasoned, hard-core management style, chiseled by the tough environments of their home markets. They are especially attractive if they are already a part of your organization. Sara Lee Household Products brought in an Indian from its Singapore office as managing director in the early 2000s. He was followed by the company's Indonesian general manager, who relocated from Jakarta. They both were able to bring deep internal company knowledge combined with street smarts in Asia's emerging market economies.

Locally based mainland Chinese: A group growing in numbers is experienced, locally based mainland Chinese—those who have worked for other foreign invested companies. Given the 10-15 year development period since China more fully opened its doors to the West, this pool has expanded and matured, providing a group of more seasoned middle to senior management. However, these staff members are more expensive than local Chinese without foreign company experience and can be prone to job hopping. Additionally, we have often seen situations where local talent has been promoted beyond their abilities. One can find resumes of local Chinese that have all the right words and titles on them but, when you dig deeper, their experience is rather thin.

Returnees: There is now a growing pool of returnees—Chinese nationals who have gone overseas for an education but are now coming back. Many of these returnees also have solid work experience in China to go with their Western education. And while they expect higher compensation, their costs are generally more reasonable than managers from other Asian countries, and certainly less than Western expatriates. We have found this group to be an excellent source for country manager positions with SMEs or as a first lieutenant to an expatriate, with the aim of being the successor in a few years. Educational institutes such as Thunderbird in Arizona (Garvin School of International Management), the Shanghai-based business school CEIBS, and Nanjing Hopkins in China are examples of schools with specific programs for these managers and fertile places to look, as are other major international business schools.

Localized expatriates: This last pool of management talent is just now emerging. These are Western managers who have worked for multinationals in China and wish to stay long term. They are willing to work on a localized package, such as a reduced menu of typical expatriate benefits. They often live a less expensive lifestyle, do not have kids in school, and have integrated to a degree into the local community. These managers offer a combination of deep China experience and Western business knowledge, but at a cost lower than a typical, more transient expatriate, and with the prospects of a longer tenure in China. We sometimes call these individuals "half-pats" because of their Western roots, China experience and willingness to live more locally. In fact, a number of the more progressive multinational firms are developing hybrid compensation packages for these individuals to transition the organization to a more locally staffed operation without the shock of going directly from foreign to local Chinese management.

Figure 6.4 summarizes these different resource pools and highlights their typical advantages and disadvantages. You need to carefully overlay these options with your management position assessment to find the best balance of effectiveness, availability and cost. The challenge is structuring your China management operation with the right mix of both internal and external resources, recognizing that this mix will likely transition from expatriate to local talent over time. It is important that you carefully consider each position against the anticipated needs of your organization.

FIGURE 6.4: SOURCES TO BUILD YOUR CHINA MANAGEMENT TEAM

Talent source	Advantages	Disadvantages
Internal (expatriate)	• Knows company culture • Connections to home office • Set up speed • IP protection	• High cost • Opportunity costs • Shorter China term • Lack China experience
Other ethnic Chinese (outside of Mainland China)	• Some language/culture experience • Less cost than western expatriate • May have market experience	• Limited China experience • Acceptance in China • Can still be costly
Non-Chinese Asian	• Typically lower cost than Western expatriate • Relevant emerging market and/or internal company experience	• Lack direct China experience • Cultural fit/language
FIE experienced local Chinese	• Western experience • Local market savvy • Relatively cost effective	• Retention • IP leakage • Rising costs
Chinese returnees	• China experience/ connections • Much less cost than Western expatriate • International exposure/ experience	• May have limited management experience • May want more money than they're worth
Localized expatriates	• Less cost than traditional expatriate • Deep China experience • Longer term commitment to stay in China	• More costly than local options • Limited (but growing) pool

A word of caution for companies entering into a joint venture with a local firm. It can be tempting to allow your partner to fill many management positions with its seemingly deep pool of staff who, by definition, are Chinese and familiar with the lay of the land. You need to carefully consider the staff that will fill these positions. There is no substitute for your own, direct insight into the day-to-day operation—no matter how trusted your partner may be. Even if key positions in the venture should be staffed by members of its team, you need to be involved in the personnel screening process, as if you were doing the hiring yourself (which, in effect, you are). Frequently, bringing in an outsider vs. one of your partner's staff can avoid problems of misapplied loyalties or residue of internal conflicts. Staff members who are free of a "history" are likely to be more equally loyal to both parties. In any case, get directly involved in the due diligence in all aspects of staffing for the venture.

Figure 6.5 suggests a simple audit template to help you sort these tasks out and plan your human resource needs.

FIGURE 6.5: SAMPLE CHINA MANAGEMENT AUDIT

Function	Phase of China strategy		Notes
	Startup	**Operations**	
General manager	Expatriate	Local	Hire replacement at startup as second lieutenant, taking over in two-three years
Finance	Non-China Chinese	Same	Support with frequent trips by corporate CFO
Manufacturing	Local Chinese hired from competition	Same	Support with frequent trips by corporate Ops director
Technology	Non-China Chinese	Local	Support with frequent trips by corporate technical staff
Sales / marketing	Expatriate	Local	Hire second lieutenant at startup to take over in two-three years
HR	Local with MNC experience	Same	Local hire understands China HR practices
Distribution/ logistics	Local with MNC experience	Same	

As with any NBA team over the course of the season, you will no doubt contend with injuries, poor performance and recalcitrant players. You'll need some good bench strength, not to mention a wise coach on the floor. Your success will depend directly on the overall talent on your roster, the ability to fill key skill positions with the right people, adept management and solid execution of the game plan.

CHINA EXPERIENCE

We have completed the main structural elements of our organizational pagoda by putting in place the pillar of management sponsorship and the supporting structure of the management team. We are now ready to add the aesthetic features that make it complete and worthy of admiration. These include layered eaves, gold plating, statues and decorative carvings. These features—simultaneously both aesthetic and functional—relate to your existing or accessible China experience, which you will have touched on during your review of organizational depth and management team. The benefits to your initiative of having previous China experience are obvious. This experience can help you to avoid many mistakes (as I am trying to do in this book), leverage existing relationships, fast-track your China initiative and more readily transfer your company DNA.

We have a saying in our consulting practice: "Life's lessons can be stir-fried but not microwaved." Certain life experiences can be like the rapid-cooking process of stir-frying, teaching you lessons faster than others (for example, the "high temperature, stir-it-up" environment of on-the-job training is a few speeds higher than classroom learning). However, rarely can one learn a lesson overnight—reducing to seconds in a microwave what might take minutes or hours in conventional cooking. A company's "life lessons" in international business, specifically time spent working in Asia and China, will enhance the organization's readiness to plan and implement the China strategy.

"It must be a nightmare for companies coming to China without any international experience," commented the head of a major U.S. financial institution in China. Executives without international experience frequently fall prey to the "airport abduction" scenario—they are picked up by a local contact the moment they land and are chaperoned until the second they get back on the plane. While in China, they are enveloped by their captors and made to think that the only way they can navigate the complex maze of China is by their protector's side. It goes without saying that these captors will have close connections with the local vice mayor, have access to cheap land and may just happen to know (or own) a company with which you can set up an attractive joint venture, coincidentally from whom they will be getting a large referral fee. China is a complex, intimidating and uncomfortable place for an international business novice—but it is supposed to be! It is natural for these inexperienced business people to fall under the protective spell of an aggressive local group that shows a friendly face and will assign an attractive young person to stay by their side to translate, explain the local menu and recommend appropriate gifts for their special someones back home.

When I first met the managers of one of our SME clients, a Midwest-based maker of precision electronic components, I found them in the lobby of a Shanghai hotel comfortably ensconced by one of these friendly young people (in this case, an attractive young lady with excellent English and an engaging smile). She didn't say much in our presence and when I inquired who she was, the client CEO explained she was the daughter (or niece—he wasn't sure) of the owner of the company negotiating with them to invest in their China facility. She had shadowed him the entire trip. After a little due diligence it became clear that this Chinese company was probably not right for our client, and certainly the deal they were proposing was unattractive. Despite what we thought was clear evidence to this effect, the CEO was still drawn to the deal and the Chinese company. "We feel comfortable with them", he would say—no doubt, given our client's utter dependence on them when they were in China. Being trapped in this type of comfort zone can anesthetize you to other realities, and other potentially better opportunities. If you are new to China and are totally comfortable in the learning process, then there is probably something wrong: You should assume that a certain level of discomfort will accompany your China expansion efforts! You need to work through this phase without becoming totally dependent on advisors or prospective local alliances.

Another SME client exemplifies the right way to go through this learning process. His first visit to China was 15 years ago and was now a distant memory. He somewhat reluctantly returned recently to directly explore opportunities uncovered through external market research. His plate was full on the domestic front and the prospects of setting up a complicated new operation in China were a bit overwhelming. On his first trip back to China, he came with his suitcase full of bottled water, biscuits, diarrhea pills, a first aid kit and other medical supplements. He was dutifully escorted to meetings with prospective customers and suppliers, and willingly traveled by trains, planes and automobiles around remote parts of the country. He learned a great deal and further validated market opportunities, and his excitement about the prospects China offered rose accordingly. Importantly, on his subsequent follow-up trip, he chose to do more of his visits on his own, staying in $30 a night local hovels as opposed to the luxury of a five-star hotel. His previously stuffed suitcase now became a slimmed down back-pack with only the bare necessities. He had many uncomfortable moments, inedible meals and very tough and sometimes awkward discussions with local companies, but his learning curve escalated dramatically—not to mention leaving China with a diary full of adventures and hilarious stories. He was able to "stir-fry" his learning curve, condensing what would have been two to three years of learning into six to 12 months, empowering him to make objective judgments on his own regarding opportunities and partnerships rather than become overly dependent on advisors.

On the surface, inventorying your China experience may seem quite simple: Either you have it or you don't. But just as in the other dimensions we have reviewed, there are more subtleties here than meet the eye. Your company's readiness in this area can be measured by the depth and breadth of experience and access to resources on several levels.

- **Management with direct China business experience:** The company has China-experienced personnel who can translate company objectives to China and China realities back to the company.
- **Existing value chain networks:** The company has an existing Chinese network of contacts within its value chain from which it can obtain China experience.
- **Indirect China resources:** The company has access to other China- or Asia-based resources outside its direct control that can provide experience.
- **International business experience:** The company has prior business experience elsewhere in the world that might help its understanding and execution of a China initiative.

Let's look at each of these areas in a little more detail.

Having management with China experience is naturally a tangible benefit to your readiness to execute a China strategy. This experience can be direct, such as having set up or run a China operation in the past, or indirect, through frequent travel to China or even dealing long distance with Chinese customers. We see this management competence frequently in high demand, especially for companies inexperienced in China. One of our clients in the heavy-duty truck component market clearly saw on the horizon its need to go to China. During its next CEO hire, deep China experience was a key criterion on the qualification list. Another industrial conglomerate anticipating more China activity created a new position, international business development director, with a priority qualification being past China experience. As a result, this new director was able to guide the company's multiple small divisions in their China planning and business setup. If China is or will be a critical part of your future strategy and you don't have this depth of China managerial experience, I suggest you look to bring it in-house.

If finding and funding such a position is not feasible, you may have access to China experience within your value chain that you can leverage. It is fruitful to exploit these connections whether you have in-house China experience or not. If you are doing business with China today, even indirectly, you likely have some viable resources to tap in this regard. Customers, suppliers and distributors can often provide friendly — and free — counsel on doing business in China. It is becoming almost common to see customers and suppliers in North America exploring China together, typically one of them leading the other on the learning curve. This cooperation can be informal, in the form of advice, relationship networking and information sharing, to formal, such as sharing a facility or even joint venturing. I previously mentioned PPG's relationship with Nanya and how its Taiwanese venture relationship was extended into China. PPG frequently works other relationships in its value chain to further its own welfare as well as that of customers and suppliers by sharing its experience and resources in China. Delphi, with its extensive resources and *guanxi* in Anting, the well-known automotive city outside of Shanghai, frequently offers help to many of its North American suppliers seeking to come to China. Their experience and considerable local influence can help their suppliers more easily set up there, creating a win-win result.

If you don't have any direct value chain resources to tap, consider your wider circle of advisors. Board members, accounting firms, banks, lawyers, and consultants can provide valuable connections–some of which could lead to direct partnership relation-ships. It is likely that you have at least some level of indirect China experience and resources in your existing network that can be exploited. Our firm often gets referrals from senior management clients who are on the boards of other companies, asking us to do for that company what we did for them. There are also a host of other support organizations such as the U.S. Consulate offices, state international trade boards, industry associations and local American chambers of commerce. These organiza-tions are designed to support your activities in places like China and should be fully utilized as a first step.

Lastly, don't underestimate the value of other international experience on your management team. "It is very important that senior management have overseas experience, even if it is in a non-Chinese, non-Asian environment," advised the China general manager of a German chemical giant. "Any time spent in another culture is very important." As in learning a foreign language, once you have mastered the first one, your familiarity with the learning process makes the second one come more easily. You expect and more readily recognize idioms in speech, variations in grammar and slang expressions—making it less likely you will put your foot in your mouth, or more able to extricate it gracefully when you do. The same concept applies to international business experience, particularly in developing countries. Past experience in coun-tries such as Brazil, Russia or Poland will make you more alert to differences in how China business operates.

FIGURE 6.6: INVENTORY OF YOUR CHINA EXPERIENCE

Experience area	Potential contacts	Follow-up responsibility	Areas in which they can provide assistance	Priority level
Management experience				
Value chain network				
Indirect China resources				
International business experience				

Fully inventorying your existing and potential China relationships can enhance your managerial preparedness. Completing Figure 6.6 with your management team can help you identify critical *guanxi* of your own that you can leverage in your China expansion. There is no need to go into the process as a "China newbie," so find a way to beg, borrow or steal this experience in some form.

RELATIONSHIP MANAGEMENT

The final piece to our pagoda structure is its steeple. In Lingxiao, which means "reach to the sky" in Chinese, the steeple is capped by an iron tip more than 40 meters high. The steeple not only serves as the crowning image of the pagoda, visible for miles in the surrounding countryside, it also provides functional stability and support. Like relationship management for a Western firm, the steeple communicates the existence and character of the pagoda to the outside world. The steeple even protects the pagoda from rain leaking into the building, just as relationship management serves to manage the outside elements that pound on an organization.

In chapter two, I described the unique characteristics of relationship management in China and how important it is to your effectiveness in the marketplace. I reviewed the complexity and opaqueness of relationships in China and how they affect all levels of the value chain. We will now explore what it means to be ready to implement effective relationship management in China. "It is important that the top people get involved in managing relationships," pointed out the general manager of a Fortune 100 U.S. company with a long history in China. "Americans tend to underplay the importance of relationship building in China. Other Asian cultures know this better." To many Western firms, the issue of relationship management seems peripheral—so corporate management underestimates the level of effort needed to do it right, providing no support or guidance. As I noted before, just the opposite is true: Relationships in China are crucial.

Being ready to implement effective relationship management requires that your company has experience not only in working closely with players in your value chain but also with government (at multiple levels) and institutes or regulatory bodies. It starts with your experience in your home markets:

- Are you now frequently dealing with local government and regulatory authorities or using third parties to assist you in developing business, as in the case with Caterpillar?

- Does senior staff spend significant time communicating with industry, regulatory or government offices?
- Do you have a defined process to cultivate and monitor these relationships?
- Do you work intimately within your value chain at the customer, supplier and intermediary levels?
- Have you worked in partnership relationships with other value chain participants?
- Have you done co-development with any of your customers or suppliers?

While there certainly will be issues specific to managing relationships in China, the principles you use at home can be a good foundation.

To help you explore your preparedness in relationship management, we will review three main areas:

1. **Understanding** the scope and intricacies of relationships in China
2. **Developing** a process to monitor and manage these relationships
3. **Empowering** local management at all levels to participate in relationship building

UNDERSTANDING RELATIONSHIPS IN CHINA

Equal to their importance to effective business conduct are the complexities of relationships in China. Figure 6.7 provides a picture of the myriad levels of relationship connections possible. This picture is both complex and dynamic. Staff at all levels can be touched by internal and external points, some hidden in terms of their relevance and importance to your business, like the dreaded "sleeper 8 pin" in bowling.

As an example, one of our clients, a leading European pharmaceutical company, had a problem with a local Chinese firm that was copying one of its products. This local firm was even in the same township as our client, which, because of its size and notoriety, seemingly had quite a bit of influence with local government. When the product copying was identified, the European firm immediately sent a team of lawyers to China to stop the piracy. After six months and more than $250,000 in legal expenses, they had gotten nowhere. Finally, the general manager threw up his hands in frustration and lamented the dilemma to his mid-management team. Not long afterwards at a local city banquet (these occur almost on a weekly basis), one of his mid-level managers took it upon himself to speak with a personal acquaintance of his, a mid-level government official in the township in which they operated. He explained the situation and the angst of his GM, reiterated the fact that his firm was a big investor in the township and said they would "appreciate" any help in resolving this unfortunate situation. Within two weeks, the local firm copying the product was shut down. It took a simple, mid-level connection to get done what a team of expensive lawyers could not do (maybe this fact is not so shocking to you!).

FIGURE 6.7: COMPLEXITY OF RELATIONSHIPS IN CHINA

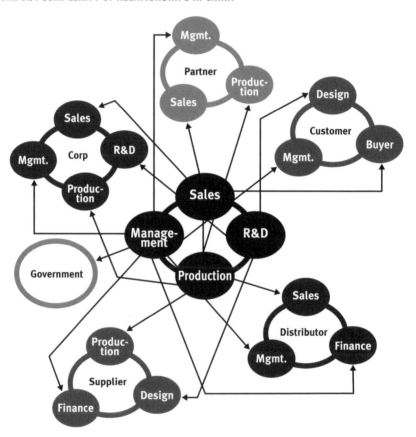

As this case demonstrates, these relationships are often direct facing and very personal. They can lack transparency, making it difficult to know which relationship has what power or influence. They are very time-consuming to build and maintain and, too often, doing so is unfortunately viewed as a discretionary function for top Western management. Chinese government organizations tend to function in silos, so lateral connections are often difficult and painstaking to make. Even your own staff can be hesitant to share knowledge, which is considered power in China. As a result, good insights can go into a black hole and become irretrievable when needed.

BUILDING A RELATIONSHIP MANAGEMENT PROCESS

To both understand and leverage your China relationships, we recommend you construct a relationship map, a blueprint by which you can optimize your relationship management activities in China (I gave an example of such a map in chapter two). The process identifies the important external contacts and inputs to your organization, qualifies their relevance and importance while determining the critical connect points between contacts. Further, it provides a mechanism to monitor, capture, evaluate and disseminate insight to the right points in your company. "We had a culture of relationship building in the U.S., so we took this approach to China," said the China head of a U.S. food ingredient company. "However, China requires more time investment in developing the soft issues—but the payback is bigger than in the U.S." Recognizing the importance of relationship building, that company developed multi-pronged partnerships along its value chain from the outset, as described below.

- Set up a close relationship with the Food Standard Bureau in Beijing
- Developed one key distributor relationship and provided extensive management support and training to help the distributor's business, then used this relationship as the foundation and model to expand to other distributors
- Established a close rapport with local government, at the Foreign Exchange Bureau, tax bureau, etc.
- Established a partnership with a key Japanese raw material supplier that had manufacturing in China—eventually extending this relationship globally

In another case, the China head of a leading U.S. bank spent 45-50% of his time in the early years dealing with government officials. He recognized the need to build multiple local relationships in the early going of their China expansion. In order to seed the company name and image among the growing pool of Chinese bankers, his company set up an MBA program at Fudan University in Shanghai and was active in training Bank of China employees. "In the short run, there were very little direct benefits from doing these things, but in the long run, this was good for publicity, recruitment and to gain favor with the government," the executive said.

In China markets where your technology is in an embryonic or early development phase, establishing relationships with key influencers can have excellent mid- to long-term payback. One of our clients selling steel H-beams in the concrete-oriented world of China's construction industry worked hard at multiple points of the value chain to teach the benefits of steel vs. concrete construction techniques. The company needed to go to the specifying source, such as design institutes and even local civil engineering schools, to promote its technology and process. This type of approach takes patience, as there is no shortcut to meaningful results—another reason why stakeholder support is critical. Figure 6.8 outlines some key steps to implement, internally and externally, to strengthen your relationship-building process in China.

FIGURE 6.8: KEY STEPS IN BUILDING A RELATIONSHIP-MANAGEMENT PROCESS

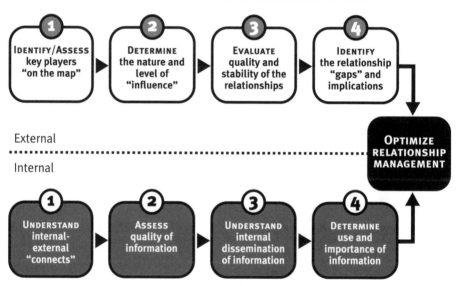

Implementing this process successfully will achieve several important benefits:

- **Identify** the importance of these relationships and how well you have them covered
- **Monitor** the flow of activity throughout the map
- **Capture** the insight from this activity
- **Evaluate** the importance of this insight and who else on the map needs it
- **Communicate** this information in a timely manner internally to those who can effectively use it

EMPOWERING YOUR TEAM TO BUILD RELATIONSHIPS

As the market matures in China, you will need to devote less time to government relations than you did at first. However, the task can still require 20-30% of your senior manager's time on an ongoing basis. Government relations are becoming more complicated as officials get more sophisticated, harder to reach and less easy to impress or influence. You need to empower other employees and develop an effective relationship-building system to relieve the burden on top management. If your senior staff are expatriates and cycle in and out of China, it is all the more important to delegate relationship building down your management hierarchy. The case of the European pharmaceutical firm noted above demonstrates the importance of having your whole team involved: Its mid-level manager did what a team of very expensive lawyers could not do.

Part of this empowerment involves a flexible decision-making approach. Your company's decision-making culture must allow for the unpredictable and occasionally critical decisions that often need to be made in a timely manner, sometimes at lower levels of the management hierarchy and likely with less information than you are accustomed to having. To lift a line from the movie "Jerry Maguire," managing a China expansion is a "pride-swallowing, day-in-day-out siege" and it will take a significant portion of your key management's time and effort. A decision-making system that requires multiple layers of validation and approval back at headquarters can unduly bottleneck the process. Give enough rope to the local team to enable them to react to market dynamics in a timely way, but build safeguards in to protect the company—not an easy balance.

As I have mentioned previously, out-of-the-box thinking is an important attribute in a fluid and changing market landscape. Handcuffed local or regional management, or a company with a highly centralized and closed management style, will be at a disadvantage in a fast-changing, complex market. In the 1990s, my partner Kent worked for a mid-sized IT company, selling and supporting manufacturing information systems in China. Some of his competition included the leading software giants of the world, all of which had large organizations and complex decision-making structures. Kent and his sales team were empowered by their U.S. management to make decisions on product and pricing. On more than one occasion, he and his sales team won business away from their much larger competition simply because they could make decisions quicker and respond better to local conditions.

In one instance, Kent and his team were on the verge of closing a deal with a general manager at a foreign-owned manufacturing company in China. Before signing the deal, the local GM had one sticky issue. "We have one problem," he said. "The manufacturing software system you offer is great, but I really need a new office chair—mine broke the other day." Kent's sales guy was a bit confused. "So go buy an office chair," he said. "Well, I would," said the general manager, "but I need headquarter approval for both the software system and the chair, and I know that my boss in the States will not approve both of them. You see, our HQ is on a cost-cutting kick and, despite the value difference, he is going to look at both requests in the same way ... both cost money that HQ is loath to give up." Thankfully, the sales person was quick on his feet and said, "Well, how about I include an office chair in the package and call it 'hardware'?" "Excellent!" cried the GM, extending his hand, "you have a deal!"

CHAPTER SUMMARY

MANAGEMENT PREPAREDNESS

To be fully prepared to put in place, execute and manage a China strategy, you need a combination of strong and ongoing management support; sufficient management depth to simultaneously staff your China team while maintaining a capable organization in your core operation; enough China-related experience and resource to jump-start your local operation; and a flexible and responsive management style to effectively deal with China's unique and dynamic business environment. I compared these management requirements to the structural and aesthetic elements of an ancient Chinese pagoda whose features come together to form a solid and functional edifice with high visibility and impact in its surrounding area.

Strong **management sponsorship** means that your company's stakeholders are fully behind your China initiative and will actively support it even in difficult times. A lack of substantive and ongoing management support has been identified as a major weakness of many Western companies' investments in the 1990s. Effective management sponsorship is characterized by three key elements:

- A clear understanding by top management of the implications of a China investment to the company's existing operations as well as the opportunity costs.
- Specific endorsement of the China initiative by key stakeholders with relevant assurances of resource support.
- The assignment of a champion or specific sponsor in the home office who has both the power and motivation to support the China venture over time.

Sufficient **management depth** means that you have enough available management talent to staff critical positions in the China operation for the needed timeframe without weakening your core operation. Companies often take the most expedient path to staffing the China operation without sufficient due diligence. In their hurry to move ahead or due to underestimating the complexity of the job, many companies assign the wrong people to fill critical positions in the China organization, sending in the B team to do an A team job. On the other hand, some companies have too quickly hired the first "China face" that comes their way, not fully assessing the breadth and depth of this person's real experience. It is important to carefully think through two main staffing questions:

1. What key positions need to be staffed by your existing management team?
2. Where are you going to obtain staff to supplement these key positions or, in some cases, fill the critical slots where using existing staff is not feasible?

I also noted the expanding pools of China talent that are emerging to support a Western company's China team.

Having relevant **China-related experience and resources** has been determined as almost necessary to ensure the operation sets up smoothly, in a timely manner and with the least amount of hiccups. Companies often do not realize the breadth of available China resources to which they have access. Companies can find valuable experience and resources in a variety of places:

- In-house managers who have been doing business in China
- Within your value chain at the customer, supplier and even indirect competitor levels
- Among your wider circle of stakeholders and advisors
- In-house managers with valuable experience in other international markets

Fully inventorying and then exploiting these resources can yield a cumulative China experience (or your own *guanxi*), which is significant and can strengthen your China activities. I also mentioned the importance of building your own base of experience, the benefits of "stir-fried" experience and the need to spend time in the trenches yourself to extend and deepen your learning curve.

Relationship management is a subtle but powerful factor in setting up and operating a China business. Companies need to be prepared to operate under different rules and with a more flexible style if they want to be effective. Western firms are often caught off guard by the amount of time and energy needed to both understand and manage relationships in China, especially at the senior level. Companies with solid experience in the West or other international markets in relationship building with government, customers and suppliers need to proactively transfer these competencies to the China organization. I spoke of having:

1. A good understanding of the scope and intricacies of relationships in China
2. The importance of developing a process to monitor and manage these relationships
3. The need to empower your management team at all levels to be involved in working your firm's network of relationships

The complexities and dynamism of China's market require flexibility and speed. These should be coupled with out-of-the-box thinking to fully exploit China's opportunities.

In sum, if you build your organization with the integrity, skill and appeal of the ancient pagoda designs, your China organization will thrive in its surrounding community, withstand the elements that come against it and last for centuries (or, for a long time)!

Chapter 7
Financial Preparedness: Making it Happen

> *It's a very personal, very important thing. Hell, it's a family motto. Now are you ready? Just checking to make sure you're ready. Here it is: Show me the money. OHHH! SHOW! ME! THE! MONEY! Doesn't it make you feel good just to say that, Jerry? Say it with me one time, brother!*

'Jerry Maguire' (1996)

In the 1990s, many Western managers left their financial business sense at the border when they came to China to explore investment. Sure, the market was embryonic, there were few precedents to use as benchmarks, regulations were lacking, entry options were limited and changes were occurring daily on the market's landscape. These conditions made for a tough investment environment, even with the most rigorous feasibility assessment. Management often had little choice but to, as the Chinese saying goes, "cross the river by feeling for the stones." But if you add to these challenges the half-hearted due diligence done my many companies in their invest-ment planning, it is no wonder that many failures occurred.

Today, China is not necessarily an easier market in which to make money, but the challenges and risks of being successful are much clearer, making preparation more possible. While companies in the 1990s had to deal with many unknowns, today these have been replaced by very evident and tangible challenges such as extremely intense competition, a more demanding customer base, more complex distribution, rising costs and shortages of skilled labor. Because these challenges can be better understood today with in-depth market investigation and due diligence, the benefits of preparation are higher — now, at least, you know what to be prepared for! Frankly, there is no excuse to enter China naïvely in today's environment. It will be tough enough to make money even when you are well prepared. As the old proverb goes, "Ignorance may not kill you, but how can you be sure?"

The last of the dimensions we will consider in our organizational readiness framework is Financial Preparedness. At the end of the day, it is the financial issues that make their way to the top of the pile. Without resources and a willingness to use them, you will not be able to transfer your key operational competencies or build the necessary management team to utilize them. Grandiose plans and good intentions melt away if they are not sustained by sound financial support. Simply stated, financial preparedness means the company's financial condition is stable, resources are sufficient to risk a China growth initiative and the will exists to actually make and sustain required investments.

To measure the financial preparedness of a company, we use four main indicators:

- **Financial health:** The company's core financials are strong and can provide ongoing resource allocations to support a China expansion.
- **Willingness to spend:** The company is willing and able to spend, often as discretionary expense, the money required to explore and establish a China initiative properly.
- **Level of risk tolerance:** The company can, if needed, absorb a failed or underperforming China investment.
- **Expectations on returns:** The company is flexible in its measurements of return on investment and ongoing P&L performance, which will accommodate the less predictable and often longer timeframe requirements of a China expansion.

As in the other dimensions, and the China Readiness Assessment itself, these indicators are highly related. In considering how best to describe this interrelationship, I am reminded of the renowned Chinese art of acrobatics, which has been in existence for more than 2,000 years, continually evolving in skill and creativity. The acrobats defy gravity with amazing displays of contortion, flexibility and balance, showcasing tremendous dexterity and grace. They are truly masters of agility. So, too, is a successful Western firm investing in China: flexible, comfortable with contortion and able to perform feats of astounding balance!

The key indicators of financial preparedness often do stack up like Chinese acrobats enacting what is roughly translated as the "piling the Buddhas" routine—although financial professionals may cringe a bit at a metaphor involving juggling. This feat comprises a number of acrobats precariously balanced on each other, as pictured in Figure 7.1. We can look at the acrobats as providing three fundamental parts: the foundation, the height and the trick. The foundation is formed by several strong and steady acrobats, providing a stable base for the others. The middle section provides the height and grandeur—the greater the number of acrobats in the middle, the grander the feat. The top acrobat crowns the effort by performing a trick, juggling fire, spinning plates, contorting his or her body, or all of the above, eliciting oohs and ahs from the audience.

A company's financial preparedness can be compared to these three elements. The foundation is formed by financial health and willingness to spend, each providing a steady and stable base for the China investment. The height of the feat is gained by a company's level of risk tolerance—the higher the risk tolerance, the higher the feat; and the trick is accomplished by a company's expectations on returns.

FIGURE 7.1: "PILING THE BUDDHAS" OF YOUR FINANCIAL PREPAREDNESS INDICATORS

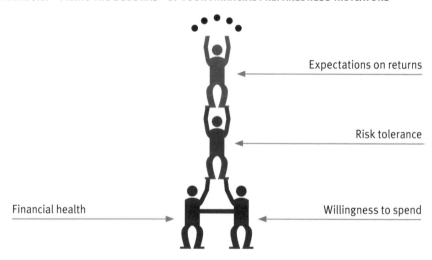

As we review each of these indicators, keep their interrelationships in mind. They will influence companies differently and in varying sequence—alternative acrobatic formations, if you will. For instance, your organization's financial health will directly affect your willingness to spend. Your risk tolerance will impact your acceptable level of expected returns on this investment. Then again, your financial health will influence your risk tolerance, which could constrain your willingness to spend money—somewhat like the old song, "the hip bone's connected to the thigh bone; the thigh bone's connected to the knee bone ..." and so on. As you build your own financial preparedness profile, it will become apparent how you need to "pile your Buddhas."

FINANCIAL HEALTH

It goes without saying that Chinese acrobats need to be in tip-top physical health. In particular, the acrobats holding up the rest must have strong and steady legs in order to support the stack. An acrobat with an ailing leg will be sidelined until he heals— performing with such a weakness could not only further hurt the athlete but put in jeopardy the teammates he is supporting.

Just as strong management sponsorship provides a necessary foundation to your managerial preparedness, the condition and stability of your company's financial health will be an important support to hold up your China initiative. Investing in China with a weak financial profile is a bit like "piling the Buddhas" on an acrobat with a bum leg: You are limited in the amount you can pile on top of this weak foundation and the entire troupe is handicapped in its flexibility to perform. For some companies, the lack of strength in their financial picture is obvious—their base acrobat comes onto the stage with a noticeable limp. For other companies, their weakness is not so apparent, more like a trick knee that is fine most of the time but can unexpectedly give way when too much pressure is applied or it is twisted the wrong way. Often, we see companies whose financial picture seems fine on the outside but when the pressure of a China initiative comes to bear, the "bad knee" gives out and the structure collapses.

So let's play the role of a sports doctor for a moment and look at some ways you can diagnose the condition of your foundational financial health (Figure 7.2). A weakness in any of these areas raises a red flag and needs to be explored further. The exercise is not complicated but needs to be done thoroughly and objectively. Difficulties typically arise when management is not honest with themselves or each other about their situation or are wearing rose-colored glasses with respect to the China investment scenario.

FIGURE 7.2: DIAGNOSING YOUR FINANCIAL HEALTH TO INVEST IN CHINA

Financial health check			
Parameter	**Weak**	**Adequate**	**Strong**
Key financial ratios are in line with industry standards			
You have access to sufficient cash to fund the investment			
Your balance sheet can absorb the investment			
You have sufficient financial resources to fund the core business concurrently with the China investment			
The company has a good track record of healthy financials (i.e. not just coming out of Chapter 11, a failed investment or some other financial reconstruction)			
P&L can absorb less-than-expected financial performance of the China operation, at least in the near term			
The company is not in retrenchment but is actively looking to make strategic investments			
Key management and shareholders have confidence in the company's financial health			

Let's go back to our consumer products company from chapter six (with the schizophrenic management personality). As I related, management kept going back to the "China stage" with big ambitions but also with one of their legs in a cast as the company was still in Chapter 11. The China market presented an attractive opportunity; management knew—and had known for many years—that they were lagging their competition in China and had to ramp up quickly. They had been frustrated—particularly the Asia VP—at missing the growing opportunity in China. But the realities of their financial condition could not support the cash-flow requirements in the early years of the project, no matter how creatively management played with the numbers. Management's enthusiasm was not enough to overcome these hurdles and they had to go to the sidelines to heal, to return another day.

Conversely, the engine controls company mentioned in chapter six had injuries of a more subtle nature. Like the slightest pressure on a hairline fracture, the subsidiary's president felt the initial pain in the early phase of his exploration of China and quickly backed off the project before major damage was done. His company has since had "successful treatment" and is back on the stage.

Some companies, especially small to mid-size firms, that wait too long to enter the China market have already eroded their business health to the point that their financial resources are precariously low—this is more like fatigue than an overt injury. These cases often arise when a company belatedly responds to its customers' migration to China or to the emergence of Chinese competition. Its base business has declined due to customers' production shifts and a loss of market share to Chinese competitors, with a resulting weakening of financial performance. This dilution, then, diminishes the company's ability to support a China initiative and increases the risk, putting the company into a higher level of desperation. It is difficult to stop this downward spiral so early treatment is prescribed. As with our Chinese acrobats, it is better to stack them on the base acrobat when he is strong and fresh, not worn out.

Recently, our firm was dealing with a precision stamper in the automotive business that was on the fence in terms of a China investment. Its key customer was migrating to China and wanted our client there. But this same customer was experiencing a downturn in its domestic business (ironically, due to its own customers' manufacturing migration to China), which was trickling down to our stamping company. At the same time, our client needed to expand its operation in Mexico but its financial resources could not handle taking on both projects. The CEO is, at this time, opting for the apparently safer route of a Mexican expansion, a more known environment and investment scenario given the company's experience. Time will tell if his prudence was well founded or if he was too shortsighted, taking the comparatively easier path forward.

Many SMEs find themselves in this type of dilemma today. It is not easy to make objective comparisons between investments when the character of each is so different. I spoke earlier of SMEs needing to determine whether their expansion should be in "Sheboygan or Shanghai." Expanding in Sheboygan sure sounds less complicated and risky, but is it the right strategic move for the long term? A major theme of the China Readiness Assessment is that honest introspection, coupled with good external insights, is the prescribed approach.

The business scale of SMEs tends to limit financial resources, although as privately held companies they may not have the pressures of Wall Street to maintain quarterly performance. SMEs can use this difference as a strength when it comes to doing business in China. While the financial health indicator more often comes into play for SMEs vs. multinational firms, it can also influence larger companies in more subtle ways. The engine controls company case is an interesting one from this standpoint as it was a subsidiary of a profitable multibillion dollar company with a strong balance sheet. There were plenty of resources available to support the subsidiary's investment but stringent conditions to access them. The lack of financial health of the subsidiary was more of a proxy for another financial preparedness indicator—expectations on returns—which I will address later in this chapter. Because the subsidiary could not meet short-term financial goals, its freedom to develop China was constrained.

If your financial base is strong, no matter your size or ownership, you can move more flexibly in your China strategy, knowing you have the resource base to support whatever approach makes most sense. If your financial condition is strained, then, like having a hairline fracture in your leg, you need to be careful in your investment appetite, limiting your expansion options as you would your level of physical exertion.

WILLINGNESS TO SPEND

If basic financial health is the first acrobat that forms the foundation in our metaphor, the second acrobat is the willingness to spend the resources necessary to launch and sustain a China initiative. J. Paul Getty is quoted as saying, "Money is like manure. You have to spread it around or it smells." Having deep pockets and the willingness to spend large sums of money were often mandatory for survival in the early days of China investment. Companies are much smarter today but the need to invest meaningful dollars may still be necessary to prudently and thoroughly explore, design and execute your China operation.

It is relatively easy, or at least more familiar, to spend money on the hard costs of a China initiative. We all realize that equipment, building, utilities, supply chain resources, etc., are necessary to doing business and we automatically factor them in to any new initiative. What is not so evident is the need to spend on soft costs to investigate and establish a China initiative—travel, investigative research and other support resources to ensure the initiative is done right, or done at all for that matter. There are three broad categories of soft costs in which companies must be willing to spend prudently: market assessment and due diligence, travel-related costs, and implementation service and support costs. Let us briefly explore each of these and assess how a company's willingness to spend on them might impact the foundation of its financial preparedness.

MARKET ASSESSMENT AND DUE DILIGENCE

The Internet has provided companies with a tantalizing buffet of data on China: enter "China" into a search engine and an overwhelming number of sites will be returned to you (a recent Google search on China yielded more than 250 million results). These days companies do not suffer from a lack of information on China; they suffer from a lack of insight into what that information means to their China strategy. Any macro data on China, from GDP to consumer spending to broad market segmentation, should be taken with a grain of salt and a large allowance for variance. Macro data is a logical starting point but the real due diligence on the market will be done through face-to-face interactions with your value chain: decision makers at customers (potential and actual), distributors, regulators, government officials and competitors. Macro or secondary source data will not be enough. As we like to say, "Data will tell you the temperature of the water, but not the depth." If you are just learning to swim, you will get used to the temperature but you may have a difficult time coping with the depth if it is over your head! Unfortunately, taking half measures to save money and time is a frequent alternative to prudent and in-depth investigation. Taking shortcuts was a costly strategy for many firms that entered China early; management assumed China would be cheap and comprehensive due diligence was not necessary.

Over the years, I have seen a spectrum of approaches by our clients in spending or not spending to explore China opportunities. One of our clients was looking at opportunities in the area of industrial measurement devices. Before making any major decisions on investing further in China, it conducted extensive research that showed a market not much larger than the cost of the research (I am being a little facetious here, but not much). Nevertheless, the research results saved them a lot of money in what would have been unproductive promotion and staff buildup to crack a market that was in an embryonic development phase. In a similar vein, an optics company conducted detailed market assessment before launching a major China initiative. The results, though indicating a limited near-term opportunity, helped it to appropriately scale the

159

next level of investment in market development and to focus on building a strong base for its long-term business. Conversely, our electrical products and materials supplier cited in chapter five (the small subsidiary of an industrial conglomerate) uncovered a significant and unexpected opportunity by proactively exploring the market. In that case, the parent company was instrumental in getting the division to think long-term and do its homework well.

It is rare indeed that this type of upfront investment does not pay back multiple times, no matter the results. Doing an assessment and finding out there is not a China market opportunity is just as beneficial as finding out that there is one. More often than not, good upfront due diligence will help you to avoid making poor decisions and wasting resources.

One area that warrants particular attention is partner due diligence. Finding a good partner and then managing the relationship well are among the most challenging tasks in doing business in China. There are countless horror stories of unwise partner selection, amateur negotiation styles and naïve deal arrangements. As hard as it is to operate a successful alliance, you don't need the added burden of having married the wrong partner. Much anguish can be avoided by objective and disciplined due diligence. If the six Ds of "due diligence, due diligence, due diligence" don't work for you, then try the three Vs: "validate, validate, validate." There is no magic formula here. Simply turn over as many rocks as you can to uncover inconsistencies, hidden liabilities and plain old misinformation. The Chinese are generally better at posturing and negotiation than Westerners, particularly Americans, so you need to go into the deal process well prepared. Even when I leave the local Shanghai street market having acquired my goods at 40-50% of the sales clerk's initial asking price, I know in my heart of hearts that I left money on the table. The point here with respect to readiness is being prepared to take the time, and to spend the money, to research your situation in depth.

While spending money to do solid groundwork is key, don't re-invent the wheel. As mentioned before, there are many resources from which to get low-cost or even free information. Make smart use of government agencies for information, connections and trade delegations. Read as much as possible (for instance, you are certainly sagacious in reading this book!), attend seminars on China and tap your customers and suppliers for as much insight as you can. With this base insight, you can do additive and more focused exploration to confirm and expand your understanding.

TRAVEL COSTS

I previously mentioned the importance of making trips to China to get a direct view of your opportunity and the hurdles to exploit it—that valuable "stir-fried" experience. You cannot underestimate the benefit of your staff getting up close and personal with China, learning firsthand the opportunities and challenges facing them. We tell our clients to expect that trips to China will cost them up to US$10,000 per week-long trip per executive traveling. How do we get to this figure? Well, start with the actual costs: Business class tickets can easily run US$5,000-6,000 a pop; daily out-of-pocket costs (hotel, food, local travel) can run $300 per day; plus the "out of commission" costs for these executives to be away from the office and far from the day-to-day business of running their company, especially if the executive is not used to managing daily business from 13 time zones away. Recently, a major chemical company spent US$60,000 for a three-person technical team to conduct an equipment qualification exercise several weeks long. Add to this the number of trips by engineering, supply chain management, production people, etc., and the trip tab can run up to US$100,000-$150,000 before you know it.

While you need to get first-hand experience, I caution you to balance this perspective with objective research and due diligence. One sad case of imbalance was a North American bus maker that spent two years nursing a joint venture relationship with a China bus company in Dandong, in far northeast China, at the time a tortuous 10-hour train ride from Beijing. One unfortunate middle-aged executive made the trip a dozen times, spending tens of thousands of dollars and countless days. When he finally realized he needed some outside help, he initiated objective market investigation. This effort revealed that he was dealing with the wrong company in what turned out to be an unattractive market. Timely research and due diligence on the front end, before extensive travel was initiated, not only would have saved a lot of time and money, but would have prevented this tragic executive's hair from turning prematurely white over the course of his many trying adventures traveling to the outer limits of China.

IMPLEMENTATION SERVICE/SUPPORT COSTS

Once you have explored your market opportunities, identified the appropriate entry or growth strategy and been to China a time or two to do your own due diligence, it is time to implement your strategy. The legal and financial processes necessary to establish business entities in China can be complex and time consuming; but there are professionals well experienced in this type of work. From large audit and legal firms to smaller, independent ones, there are literally hundreds of service firms established in China now to assist foreign companies with these tasks.

The key to using legal and financial advice successfully is to do so only when you know what you want to do and why you want to do it—after you have done your market due diligence and strategy planning. Our company has worked successfully with several legal and financial firms where we help focus our client on the strategy (the what and why) while they help with the execution of the agreements and tax planning (the how). Unfortunately, we see many firms getting caught up with the how before they really know the what and why. This is particularly true when management feels pressed to "have a plant in China" or "set up a joint venture in China" as a result of customer pull or competitive threat. Management can get immersed prematurely in the structural discussion without proper alignment with their strategic intent. Having a factory or venture in China is not a strategy–they are means to an end, such as to have access to low-cost product, to penetrate a market channel, etc. Focusing first and thoroughly on the strategic goals can open up alternatives in how to achieve them. For instance, a better way to get low-cost product might be through contract manufacture. Our home improvement products company referenced in chapters four and five, which was working with the Taiwanese cartel, took a step back from the how (it initially was drawn into an analysis of an equity deal with a supplier) and found a better way to achieve the same, if not better, results through a simpler contract relationship.

Legal costs will come into play at various points for contract development and review, company setup, patent or copyright requirements, etc. China's high level of bureaucracy can make the most straightforward tasks painfully slow and expensive. Depending on your own governance requirements, you may need some redundant work here, both by a local firm and the company's existing legal support, whether it is internal or external. Additionally, there can be a host of miscellaneous charges relating to translations, product analysis or reverse engineering, obtaining product approvals or certifications, etc.

As one experienced China executive said, "You should spend only what you can afford to lose." In your China Readiness Assessment you need to be able to come up with this number. We like to use a shock test at the outset of this discussion with clients in the initial stages of contemplating a China strategy by suggesting that a minimum of US$200,000 will need to be spent in the exploration and implementation stages alone (as discretionary expense). If our client does not go into cardiac arrest, we then continue the conversation. If a client balks at this number, we question their seriousness and stomach to go much further. Their hesitation can be a sign that their financial health is not in a state of readiness to move on and that, if they cannot absorb this level of expense, it may be best not to proceed.

If they survive this initial test of resolve, we can then start to build a budget. Figure 7.3 outlines a representative case for the exploratory and early implementation phases of a China investment for a mid-sized manufacturer of industrial machinery.

FIGURE 7.3: SAMPLE PROFORMA FOR A CHINA 18-MONTH EXPLORATION AND IMPLEMENTATION PHASE

Cost element	Composition	Estimated costs
Market research	Full market assessment and strategy planning	US$80,000
	Negotiation of an LOI with potential JV partner	
Exploratory trip	Four executive staff, 10 days	$50,000
Implementation costs	Execute documents to create legal business entity	$50,000
	Strategic tax planning	
Miscellaneous costs	Other staff travel, phone calls, domestic legal expenses, product design changes, etc.	$30,000

This is just one example (and, as the TV commercial caveat goes, "your actual costs may vary") but it is representative of what it takes to get up and running in China. Again, soft costs as mentioned above are often difficult for companies to swallow, particularly SMEs with a do-it-yourself style. However, time and again our firm has seen how, when properly planned and implemented, this preparation returns multiple times its original investment. Here it is useful to remember the old adage, "a budget is just a method of worrying before you spend money, as well as afterward."

RISK TOLERANCE

Certainly, the performance of any individual Chinese acrobat is worthy of admiration; however, it is the height—and its associated risk—at which these athletes perform, one on top of the other, that makes them so amazing. But while this looks dangerous to the audience, and certainly there is an element of danger, it is almost second nature to the performers. They practice daily to manage the risks, diligently preparing until they are confident of their skills and comfortable in their routine. Managing the risks of a China venture can be quite similar. With careful planning, the risks of investing in a developing country can be managed. Therefore, properly identifying and assessing these risks are fundamental tasks to be done *before* investing in China.

The focus here is not to discuss general risk assessment techniques, which are well documented with many sound processes to follow. The emphasis is on understanding your risk tolerance, which will help you gauge your readiness to deal with the identified and sometimes unique risks of a China investment. We are defining risk tolerance as the **level of your flexibility to participate in an uncertain environment**. The level of uncertainty in investing in China is multifaceted and, like an acrobat preparing to enact a complicated stunt, management must be fully aware of the potential pitfalls and weak points in the routine. This preparation enables them to make dangerous moves look relatively easy. The areas of uncertainty can be organized into three basic types: macro factors, market forecast and regulatory issues.

MACRO FACTORS

Macro data includes the broader economic and political indicators that characterize the general environment in which you will operate. Such indicators are very identifiable and sometimes reasonably predictable. Certainly they are well researched, collected and published by a multitude of government and think tank organizations. Many companies, like ours, rely on these organizations to provide the inputs to assess the general environment's uncertainties. Swings in the economy, trade, currency rates, political power, etc., all contribute to a general level of uncertainty that trickles down in some way to your specific market space.

We recommend that companies scan the output of these third-party organizations and develop an *uncertainty profile*, which will flag the multiple factors you need to monitor as you develop and implement your strategy—like a dashboard of indicators. Once you have an idea of the level of uncertainty in these factors, you need to ask yourself how this uncertainty will affect *your* market and *your* company, and what level of flexibility your organization has to adjust to swings in their evolution. Figure 7.4 presents a sample uncertainty profile conducted for a chemical producer contemplating a facility investment in China.

FIGURE 7.4: SAMPLE UNCERTAINTY PROFILE ON CHINA'S MACRO FACTORS

Indicator	Outlook	Level of uncertainty	Perceived risk to China initiative
Economic growth	Steady GDP growth of 7%+ over period	Low	Negligible
Consumer income	Steady increase of consumers into addressable market	Low	Low
Import accessibility and costs	Increasing openness due WTO—tariffs will continue to decline	Low	Could make local facility less competitive
IP risks	Will remain a key problem with limited enforcement in near to mid-term	Moderate	Must assume worst case
Labor costs	Remain low overall but with steady increase, especially along east coast	Moderate	Impacts facility location
Corruption	Corruption and red tape are still endemic to culture; will take time to change	Low	Find a way to deal with it in acceptable way
Currency fluctuation	Increasing pressure to appreciate with some likely move in near term	High	Factor into cost proformas
Currency convertibility	Eventual full convertibility expected	Moderate-high	Assume conservative case for investment proposal
Political stability	Quite stable and predictable–slow to change	Low-moderate	May be some local fallout/incidents

The main objective of the chemical producer's strategy was to establish a low-cost production facility for both the local market and, eventually, exports, so this client was most concerned with factors affecting its manufacturing cost competitiveness. It paid close attention to macro factors such as labor costs, currency fluctuation and the like, which could directly affect the facility's competitiveness. Of course, these macro factors needed to be compared to other alternative production sites and be constantly updated and re-evaluated based on current conditions.

The relevant factors to consider vary depending on your situation, industry type and proposed China investment. For instance, if your China investment is primarily to support a global sourcing program and there is potential for a significant currency swing, how would your strategy be impacted? What contingency plans do you have to react to this economic change? Currency convertibility, on the other hand, may not have a significant impact on your China sourcing operation, which will not be a profit center, but could be important for a more locally oriented operation that yields dividends needing to be repatriated.

If your strategy is mainly for local China market development, then economic growth, consumer income levels, corruption and the like may be of more interest. Often, these macro factors will be evolutionary in nature, such as China's legal setting. You may need to pace your level of localization against these trend lines and adjust for a changing environment. This view of the general landscape's level of uncertainty will serve as a backdrop for your deeper analysis of the uncertainties in your own market segment.

MARKET FORECASTS

As we discussed in chapter two, the pace of change in China's markets has been, and remains, phenomenal. If my wife and I haven't been to one of our favorite Shanghai restaurants in a month, we will always call ahead to make sure the restaurant is still in business and is still located at the same place. Even this precaution may not be enough, however. For example, after confirming by phone that our favorite French restaurant was open and still at the same address, we couldn't find it, despite repeatedly walking up and down the street. The next day we called again to learn that, though they indeed were still in business and still located at the same place, they had acquired a new name and were now serving tapas—important pieces of information they neglected to mention and we didn't even imagine asking about. No doubt the French accent of the person who answered the phone dulled our normally alert senses.

Some of the widest forecast envelopes I have developed as a consultant have been for China market analyses, almost to the point of being embarrassed to present such broad gaps between low- and high-end scenarios. Markets can change on a dime in China, as we witnessed in the automotive sector in the early 2000s when, after years of unimpressive growth, it exploded with annual increases of +60% per year over a two-year period. The China CEO of General Motors—who, before the market's take-off occurred, was derided by the media regarding the wisdom of his company's aggressive facility investments in China—became a hero when the market unexpectedly took off. The line between being labeled a seer or a crackpot is rice paper thin in China. The reality was that no one could have accurately predicted the auto market's rapid rise. General Motors made its investment with a high level of uncertainty on the timing and slope of that growth, but was prepared to operate flexibly, convinced that the market would eventually evolve in a significant way and that it needed to have a major position there in the long term. Today, China is General Motors' most important market. Mario Andretti's words are apropos to many of these types of China investments: "If everything seems under control, you're just not going fast enough."

To help define the limits of your market's uncertainty, we recommend you do multiple forecast scenarios, based on the interplay of a series of predictive factors. Figure 7.5 provides an example of this approach. This case involved China's intention to go "green" by converting the transit buses in many cities to some type of alternative fuel-powered vehicle. There were plans in place to make this happen—and even commitment by a number of major cities such as Beijing—to convert the entire bus fleet to green vehicles, especially in anticipation of the Olympics in 2008. Our client would have a significant opportunity in China if these buses converted to CNG or LPG (gaseous) fuels, the clearly preferred alternative fuel at the time of our analysis. We developed an envelope forecast based on levels of gaseous bus penetration, a mid-case between these extremes being the most probable scenario.

FIGURE 7.5: EXAMPLE FORECAST SCENARIO FOR CHINA GASEOUS CITY BUSES

Scenario I: Low-end forecast	Scenario II: High-end forecast
Annual single fueled gaseous city bus production maintains level achieved in 2005 or ~15% of total city bus production	Annual single fueled gaseous city bus production expands rapidly and achieves ~40% of total city bus production
• Gaseous city buses achieve limited success with relatively poor performance and unfavorable cost results • Other "clean auto" solutions are available and compare well against gaseous • Gaseous fuel availability and infrastructure construction are still a bottleneck of gaseous city bus popularization • Result is "Go gaseous" program completed in 16 cities/regions but limited spread to other cities, except where cheap gas is available	• Gaseous experiment is successful in terms of performance and environmental goals • West-to-East pipeline project and other LNG projects secure the natural gas supply to most key cities • Gaseous station construction catches up to gaseous vehicles on the road • Gaseous solution is prioritized over other "clean auto" solutions • Gaseous bus usage spreads nationwide beyond the target 16 cities

We also created a forecast sensitivity chart (Figure 7.6), which highlighted the key factors our client needed to monitor to determine which forecast scenario would actually evolve. Sure enough, less than two years into the forecast, the market changed course as the performance of gaseous buses failed to meet quality expectations, a factor highlighted in the sensitivity analysis as a key swing variable. The market then began to change direction to a diesel engine technology alternative; our client's prospects changed quickly as the low-end forecast scenario began to look more probable. As was the case here, there often are no valid trend lines to go by. Further, non-market factors, generally expressed as the will of national or regional governments, can change the course of your market's direction much like a tsunami can change the local landscape. You will often be navigating in uncharted waters, so keeping your early warning system at high alert is critical.

REGULATORY ISSUES

Regulation can have a significant impact on a market's prospects in any country; however, in China, there are additional issues with which to contend. First, there may be no established regulation for a given industry area and new policies are constantly in the works. The only guidelines or benchmarks are often other similar international regulations such as environmental requirements, emission standards, building codes, electrical specifications, etc. Yet these international standards may present varying outlooks based on whether China adopts policies more similar to those in the U.S., Europe or Japan. Often, Chinese standards and regulations will use one or a mix of these standards as the core of its own regulations, and then add a Chinese façade. Further, enforcement does not necessarily accompany issuance. These types of regulations typically fly in the face of economic development, commercial interests often winning the battle due to the pressure to sustain growth and job creation.

FIGURE 7.6: FORECAST SENSITIVITY ANALYSIS, GASEOUS BUS CASE

Variable	Level of uncertainty	Comment
City bus forecast	Low	Minimal variation, strong trend line
Government commitment to clean air	Low-moderate	Some slippage in second-tier cities
Widespread availability of gas	Low-moderate	Pipeline plan well underway and funded
Gaseous infrastructure in cities	Moderate	Some cities will likely struggle with expense and time to build stations
Good performance of gaseous buses (cost, emissions, reliability)	Moderate-high	Not proven yet in China, but there is international precedent
Competition from other technologies	Low-moderate	Nothing imminent on horizon

A demonstration of the huge potential swing in market opportunity due to regulatory factors again draws on developments in emissions standards. The Chinese government had outlined its intentions to meet Euro III emissions standards in the truck market (and I emphasize the word intentions). The target for compliance by truck makers for Euro III was set to take effect in 2008, when all new trucks sold in China must have been upgraded from Euro II emission standards. Going from Euro II to Euro III is not an easy or cheap transition in technology, so the truck suppliers were very concerned about the reality and timing of the government's intentions. We explored this issue with all the leading truck suppliers as well as other industry observers, and the bottom line was that no one really had a clue what the government would do. As a result, all the truck manufacturers were compelled to do the development work to prepare for Euro III, but stop short of commercialization on a mass scale. To extend our acrobat metaphor, it was as if the athletes ruthlessly trained to prepare themselves for a performance not yet scheduled; a frustrating situation, to say the least.

FIGURE 7.7: ALTERNATIVE GROWTH SCENARIOS FOR EURO III TRUCKS

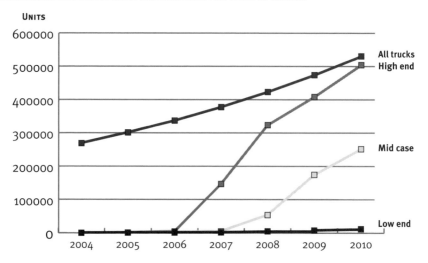

Figure 7.7 portrays the growth curve scenarios we developed based on an assessment of multiple factors surrounding when, and to what extent, the government would implement Euro III. Our client supplied a product that would come into play when the Euro III standards were put in place. Its challenge was to decide how aggressive to be in anticipation of Euro III adoption. As a minimum, it needed to be very active in the development phase with the truck makers as they prepared for Euro III compliance or it would be out of the loop. But to be competitive in the market, our client also needed to have a China manufacturing facility. Some key competitors were active in similar devices for passenger cars, which had been mandated for Euro III in China a couple of years earlier. As a result, these companies had China manufacturing facilities and could more readily extend them into the truck market, vs. our client, which needed to build a greenfield facility. While these competitors were preoccupied with the passenger car market, our client had a window of opportunity to be first mover into local manufacturing for truck applications—but at what risk? If the market evolved on

the high-end curve, the client needed to have broken ground already. But if the low-end curve evolved, a facility would not be needed for many years.

The conclusion, in the end, was to take an "aggressive middle road" position: be very active in the design phase by proactively creating business development programs with key vehicle makers, while openly advertising its intent to locally manufacture. To give credence to this intention, the client secured land in a development zone and laid out the facility design but dragged out the process while monitoring regulatory winds. The client also planned to use the China facility as a production source for offshore markets to help support capacity utilization in the near term. It was a public company but with sales well under US$100 million, so the China investment would have high impact on its financials. The board was very involved in the decision process, and management did careful due diligence to narrow the risk factors. The end scenario fell within their risk tolerance comfort zone, and they felt they had enough flexibility to manage the market's uncertainties. Because the company's financial health was sound, management was able to deal with a higher level of uncertainty than perhaps other companies of their size could have. This case demonstrates the interrelationships of the financial indicators, especially the importance of the strength of your "bottom Buddha."

To get an aggregate picture of your risk tolerance, you can plot your level of flexibility against the overall uncertainty of your market space based on these and related factors. Figure 7.8 portrays a matrix to describe your risk tolerance position and its overall implications to your financial preparedness. Your position will be the result of analysis of your financial flexibility (directly correlated to your financial health) against the level of macro environment, market forecast and regulatory uncertainty. There are a variety of methods to formulate your position through management workshops, internal surveys and factor indexing.

Our truck component client described above was squarely situated in the upper right quadrant, a positioning it determined through detailed market research and an assessment of its internal resource level and needs for the whole company. Conversely, our precision stamper, which opted for Mexico, was more in the lower left quadrant. However, management determined their positioning without any market investigation and so was in danger of misreading the uncertainty level.

FIGURE 7.8: POSITIONING YOUR RISK TOLERANCE LEVEL

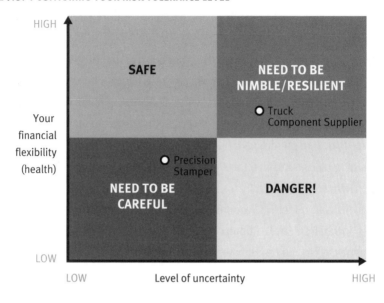

This risk tolerance positioning can significantly influence the level and nature of your investment as well as the kind of structure you select for your China operation. If you are positioned on the right side of the matrix, especially the lower right quadrant, you may need to spread the risks with a partner or be very creative in your approach, making use of less traditional investment vehicles such as a contract joint venture or marketing alliance, which require less upfront investment. Using a creative structure can provide a good balance of investment level and control and flexibility. We would encourage our precision stamper to simultaneously think through possible China scenarios that met a very tough investment risk threshold. They could set the bar as high as they like. China offers so many possibilities in approach that one should not discount the plausibility of an investment scenario that on the surface appears unlikely. A quip by Lord Rutherford is appropriate here: "We haven't the money, so we've got to think." If your Motivation dimension is at an urgent level to go to China, you may not have a choice anyway.

EXPECTATIONS ON RETURNS

A stack of people standing one on top of the other is an impressive thing. But without the trick—like a contortionist juggling scarves while spinning plates on her feet—it is just a stack of people. The top person (or people) is the "so what" of the acrobatic feat; the others are there to support them and give them impressive height. So, too, in your China initiative, you must plan carefully for the trick, or expectations on returns. Because of the strength and skill of their fellow acrobats, some companies can design a fantastic, eye-catching trick on the top of the stack, while other firms with less capable teams must have more modest expectations. Knowing what expectations on returns your company and your stakeholders can bear is the final piece to our financial preparedness dimension. Understating what your team can do will result in only tepid applause at the end of the show. Overestimating what your team can handle could result in bodies strewn across the stage—and the likely termination of the troupe's leader.

For larger companies heavily influenced by Wall Street, the issue is often not depth of financial resources or dealing with uncertainty, but expectations on their company's performance. This was the case for our client in engine controls. As noted, the parent was a multibillion-dollar entity with plenty of financial resources but was, like many listed companies, highly sensitive to the impact of the subsidiary's performance on the overall corporation, which resulted in a short leash on the company's ability to invest in uncertain markets with longer-term returns. The common fallout of this situation is mixed messages sent simultaneously to the subsidiary's management: "You have to be in China." "You have to fund this initiative out of your own coffers." "You need to make your numbers this quarter." These directives make for an almost impossible task and the result is ultimately a lack of stakeholder support. The head of our controls company tried to juggle the balls at the top of the stack as long as he could—but they turned out to be made of lead, eventually sapping his strength and tipping the pile.

As you consider your expectation on returns for a China investment, the logical starting point is your standard return ratios, however you might measure these. They represent your default expectations if no extenuating circumstances exist. For a more conventional China investment, where the scope and nature of your project are very familiar and the uncertainties have a narrower sensitivity band, you can view expectations on returns according to traditional company metrics. Western firms historically have been too quick to apply extenuating circumstances to China and have been sloppy in defining exactly what these circumstances were. Because China was an unknown emerging market in the 1990s, many firms extended too much financial grace to their feasibility assessment, going forward under any number of invalidated assumptions, such as, "China is the land of milk and honey," "we are a Fortune 500 firm and need to be there," "China has more than 1.3 billion people," "all my competitors are going there," etc. While there is merit in many of these points, companies that usually were very rigorous about their investment analyses in other markets took an almost casual approach to their China assessment. Because it was China, many firms naïvely waived prudent financial procedures.

Expectations on returns, in many ways, have come full circle over the last 15 years: from a naïve expectation that China would be a windfall or that China should have special dispensation, to today, when a China investment is expected to adhere to the same investment standards as anywhere else in the world. The more experienced companies have completed this cycle. For some companies, after experiencing failed China ventures themselves or witnessing the very public failures of their peers, the pendulum has swung a bit too far — beyond prudent financial caution to investment paranoia. Management in these firms believes "no one makes money in China," and that "China is a financial black hole." This bias can be as dangerous as financial naïveté. As I have been advocating throughout this book, a stoic balance based on a clear understanding of your motivation to go to China, coupled with an objective perception of the facts of your China investment opportunity, is the best approach.

Many Western firms today are challenged when the China initiative is based on more of a defensive strategy, notably in needing to follow their customer base or shifting more of their supply chain there to streamline costs. In these cases, the downside of not taking action can be of higher risk than making the move. As John F. Kennedy said, "There are risks and costs to a program of action. But they are far less than the long-range risks and costs of comfortable inaction." These decisions can be gut-wrenching as the uncertainty level is undoubtedly high, and the ultimate resolution or fruit of your investment may be in the distant future. A key need is for transparency in the analysis so that a proforma financial outlook can be accurately weighed against the benefits and risks of entering China, not artificially bolstered to make the deal work, or sabotaged to kill it. Companies with the phrase "the numbers do not lie" as a mantra for their domestic operations will do well to apply the same to their China businesses.

One of our clients in plastic additives agonized over a China investment for years and struggled with making a fair analysis of the situation. A local China producer had been steadily growing in scale and international market reach, resulting in both loss of business for our client and price decline in the global market. Our client's motivation for a China facility investment was purely defensive, as a means to pre-empt this competitor from eventual global market leadership. After review of many different options—from a joint venture with another local China producer to a green-field investment—the most effective investment strategy appeared to be a deal with the devil himself. After some skillful posturing and veiled threats of doing a venture with one of its competitors, our client got the attention of this 900-pound gorilla and brought him to the negotiating table. As they conducted feasibility assessments on the joint venture, the numbers did not meet our client's expectations for returns (in their case, RONA, or return on net assets). On a discrete basis, the proposed invest-ment normally would have been flushed, but the complication was that this invest-ment had to be considered in the context of a global financial picture due to the local China company's extending reach.

Some very sophisticated spreadsheets were prepared estimating financial returns using a number of potential assumptions in global market pricing, demand and supply growth, competitive material substitution, technology innovation and others. Several scenarios were developed, including a baseline status quo forecast, against which the China investment could be measured. It was a very complex exercise, fraught with the potential for manipulation as even a small adjustment, say, in global pricing assumptions, would significantly change the relative investment returns of the various scenarios. In the end, our client could not accept the lower-than-target RONA on the China investment, despite the strong warnings by some internal managers of signifi-cant deterioration in their global business if they did nothing. But it was a tough, and ultimately impossible, sell. The reality of an unattractive investment today was more compelling than the prospects of a dismal long-term future.

The increased investment in China by the Taiwanese, Japanese and Koreans is adding pressure to the typically shorter-term financial orientation of U.S. companies. For instance, the Japanese are well known for making investments with very long-term results. The case of our metals processor in chapter five (which was being drawn to

China by its largest customer) is a good example here. Its Japanese competitor took the approach of "if we build it, they will come" and did not seem to sweat so much about the short-term, or even mid-term, returns on that investment. Unfortunately, the action had a cascading effect on our U.S. client, whose hand was now forced. If our client came to China, its key customer—the one pulling it to China—would give it business; if our client did not come, the customer would likely turn to the Japanese competitor that had set up nearby. In this case, our client did not have the luxury of employing traditional return ratios in evaluating its China investment. It was forced to play under similar rules as its Japanese competitor—another reason to have a deep understanding of your competition in your market assessment.

For those companies looking at China as more of an opportunistic potential with nominal downside if they do not participate, expectations on returns can be set very high. One of our European clients in the automotive aftermarket took an extreme position in this regard. As is often common in these cases, this company had been burned badly in other international market investments, which made its chairman extremely conservative and an almost unassailable wall when it came to an acceptable investment proposal for China. Management decided to take an export-only approach to China and go after the low-hanging fruit. They fully relied on local distributors for market development, and had no intention to produce any products locally. Certainly, they will be profitable in whatever they do. We believe, however, that they may have left business on the table by this cautious approach and perhaps ransomed their long-term opportunity by not taking a little more risk and establishing a stronger position today.

Where defense of your core business is at stake, such as with our metals processor above, the financial return requirements need to be tempered; if your risks of non-action are low, as in the case of our auto parts supplier, you can afford to set higher standards. It all comes down to the expectations built on the foundation of your basic financial health and willingness to spend. Your risk tolerance will adjust how high you can go. Set your expectations correctly and you can anticipate a flawless performance and a happy audience.

CHAPTER SUMMARY

FINANCIAL PREPAREDNESS

Being financially prepared to both explore and execute a China strategy is foundational to your overall readiness and is an interaction of several factors. I compared this interaction to a Chinese acrobatic performance, one acrobat standing on top of the other, a "pile of Buddhas." Foremost, your financial health needs to be stable and healthy enough to both fund the China initiative and support its ongoing implementation. You also need to be willing to spend the necessary funds to fully explore and evaluate the market and your options, conducting detailed due diligence *before* you commit to your strategy. These two factors will form a strong foundation to your financial preparedness.

You must also be prepared to deal with uncertainties in the overall China environment as well as in your own market space and must know (and accept) your risk tolerance profile. Your return on investment may not meet normal expectations given this uncertainty and the typically longer-term nature of China investments. I compared the interrelationships of these factors to a Chinese acrobatic routine, whereby the acrobats, like your financial preparedness indicators, must be balanced adeptly and in a formation that suits your company's profile.

A healthy **financial profile** is typically part of the foundation in your acrobatic formation, its strength and stability the anchor on which the other indicators will balance. We recommend an honest financial health check that will highlight areas in your ability to develop and sustain a China initiative without compromising your core business. I likened your financial health to the physical condition of an acrobat that must support his colleagues stacked on top of him: If he is in peak condition, he should have no problem; if he has a weak leg, he risks causing the entire formation to crash down around him.

Joining basic financial health as part of the foundation (and too often forgotten as a feature of a company's financial readiness for China) is the **willingness to spend** the needed resources upfront to fully explore the opportunity or threat facing you. To conduct the proper due diligence on the market as well as prospective partners, careful and sometimes costly research is needed. This upfront investment usually entails trips to China by your management team, market and competitive research, partner due diligence and associated legal and overhead costs. The results of this exploratory expenditure never fails, in our experience, to yield abundant fruit, sometimes preventing you from making the wrong decisions as well as unproductive investments.

The third financial preparedness indicator to be measured is your company's **risk tolerance**, defined as the level of financial flexibility to operate in an uncertain environment. It is this indicator that gives your stack of acrobats their impressive height. I categorized the various factors of uncertainty into three baskets:

- *Macro environment factors*, including economic, political and general business practices. Profiling these factors will provide the backdrop for determining the uncertainty in your own specific market space.
- *Market forecasts* that comprise the specific elements relevant to your business segment that enable you to make business forecasts such as changes in market, competition, channel dynamics and the like.
- *Regulatory issues* which, in a relatively undeveloped market environment, can have a direct and significant impact on the scope and timing of your opportunity in China.

Because of the complexity and dynamics of these factors, we recommend that you conduct multiple forecast scenarios and carefully flag those factors that are most susceptible to large swings and that will have high impact on your strategic approach. The above analyses can be assimilated to position your company on a risk tolerance matrix, which will help clarify your options as well as your risk appetite.

The final indicator, **expectations on returns**, considers your financial flexibility to operate in this uncertain environment in terms of harvesting the fruit of your investment. This indicator is the acrobatic trick, the exploit that delivers the audience delight (in this case, your audience is your executives and shareholders).

I highlighted the dangers in too readily applying extenuating circumstances to your standard financial requirements just because it is China, as was often the case in the 1990s. For some companies, this lax approach to financial assessment has been replaced by a kind of paranoia or cynicism about doing business in China—management believing that no one can make money there. We advocate a balanced view in assessing expectations on returns, making allowances in return requirements where the urgency of your motivation to invest dictates that you must compromise because the risk of inaction may be higher.

Chapter 8
The China Readiness Assessment in Action — a Case Study

 The only people who achieve much are those who want knowledge so badly that they seek it while the conditions are still unfavorable. Favorable conditions never come.

C.S. Lewis

In order to show a more complete picture of the China Readiness Assessment process as well as its power to help management direct its strategic planning for China, I will end this book with an example of a client that used the process from start to finish. In fact, this company was one of the first to formally execute the process in its entirety. While the name of the company and some of the details have been changed to protect its identity, the situation is authentic, the conditions it faced were real and the conversations all happened as I describe them. Let's walk together in the shoes of some executives facing the China challenge and witness the effectiveness of the China Readiness Assessment.

ABC COMPANY'S SITUATION

Once again a memo was issued from the CEO to put together a project team to conduct a feasibility assessment of setting up a facility in China (or a neighboring Asian country). While some managers said, "It's about time," others lamented, "Not again?" When we first met senior management at ABC Company, they were deep in yet another debate on whether to pursue a strategic initiative into China. In fact, this was the fourth major discussion on "what to do about China" in as many years. The wear and tear of the previous years of indecision had taken their toll on ABC management. Nevertheless, they again assembled a China project team comprised of various department heads to assess the situation and craft a response.

ABC Company is a global leader in providing processes and products to support electronic component manufacturing. At the time of our association with them, it had revenues of about US$500 million and was listed on NASDAQ. Business in China, and Asia in general, had been steadily growing and its key customers had plants throughout the region. At this point, ABC Company was supplying its customers through exports from the U.S. In fact, the company had recently made a significant investment in a new manufacturing facility in the U.S. in a state neighboring its headquarters. As often happens, soon after this expansion the global market went into a downturn so the company was experiencing some overall financial stress at the time the China situation again came to a head.

The outward pressures regarding the China question had been apparent for a number of years. Management had done significant economic modeling on setting up a plant in China or elsewhere in Asia—the findings of which appeared to show significant cost improvement. Meanwhile, the sales department was echoing the cries of its major customers, which were voicing a clear call to "come to China." In sum, there was significant momentum building to make an investment.

However, despite this apparent evidence to move forward, top management was not convinced: The risks of the investment appeared uncomfortably high given the company's financial vulnerability and the unstable market environment in which it operated. As a result, top management was at an impasse, and as various camps within the company were taking opposing sides on the viability of such an initiative, they knew they were stuck and needed to look at the situation more objectively and rigorously. They contracted our company to conduct a China Readiness Assessment as a means to find a satisfactory resolution and clear path forward that the entire team could embrace.

THE APPROACH

The China Readiness Assessment is designed to be a first, concrete step on the road to planning and executing a China strategic initiative. Its sets the parameters and direction of the planning process and provides management with a compass to find their way to a viable and supportable path forward. The process at ABC Company began with each manager and team leader completing a China Readiness Assessment questionnaire[1], followed by our team interviewing each department manager involved in or affected by the China initiative. In these interviews, we probed management on

---

[1] An online, interactive questionnaire is referenced in the Appendix

each dimension of the model through a series of questions to uncover the drivers and inhibitors to go to China. These interviews included open sharing of the concerns—both professional and personal—they would face if the company pursued a China expansion. Following each interview, we combined all management perspectives in a matrix to refine the initial survey assessment and provide a more holistic perspective on the capabilities and experience of the organization and its management to set up and operate a company in China.

FIGURE 8.1: PROCESS STEPS IN THE CHINA READINESS ASSESSMENT

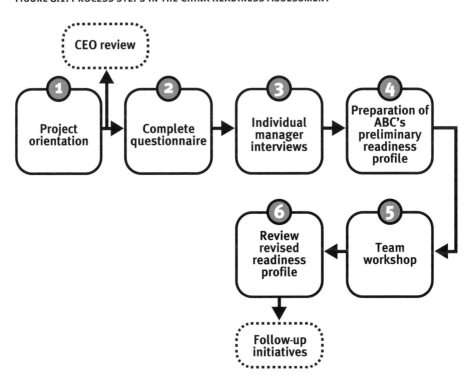

After a thorough canvassing of all internal management views, we assimilated the insights and built ABC Company's preliminary China Readiness positioning (see Figure 8.2). This profile was dissected in a two-day workshop with the entire management team. The workshop was peppered with intense moments, some humor and frequent gut-wrenching discussions. In the end—and through much hard work and soul searching by ABC management—a revised profile was developed which more accurately represented the company's true positioning on the China Readiness matrix. The shift in this positioning had a significant impact on its path forward.

Specific issues were identified for further consideration and, after four angst-ridden years of indecision on this critical issue, ABC Company's management reached consensus on a future course of action.

FIGURE 8.2: ABC'S INITIAL READINESS POSITIONING

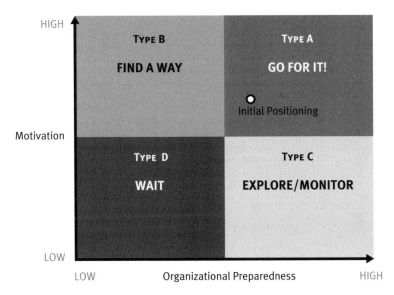

The balance of this chapter will describe the process ABC Company management went through, the issues they explored and the results they achieved. As we recount the process we will see the very human side of the China Readiness Assessment as executives struggled for the future of their company in an increasingly competitive global environment.

MOTIVATION: SEPARATING THE 'SHOULD' FROM THE 'COULD'

Over the past four years, there had been almost constant pressure for ABC Company to expand operations into China. The problem was getting a handle on the specifics of this pressure—or, in the language of the China Readiness Assessment, the Motivation. This lack of clarity was at the heart of ABC management's indecision over China: Just what was pushing or pulling them to take this big step and how should they respond? Until they could better articulate the primary motivations, they felt uncomfortable making any investment.

Senior management's response to the initial readiness questionnaire resulted in a Motivation profile (Figure 8.3). In order to flush out what was behind these initial responses, we initiated a sequence of probing interviews with individual senior managers at all key functional levels. The first, and one of the most revealing questions we asked was, "Why do you think ABC needs to do something more in China?" Despite its simplicity, it elicited many furrowed brows and qualified responses. While there were several areas of consistent agreement among management, there were also deep rifts exposed in the differing opinions on where ABC was with respect to a China opportunity and what should be done about it. These divides kept management from taking a confident step forward. Let's review how ABC management worked through each of the Motivation indicators we outlined in chapter four.

Most ABC executives were clear that one motivation to being in China was obvious cost savings in manufacturing their products there. As suppliers to major OEMs producing computer and consumer electronics, ABC was under constant price pressure. "I am always being asked by our customers what our 'China price' is, and I really don't know what to tell them," the vice president of sales said at the time of the assessment. "Do we even have one? *Should* we have one?" Even a cursory analysis of ABC's financials would have revealed that lower labor rates and facility costs in China, to say nothing of a shorter distance to customers throughout Asia, would have made for cost-per-part savings of five to ten cents, "a huge advantage in our business," the sales VP said. Another manager added, "I would estimate that cost savings is 80% of the reason that we are considering this move."

FIGURE 8.3: ABC COMPANY'S INITIAL MOTIVATION PROFILE

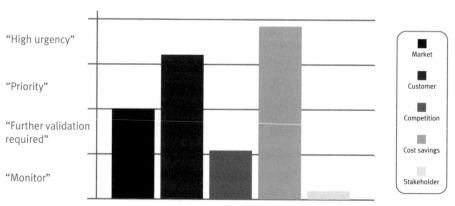

In ABC's business, being cost competitive was becoming more urgent. While its products were not yet commodities, ABC was finding it more difficult to differentiate itself on technology and service alone. Irrespective of these valued provisions, customers were demanding lower prices—but there is "a hard floor to how much we can shave off our price by manufacturing in the U.S." said one manager.

FIGURE 8.4: ABC COMPANY ASSET LOCALIZATION

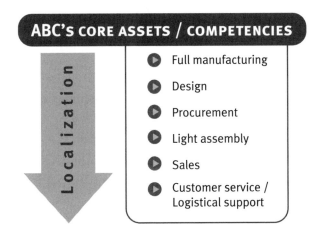

Management had to determine precisely what manufacturing resources needed to be transferred to China to optimize cost savings while being technically feasible from an operational standpoint—and this is without yet considering risks in intellectual property. To this end, we completed an asset localization chart (Figure 8.4) and discussed each asset's contribution to cost reduction. Certainly, the ability to manufacture locally and ship to nearby customers drove any savings—on this point there was universal agreement. In order to gain substantial production cost improvements, however, ABC would have to go deep into its bill of material, all the way to full manufacturing. In effect, the manufacturing equation appeared to be an all-or-nothing proposition. This raised the bar on several issues. From the technical side, there were concerns whether or not ABC could find qualified manufacturing personnel and production management locally. On the investment side, it would need a full-fledged facility. The support necessary from the U.S. during and after startup would be significant. The fact that the company had difficulties in this regard with its new U.S.-based facility expansion shed doubt on the project's feasibility. Many of these points were carried forward in the session on *transfer of operations* later in the workshop.

Most ABC executives identified another urgent motivation as *customer pressure* for the company to have a more direct presence in China and more broadly throughout Asia in order to better serve the needs of customers in the region. Most of ABC's customers had moved manufacturing operations to Asia over the last several years, with the most important ones locating in China. "The perception around here is that our customers are telling us, 'It would be better if you were in China,' " the vice president of sales said at the time. Another ABC manager was concerned that they could not adequately serve Asia-based customers from the U.S., saying, "We need to locate more decision-making power over there in order to serve our customers better. We are too far away here."

ABC Company found connection with all four customer pressure points identified in chapter four (Figure 8.5). Certainly, customers were looking for lower costs and closer logistics. If ABC continued to manufacture only in the U.S., it would have a very difficult time convincing customers that it was offering the lowest possible price. In other words, there was both the *actual* cost savings and the *perception* of lower costs as assumed by the customer. During the workshop, we had a lively debate on whether this was a manufacturing issue or a communications issue. One executive said, "Well, if we can convince them that keeping manufacturing in the U.S. is in their best interest, then why do we need to move at all?" It was a perceptive question and one that would come back into play on the last day of the workshop.

FIGURE 8.5: NATURE OF CUSTOMER PULL ON ABC

Customer Driver	Perceived level of 'pull'	Key issues to consider
Lower Costs	Strong–customers assume cost reduction due to 'China price'	Reality vs. perception Net gain or loss to ABC?
Logistics	ABC needs to be in same time zone JIT requirements/reliability that ABC will supply	Extend ABC's current logistics in region More senior staff in China/Asia
Technology/design	Highly valued–want benefits in China, not second best	Service and design issue, not manufacturing
Relationship	Highly valued asset of ABC Too far away	Perception issue–must show local face

One of the primary requests from ABC's Asia-based customers, however, was to have closer access to ABC's design and technical capabilities. While ABC had been very good about parachuting in technical service resources, often at a moment's notice, there was general agreement that the customer would simply feel better having ABC's technical expertise in the same, or at least a nearby, time zone. "There is something comforting about having your supplier close," the CFO said, "and right now, we are not that kind of supplier to our customer." This comment summed up ABC's final pressure point of simply needing to build closer relationships with its China- and Asia-based customers. "Because we are not really there, we are often questioned whether or not we really know our customers' China needs," one ABC executive admitted. "Certainly, we feel we know their needs, but this is a game of perception and if locating more resources in China will help us gain in this area, we should seriously consider it."

Next, we discussed the possible motivation of finding new, incremental opportunities in the China market. In other words, would establishing a greater footprint in China give ABC access to *market opportunities* that it would not otherwise have? As a public company, ABC was under constant pressure to grow the top line. If China could present some addressable incremental growth opportunities for ABC, this would be a tangible incentive to expand there.

However, at the time of our workshop, ABC executives were stuck in the classic "build it and they will come" dilemma: Was there a period at the end of that statement (as in "yes, if we build it, they will come") or a question mark ("if we build it, will they really come—and can we afford to wait until they do?")? Available data indicated that demand for ABC's customers' products, including computers and consumer electronics, was experiencing double-digit growth in China and globally.

One executive was sure that "if we were there, we could pick up other orders" but others were not so confident. "I don't think buying decisions are localized in China quite yet. They are still being made here," another executive said. There was consensus among the group regarding the location of ABC's growth appetite (Figure 8.6). The horizontal axis suggested that ABC was hungry for growth. Said one candid executive: "Shareholders demand growth, individual compensation plans are tied to growth and life is generally better when we are growing." However, ABC's appetite for growth was off balance in regards to its appetite for risk, which was not commensurately large. This positioning indicated to the group that ABC was not willing to invest ahead of incremental demand; it must first find and even secure the growth opportunity and then it would build to satisfy it.

FIGURE 8.6: ABC'S GROWTH APPETITE

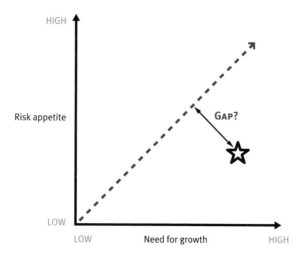

Some executives were very concerned about key *competitors,* all of them foreign-owned, which were already in China or at least elsewhere in Asia: "They are already there and that might mean that we should be there, too," the VP of sales said. However, he also admitted that they did not know enough about the local capabilities of their competition and what assets they had in the region. Other ABC management posited that keeping manufacturing in the U.S. was actually a competitive advantage. Said one, "We know our competition is having problems getting the quality and consistency in their manufacturing in China. If we move over there, are we just going to be falling into the same trap?"

No one on ABC's management team was naïve about the stability of customer-supplier relationships in its industry. "There is very little in the way of loyalty in this business," one executive said. "If you provide quality, cost and delivery, you get the business. If you don't, someone else will get the business, plain and simple."

While ABC's proprietary technology gave management some competitive advantage, it was uncertain just how long their technology could protect them. Constant advancements in the industry meant everyone had to run hard just to stay in place. There was little confidence that resting on a technological advantage would protect them in the long run. If another supplier even partially closed the technology gap and offered a lower price, ABC would be vulnerable. "Price could beat technology," the VP of sales said. "We are not yet in a commodity space but it is close enough where price really can make a difference."

In our "losing business to the Chinese in five easy steps" scenario described in chapter four, ABC's value chain was deep into steps three and four, and about to creep into five: the OEMs had localized, first-tier suppliers were following or being pressured to follow, and the OEMs were just beginning to qualify local China companies for global supply. Unless ABC could confidently identify a point of competitive differentiation by remaining in the U.S., it would have to seriously consider a deeper China play merely to stall competitive threat. "Who would have thought it would come to this," ABC's CTO said, "when we are looking to China as a source of serious competition. China is not just the land of cheap toys and clothing manufacturers any longer!"

As a publicly traded company, the *stakeholder push* motivation was always lurking over ABC management. We probed this issue, most specifically with the CEO, asking whether or not he was feeling pressure from Wall Street or his board of directors. "To the contrary, actually," he said, "My board is very cautious about our expanding manufacturing beyond U.S. borders and, frankly, I agree with them." We were quite encouraged by this point of view, as stakeholders with an itch for China and a casual interest in the facts can create a dangerous motivator.

As for Wall Street, that one was straightforward, if not necessarily easy, to manage. "We need to properly organize our thoughts, and that is why we are doing the China Readiness Assessment," the CEO said. "Once we know what we want to do and can articulate it, our performance will speak for itself to Wall Street." While impressed with his confidence, the group did not necessarily share it; many believed that analysts and investors favored companies leading a push into China.

CONCLUSIONS ON MOTIVATION

The Motivation section of the workshop qualified the pressures ABC was feeling to expand into China, poked holes in some reasons and supported others. In each of the Motivation indicators, we identified what questions remained to be answered in order to confidently rate them.

For example, we highlighted the issues around cost savings through operational efficiencies to identify which were valid drivers and which needed to be further qualified:

- ABC identified the cost saving motivation as the primary driver to reduce manufacturing costs, particularly labor, and increase margin.
- ABC's manufacturing value chain was (or soon would be) in China and throughout Asia, so all shipments of ABC products would go to the region, regardless of where they were purchased.
- We agreed that improvement was possible by moving to lower-cost manufacturing, but how much margin was "enough" (10%? 5%? 2%?) and did ABC really trust its financial planning models? There was enough debate around past experiences to indicate ABC did not have a stellar track record in this regard.
- If there was to be an investment in a China operation, how soon did ABC have to reach ROI? Management generally disagreed on what this hurdle should be and recognized that the board would be a tough sell. We tabled some of these discussions to address later in our Financial Preparedness review.

We also identified questions of customer pull to explore before we could confidently say how to respond:

- Where are the customers' purchasing decisions made, in the U.S. or China? Where is the power balance today and how is it shifting? (This refers to the power loop described in chapter two.)
- Many customers have said they want ABC in China, but what assets do the customers think are most important for ABC to localize: manufacturing, design, service, trouble-shooting, inventory, etc.? What can be realistically addressed from the U.S.?
- How much is ABC willing to bet that its presence in China will result in more sales to existing customers? What is the time frame to develop this? How can this be validated?

- What is the possible perception by customers that they will get a lower price if ABC is in China? Is this perception a reality? Will ABC lose margin on a net basis after price adjustment?

Our initial analysis of incremental growth opportunities in the China market showed a gap between what ABC wanted in terms of growth and what it was willing to risk in terms of investment ahead of that growth curve. After much discussion, it was concluded that, while management believed in mid- to long-term opportunity in China's market, there was not enough confidence in near-term incremental growth opportunities to warrant closing that gap. Therefore, ABC management decided to table the China market driver, at least in considering the current investment equation. If ABC's management could validate that enough motivation existed among the other factors, then they could consider incremental opportunities as gravy but, for now, they believed it would unduly muddy the waters. We applauded this decision, noting that too many companies are seduced by unproven incremental growth opportunities; taking it off the table now eliminated a potential distraction.

Management also concluded that ABC needed some on-the-ground intelligence to better qualify and measure the competitive threat from locally based players. As a result, a specific initiative was developed to evaluate the top competitors. Some of the issues to probe included:

- What are competitors' local capabilities and how will they likely expand in the next few years?
- What technologies are competitors taking to market today? In the future?
- What do the competitors see as attractive local market opportunities and how are they organizing to go after them?
- Where has the bar been set by competition in terms of what customers, actual and potential, expect a supplier to provide?
- What are the internal drivers and constraints on these companies with respect to being in China? What are their limitations to respond to the China challenge?
- Are there any gaps in customer expectations that are not being met by competitors' China strategies? Can ABC exploit these gaps from a base in the U.S. or must it be more local in China?

Lastly, it was very clear that stakeholder push was not a driver. In fact, management knew they would have to deal with stakeholder inertia instead. The board was in full agreement on the growth-risk perspective and was not going to be easily swayed in closing that gap: "Any investment proposal brought before the board would have to be bulletproof," ABC's CEO said.

Two comments made during the workshop on Motivation summed it all up for ABC management. The first one came from the CFO in the middle of our discussion. Remember that one of the primary motivations going into the assessment was cost savings. At the height of our discussion of this topic, the CFO said, "I am all about cost savings—but we need to find motivations *beyond* just cost savings. It needs to be about something other than lower-cost product." His purpose was to focus the team, reminding everyone that the single motivation of cost savings was not compelling ABC to respond; rather, it was the interplay between this one motivation and others.

The second comment came from the head of operations: "The reason our customers like us is that we are really good at what we do, from our manufacturing to our design, our sales and our customer service," she said. "And the fact is, we are good at doing it here in the U.S.; I would be concerned that, if we were to move this out of the U.S., could 'we' still be 'us'? Could we operate there the way we operate here?" The CEO echoed this point by saying "Right. Can we do our magic over there without losing our secret recipe?"

They both hit the nail on the head. A company's China Readiness is not only about motivation to expand to China; rather, it is about its motivations combined with the ability to execute on these motivations.

The Readiness exercise brought both clarity and change to the initial perspective on motivations to invest in China (Figure 8.7). The China market opportunity indicator dropped down and the stakeholder push indicator stayed down.

Although still critical, cost savings dipped; management's initial confidence in its value began to wane as they started to determine exactly how much could be saved and how much would be enough. The customer motivation became slightly more important as the group came together to share customer concerns and realized that a lot seemed important but that they did not know enough detail behind the customer's demands to respond effectively. The competitor motivation shot up when the management team realized they were facing potential exposure to competitors already in China— companies they did not know enough about.

FIGURE 8.7: ABC COMPANY'S REVISED MOTIVATION PROFILE

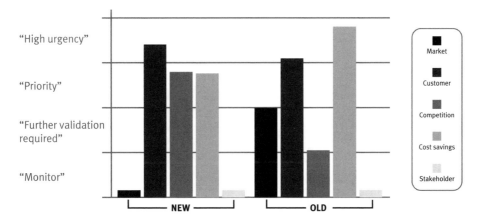

The workshop resulted in the establishment of a set of initiatives to further validate the key assumptions behind the motivations and to better position the type of responses needed (Figure 8.8).

The exercise in Motivation was open to a diverse set of views by management with different levels of experience, power and agendas, all the while focusing them on the main task: Identify just *why* they would pursue a China initiative. The CEO's "forced discipline" to work through the issues objectively enabled ABC management to get unstuck in the process and to move forward in an effective and united manner on this dimension of the readiness process, with prioritized issues and defined initiatives to address them. They were now in a position to evaluate how prepared they were as an organization to pursue these motivations.

FIGURE 8.8: ABC COMPANY'S REVISED MOTIVATION ASSESSMENT

Motivation	Initial positioning	Workshop outcomes	Key initiatives
Cost savings	• Main driver with moderate-high urgency to achieve substantial cost savings to remain competitive	• Net savings after price givebacks could be negative • Validity of cost model/assumptions considered "thin" (wide distrust of their ability to model costs) • Perceived high level of risk in implementing China initiative • IP risks could outweigh any gains	• Make cost model more robust and test key assumptions • Develop operational plan to uncover implementation risks • Explore availability of local resources to replicate company competencies
Customer pull	• Main driver with high urgency to respond to vocal requests from key customers to be "in China"	• Lack of clarity in what customers really want • Threat as a result of giving no tangible response to customers • Identified a spectrum of responses to be considered with varying levels of risk/reward	• Conduct formal research with key customer management in U.S. and Asia/China to: – Understand geographical power – Future plans – Presence of competition – Need for supplier support in China
China market potential	• Low motivation—no apparent attractive opportunity in near term	• Emerging opportunity considered likely • Impact only in mid-term	• Monitor market evolution through local Asian team
Competitive threat	• Unclear–competition present in Asia/China but strategies not well understood	• Level of threat could be serious and needs better understanding • A competitor's pre-emptive move could change competitive landscape	• Conduct formal research to evaluate competition's current activities and future strategic direction • Train marketing staff on competitive intelligence gathering techniques and strategies • Consider potential alliances in Asia
Stakeholder push	• Low–supportive of China investigation but too skeptical or risk averse to take action	• Depth and nature of stakeholder cynicism uncovered	• Add significant rigor to analysis and investment proposal

ABC's Operational Preparedness: a rough road ahead

In chapter five, we described operational preparedness, the ability to transfer or replicate the core competencies of your business to support the realization of your defined
motivations for China. This characteristic of a company's Organizational Preparedness
is measured by four indicators:

- Transfer of key operations
- Protecting intellectual property
- Business structure
- Alliances

These indicators posed some significant challenges to ABC Company.

Transfer of key operations: Because ABC's primary motivation was cost reduction
through establishing a manufacturing facility in China, transfer of key operations was
critical to its success. ABC's proprietary manufacturing processes and technology
were at the heart of its core value proposition. Therefore, management needed to
transfer these capabilities intact to maintain competitive advantage. This transfer
had to be made in an industry sector subject to rapid change and pressure to commod-
itize the product. ABC could not afford to slip backward in technical sophistication or
productivity in the China operation. Management was unanimous in their view that
maintaining their technical competence in a hostile manufacturing environment such
as China was a significant challenge. ABC's manufacturing processes were unique
and required not only specialized equipment but well-trained and experienced shop
floor personnel. Recall that the CEO questioned whether ABC could transfer its operations to China and still keep the "magic" that made it valuable to its customers. This
was the key challenge for ABC to address in the China initiative.

We then worked through some of the parameters on transferring operations as
reviewed in chapter five. ABC passed with flying colors in terms of *stability* and
process documentation. It was qualified on a number of ISO certifications and had
its processes documented in minute detail (even translating some into Chinese just
to see if they would convert well, which they did). However, this evaluation strength-
ened management's resolve to not compromise manufacturing stability in any transfer
of those operations.

Over the years, ABC had slowly introduced technology to make its manufacturing processes more automated, increasing the quality of manufacturing while reducing the cost by removing expensive labor. When we discussed how *flexible* these processes were, the immediate response was, "They are not. They must be done this way." After further probing, one of the more seasoned executives, who had spent many of his early years on the shop floor, said, "Wait a minute. Why can't we return to some of our more manual processes like we used to do? Sure, we will have to be more careful of quality, but if labor cost is not so much of an issue, why can't we put that back in?" It was a poignant question to the group but elicited groans from some managers who envisioned moving backwards in manufacturing technology.

There was initial agreement that, while the processes they had now were far superior to anything used in the past, at least a little flexibility in their setup was possible by selectively introducing some of the older, more manual methods to fit better with conditions in China. However, further discussion raised additional concerns. On a fact-finding trip to China the previous year, ABC management explored the level of manufacturing expertise in the region in order to determine if skilled labor and management were available to successfully replicate their manufacturing processes there; or, in the language of the China Readiness Assessment, to discover how *supportable* its operations would be. The findings were not encouraging. One manager said, "It was very difficult to even find craftsmen that could make tools to our tight tolerances." Additionally, raw materials such as high-quality metals and electrical connectors were not available locally, and importing them added to costs and manufacturing cycle time. Therefore, the team's ranking of their operation's supportability was low, which cast doubt on the real cost savings they would be able to achieve, not to mention if they would be able to inject more manual labor into the process.

Overall in the transfer of operations indicator, ABC found itself in the upper right-hand corner of the transfer risk matrix (Figure 8.9), indicating a high level of exposure.

FIGURE 8.9: ABC COMPANY'S OPERATIONAL TRANSFER RISK MATRIX

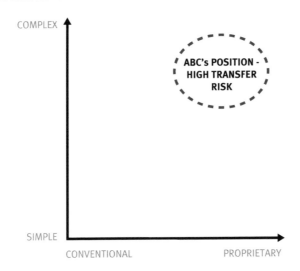

ABC management would have to think carefully through the feasibility of setting up a low-cost but highly productive operation in China with these handicaps.

Protecting intellectual property: As a company working in high-tech electronics manufacturing, protecting intellectual property was crucial and the main defense against commoditization of its business. ABC had important patents in both technology and manufacturing processes and was naturally very concerned over the poor level of IP protection in China—in fact, the company at that time was involved in a legal dispute with a China competitor over some technology ABC believed the competitor acquired illegally. One manager said, "We are already exposed in China because we ship product there; can we afford to be even more exposed by manufacturing it there?" Another manager asked the group, "Are we willing to compromise our IP for the assumed economic benefit of manufacturing in China?" This question elicited significant discussion and debate during our workshop.

The group worked through the four-step process to evaluate IP risk.

1. **What IP needs to be transferred to China?** As concluded in the discussion on transfer of operational assets, ABC would need to move its key arsenal of technology and processes to China to support the setup of a low-cost and high-quality facility. Its IP inventory checklist reflected this condition (Figure 8.10).

197

2. **What are the risks in this IP transfer?** It was clear that ABC could not retain its key competencies in the sanctuary of its U.S. operations but needed to fully expose its core capabilities to achieve success. Unless it could build strong defenses around its technology and processes, ABC would be at high risk.

3. **How can we protect IP?** Given this risk exposure, we diligently explored the protection tactics listed in chapter five to see how to insulate ABC's IP in the transfer of its operation to China:

   - ABC had already registered all its patents throughout the region. This gave it the basis for legal recourse against the patent infringement from China the company was fighting at the time, although registering the patents had not been enough of a deterrent to prevent someone from attempting to steal its technology.

   - We discussed ways to black box or fragment ABC's processes throughout the facility, but this was difficult as crucial IP was dispersed widely throughout the manufacturing processes. ABC could not put up a curtain around one key process. It would have had to segregate the entire manufacturing operation—an impractical approach.

   - We also searched for ways to stratify ABC's manufacturing processes, leaving some of the key IP back in the U.S. However, to fully realize its key Motivation—proximity to customer and cost reduction—an "all-or-nothing" localization of its manufacturing was required. In fact, anything less would actually add cost and time to the customer.

   - There was no doubt that ABC would send along a guardian to protect its technology and processes. In fact, the level of IP risks would require more operational personnel being sent from headquarters, with commensurate increases in the facility's overhead.

   - ABC had well-defined policies and procedures to protect its technologies in its U.S. facilities. These would be dutifully applied to the China operation.

FIGURE 8.10: ABC's IP INVENTORY CHECKLIST

Asset	Description	Relevance to China strategy
Brand	Not an issue	None
Formulation	Not an issue	None
Process	Highly proprietary precision tooling and assembly	Core to success
Technology	Industry leader in its patented technology area—the company's crown jewels	Core to success
Experience, trade secrets	Broad and deep experience in applying technology—strong contribution to its competitive advantage	Process know-how needs to accompany technology
Reputation	Industry leader in technology and quality	Failure in China would have significant backlash
Customer relationships	Strong position among industry leaders, provides high credibility	Easily transferred to China
Territorial rights	Had global rights to technology offering	None

4. **What is the net risk-reward of making the IP transfer?** ABC's net risk-reward position in making the IP transfer was in the danger zone (Figure 8.11). As this risk-reward ratio began to look more questionable, ABC management shifted its discussion to focus on ways they could satisfy customer needs without unduly exposing IP. This discussion uncovered some constructive options, which we tabled to review later in the workshop.

In sum, IP concerns added another cold reality to ABC's successful setup of a China manufacturing operation and caused the company to revisit the key motivations compelling it to take action.

FIGURE 8.11: ABC COMPANY'S IP RISK POSITIONING

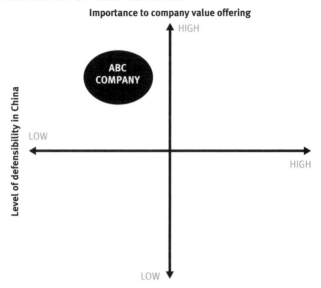

Business structures and **alliances:** The other two indicators of Operational Preparedness, openness to business structures and alliances, were of less importance compared to transfer of operations and IP protection. In reviewing ABC's openness and adaptability regarding business structure against its key driving forces to pursue a China initiative, the viable options appeared limited (Figure 8.12). The need to have tight control on all key aspects of the operation, exacerbated by the identified IP risk, made a wholly owned foreign enterprise (WOFE) the only acceptable alternative. Despite this limited choice of structures, there were no impasses to setting up a WOFE to suit the company's requirements.

Management further validated the conclusion on business structure by reviewing its abilities, experience and need for alliance partners in China. ABC executives considered the company to be an excellent partner, a trait well recognized among existing customers and suppliers. The company had even come close to establishing a joint venture with an Asian partner a few years ago but eventually backed out due to concerns about exposing its IP—not unlike the China situation.

FIGURE 8.12: ABC'S KEY DRIVING FACTORS FOR A CHINA BUSINESS STRUCTURE

Driving factor	ABC status
Investment level	Although management was concerned about making additional capital investment given the company's recent expansion in the U.S., they had the resources to support it.
Market access	Not an issue, as they would serve the same customer base as currently from the U.S.
Legal restrictions	None in their industry sector.
IP protection	*Major concerns about having an equity partnership due to technology leakage.*
Flexibility	Desirable given the high level of flux in their industry.
Control	*Critical to ensure high quality and protect technology and processes.*
Speed to market	Not important.

When we completed the asset control profile (Figure 8.13), ABC appeared to need to own virtually all its key assets, if not right away, then at least eventually. In no area was a local partner considered necessary or even contributory to ABC's needs. Management's openness to outsourcing any key asset was considered out of the question. So, despite ABC's seeming cooperative nature, it was clear that it would go it alone in China, or not at all.

FIGURE 8.13: ABC COMPANY'S ASSET CONTROL PROFILE

Asset or competence	Need to own it?	Need local partner?	Can outsource?
Production	Yes	Lack capabilities	Never
Brand	Yes	No perceived value	Never
Distribution/ logistics	Probably—JIT key competence	Maybe	Questionable
Sales Force	Absolutely—core competence	Some value add	No—too technical
Market Knowledge	Absolutely— dynamic market	Would be supportive	Never
Customer/Channel Access	Absolutely—intimate relationship	Some value add	Never
Guanxi	Ultimately	Would be supportive	Not relevant
Technology	Absolutely	No added value	Never

At the core, ABC was a do-it-yourself company. From its foundation in a small garage forty years ago, management had made its own way through organic development. The more we wrestled with these issues, the more ABC management realized that, while it was certainly an advantage in many situations, the do-it-yourself approach could also dilute their effectiveness in China. Cooperation and partnership were almost imperative to get things done there, even if ABC created a WOFE operation. A strength in its home business culture could be a liability in China if not managed carefully.

OPERATIONAL PREPAREDNESS SUMMARY PERSPECTIVE

Figure 8.14 shows the overall Operational Preparedness of ABC Company. Virtually all the indicators exposed key issues, notably in transfer of assets and IP protection. The other two indicators were closer to center, but could still cause problems in China. As a result, its overall operational positioning (the star) was dangerously close to the outer edge, indicating that ABC would face some significant risks should it pursue a China initiative. Management clearly had work to do.

FIGURE 8.14: ABC COMPANY'S OPERATIONAL PREPAREDNESS

O1	Transferability of key operations
O2	Exposure of products/processes
O3	Openness to new business structures
O4	Alliances

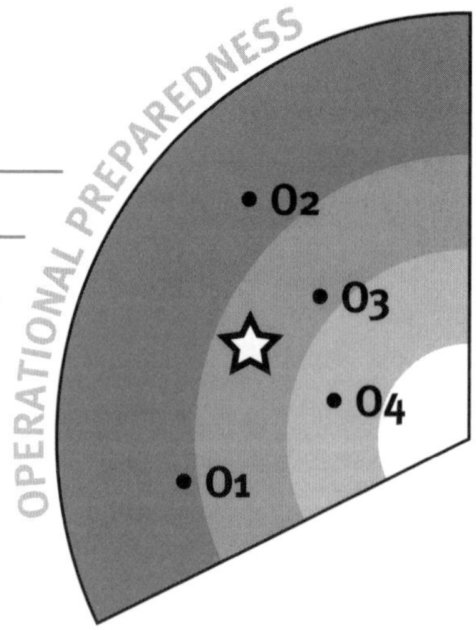

Closer to center indicates higher readiness
☆ = Composite readiness

ABC's Managerial Preparedness: a classic pagoda

With a sobering view of their Operational Preparedness, the ABC team pushed onward into the human resource side of establishing and managing a China operation. Overall, ABC was fortunate to have a solid and deep management team as well as sound human resource policies and practices. These would serve management well in supporting an expanded China initiative, should they decide to pursue it.

We reviewed the four main indicators of managerial preparedness as presented in chapter six:

- Management sponsorship
- Management depth
- China experience
- Relationship management

Management sponsorship: ABC scored well on the center pillar of management sponsorship, with strong support at the upper levels of the organization—necessary to weather the inevitable storms that roll over a China business. When we reviewed the stakeholder questions outlined in chapter six, answers were clear and confident. Top management was going into this program with its eyes wide open and with high resolve. The company had a clear practice of assigning a champion to any meaningful new project. Management explained that every new initiative is presented to the senior management team in order to "sell" them on its merits, a rather standard practice. But not only must senior management agree that the initiative meets all the financial requirements to be funded, one of the senior managers must agree to sponsor the program—to put his or her stock behind it to make sure it has the right visibility and support within the company. In other words, ABC senior management would not view any issues that emerge as "their problem"; they would be "our problem" and, more importantly, "my problem" from the perspective of the senior executive champion.

Similar clarity and confidence came out when we wrapped up our discussion on this indicator with a review of the sponsorship checklist (see chapter six, Figure 6.2). ABC management was confident that, should they pursue a China expansion project, there would be strong and consistent sponsorship from senior staff at the home office.

Management depth: ABC Company also had a rich roster of talented executives making for significant management depth. They had a senior team that had been with the company for many years and risen through the ranks to their current positions. We discussed the various staff that would be involved in a China initiative (in their case, the point people on the project included a leader in the manufacturing group and a VP of business development) and how ABC would back-fill those positions in the U.S. operation.

We were encouraged to find that many of the managers had cross-trained in other divisions and departments so ABC had a range of options to fill holes left when these two key leaders began to focus on China. In fact, there were some heated (but constructive) exchanges between managers over issues in each other's departments with respect to a potential China initiative. The operations manager had come out of a supervisory position on the shop floor while the CEO had started in the tool shop more than thirty years before, so both intimately understood the day-to-day issues manufacturing was facing. In a collegial banter between the operations and production managers, the ops guy said, "Aw, I could do your job in my sleep," to which the current production manager quipped, "You did—for five years!" The group was confident that ABC could plug management gaps left open in pursuing a China initiative.

While ABC had not put together a China staff before, it had experience in hiring personnel elsewhere in Asia. As most firms do, management made some hiring mistakes but had captured the lessons learned and felt comfortable about building a team to run a China operation. They had rigorous procedures for hiring and were committed to be very involved in the process. In fact, they intended to have their more seasoned Asian-based managers directly involved in the China business setup.

As with management support, the group went away feeling pretty comfortable with their readiness to put an effective China team together.

China experience: ABC Company was also reasonably deep in terms of past China experience—and general Asian experience, for that matter. For a number of years it had been serving customers in Southeast Asia and in China, visiting them regularly and shipping product to customers' Asian locations for further processing. ABC had a two-person customer service team in Singapore to field issues and problems from the region and pass them to those responsible back in the U.S.

Further, all senior and most middle management had traveled to China and throughout Asia, and the sales and technical service management and staff visited the region on a regular basis. These street smarts were very helpful in the workshop, allowing us to use some shorthand to discuss issues including the challenges of finding local sources, Chinese styles of relationship management, dealing with corruption, etc. Additionally, ABC was experienced enough to know that any decision to pursue a deeper China play could not be made lightly; they had all witnessed other Western companies crash and burn in China and were determined not to make the same mistakes.

ABC also had an Asian value chain rich in business contacts, which had been developed over many years of supporting its customer base and sourcing components in the region. However, as we began to inventory and probe the quality of these relationships (see chapter six, Figure 6.6), opinions differed on how valuable these contacts would be in advising or directly assisting ABC in its China project. It was concluded that, while ABC management felt the intimacy level of customer contacts in the U.S. was high, their relationship depth in Asia was uncertain. Management was not sure whether the local Asian executives of its key customers knew their company well enough, or were trusted enough, to offer valuable insight and direction. Some work would need to be done to build up this network and get closer. The team scoped out some specific issues and customer targets to explore further—which became part of the customer interview probe outlined in the workshop session on Motivation.

Relationship management: The most intangible of the Managerial Preparedness indicators is also one of the most important: relationship management. As a public company in a high-tech market space, ABC senior management were accustomed to spending significant amounts of time liaising with outside organizations: Wall Street, regulatory offices, industry organizations, key distributors, global OEMs and others were all on their relationship "hit list." ABC management saw that nurturing such relationships was key to their success. It was not just about creating great products— ABC had to *build the road* to deliver these products as well as its value proposition. ABC company practice was hard-wired to deal in this area: Each senior manager, especially the CEO, was assigned key *guanxi* to manage and nurture. This practice would come in very handy in any China initiative where so much of management's time is spent massaging relationships.

The discussion on China experience and the quality of their relationships in Asia prompted the team to consider ways to formalize a relationship management process. This discussion was the genesis of a seminar held in Asia the following year on business intelligence gathering. ABC brought in its entire Asia management team (by then, more than 20 staff members from six countries), in addition to U.S. staff, for a day-long workshop on practices to gather, assimilate and disseminate market and competitive intelligence. We had the privilege of designing and leading this seminar and could see the maturity of their Asian business team enhanced in a short amount of time.

ABC was also well suited to the nimble decision-making requirements needed in China's market environment. Because it was in such a volatile industry where technological advances could completely overturn their industry in a year, ABC management was accustomed to looking ahead, reading the tea leaves and making timely decisions. They were not susceptible to hand-wringing over decisions made; once management agreed on what to do, everyone jumped on board and focused on the road ahead. We discussed how important this attribute was in their China initiative. Inevitably, a shadow of doubt will fall over a new China play, if only for a time, and management needs to feel confident in their decision and stick with it.

MANAGERIAL PREPAREDNESS SUMMARY PERSPECTIVE

ABC's solid leadership team and management practices at home would be a valuable contribution to any China effort. The conclusion from the workshop on this dimension was that ABC's experience was most certainly "stir-fried": They had learned a lot about China business in a high-temperature environment. This was solid experience, not "microwaved"—ABC had been doing business in Asia in some form for a number of years and had gained a great amount of respect for the challenges of the path it was considering taking.

While there were still key concerns about the transfer of their core assets to China, ABC management could at least feel confident in their managerial preparedness. All of the indicators were relatively close to center, resulting in a very strong overall positioning. While ABC management did not consider this strength a solution or justification for pursuing a China initiative, they took comfort that they could find a way to get it done well, one executive concluding, "Okay, we are a management team smart and capable enough to figure this out. Let's keep going."

FIGURE 8.15: ABC's MANAGERIAL READINESS POSITIONING

M1	Management sponsorship
M2	Management depth
M3	China experience
M4	Relationship management

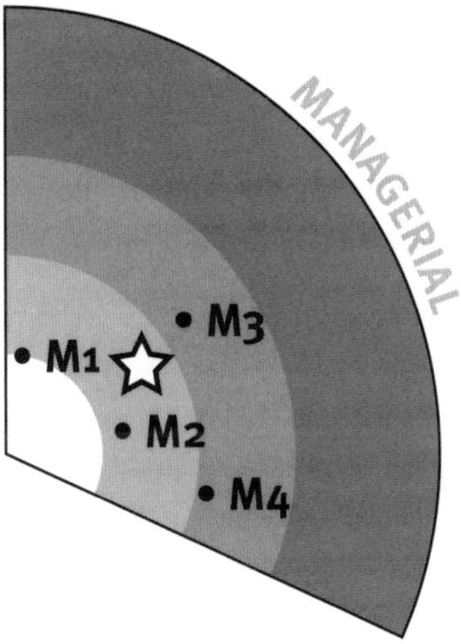

Closer to center indicates higher readiness

☆ = Composite readiness

ABC's FINANCIAL PREPAREDNESS—AN UNSTEADY 'PILE OF BUDDHAS'

With some positive momentum from our discussion of Managerial Preparedness, we plowed into the very critical area of financial indicators. When capital requests and budgets come into play, everyone gets very serious. If a company does not have the financial resources or the leeway to use them, then a sound strategy, strong management team and even a high degree of passion won't be enough.

The exercise on Financial Preparedness exposes a company's realities in four highly intertwined factors:

- Financial health
- Willingness to spend
- Risk tolerance
- Expectations on returns

Clearly understanding these realities will help you design the right approach, structure and scope of your China strategy. When combined with your profile on Operational and Managerial Preparedness, they give you a complete picture of the risks involved in pursuing your defined motivations. For ABC Company, this final exercise helped management find its ultimate positioning on the overall readiness matrix.

Financial health and *willingness to spend:* We first considered what we called in chapter seven the "foundational acrobats," ABC's financial health and willingness to spend. As a public company, ABC was subject to rigorous review of its financial health and performance. At the time, ABC had just completed two investments—one in a domestic facility and the other in a new technology—that had not yet seen a return. Additionally, the industry had just experienced another technology transition which had cut the legs out from under many of its competitors. Wall Street seemed confident in ABC's ability to survive; however, it was also sensitive about ABC taking on any further investments. Even its customers, which depended on ABC's consistent high quality and reliable supply of critical components, expressed concern over the company's delicate financial condition.

We evaluated ABC's basic financial situation in the financial health diagnosis introduced in chapter seven (Figure 8.16). As you can see, most of the indicators are in the "adequate" category: There are no flashing red lights around ABC's basic financial health. The company's condition was okay but borderline in terms of its ability to absorb a failed new venture. It had a thin margin of error and its profile could quickly go south if it made a serious mistake.

Notably, ABC's P&L could ill afford to absorb a hit should the performance of a China operation fall below expectations. This condition suggested that any targets on the performance of the China investment should be very conservative—setting the bar a bit higher to create some cushion for error.

In terms of their willingness to spend, ABC management knew they had to allocate substantial discretionary money on a China strategy, both to explore it and then, if necessary, to execute it. Time and again, we have seen companies try to get into China "on the cheap." You may find bargains on clothes in the open-air markets, but everything else costs real money. ABC management set a sufficient amount of funds aside in their budget for this effort. Even before they engaged us to do the China Readiness Assessment, they had already expended significant dollars. Several years before they had explored doing an alliance with a China-based supplier and spent nearly $300,000 on the exploration phase alone, including legal fees, numerous trips and other costs. Their prior spending on exploration—and their willingness to continue to invest in both hard and soft costs in a prudent manner—were signs to us of a healthy attitude towards their commitment to exploring a solution with proper due diligence.

FIGURE 8.16: ABC'S FINANCIAL HEALTH CHECK TO INVEST IN CHINA

Financial health check			
Parameter	**Weak**	**Adequate**	**Strong**
Key financial ratios are in line with industry standards		X	
You have access to sufficient cash to fund the investment		X	
Your balance sheet can absorb the investment		X	
You have sufficient financial resources to fund the core business concurrently with the China Investment		X	
The company has a decent track record of healthy financials (i.e. you are not just coming out of Chapter 11, a failed investment or some other financial reconstruction)		X	
Your P&L can absorb lower than expected financial performance of the China operation, at least in the near term	X		
Your company is not in retrenchment but is actively looking to make strategic investments		X	
Key management and shareholders have confidence in the company's financial health		X	

Risk tolerance: In our acrobat analogy, risk tolerance is the next-level performer. Based on its scrutiny by Wall Street and somewhat tenuous financial position at the time, ABC's risk tolerance was rated low. All its executives were very aware of the impact that a failed China initiative would have. Additionally, ABC operated in high-tech consumer and industrial electronics, an industry sector with regular technology and consumption swings and an inherently risky space in which to play.

While ABC had to be relatively risk-averse in its approach to a China investment, management also had to consider the downsides of taking no action. One executive spoke up during the workshop: "What potentially bad happens if we don't go to China? Is there risk in not going?" These questions spurred some discussion as the group internalized the impact of this line of reasoning. Given the inherently risky nature of ABC's business, would the benefits of a China initiative actually reduce its overall risk? It was logical that gaining price advantages, proximity to customers and participating more directly in the company's value chain—even in a place like China—would actually mitigate its overall risk, if management could pull it off.

FIGURE 8.17: SAMPLE PERSPECTIVE ON ABC'S MACRO FACTORS

Indicator	Outlook	Level of uncertainty	Perceived risk to China initiative
Economic growth	Steady GDP growth of 7%+ over period	Low	Negligible
Electronics market sector growth	Steady growth of 15%+ (as compared to low single-digit growth in mature markets)	Low	Low
Import accessibility and costs	Increasing openness due WTO—tariffs will continue to decline	Low	Could make local facility less competitive
IP risks	Will remain a key problem with limited enforcement in near to mid-term	High	Must assume worst case
Technology volatility	Market sector will continue to be hit with waves of technological improvement	High	Assume many changes
Labor costs	Remain low overall but with steady increase, especially along East coast	Moderate	Impacts facility location
Corruption	Corruption and red tape are still endemic to culture—will take time to change	Low	May be high, may need partner to help
Currency fluctuation	Increasing pressure to appreciate with some likely move in near term	High	Factor into cost proformas
Political stability	Quite stable and predictable—slow to change	Low-moderate	May be some local fallout/incidents

To consider these points further, we looked at the macro factors outlined in chapter seven (Figure 8.17). Several parameters had a high level of uncertainty and commensurate risk to the China venture. Technology volatility, a weak legal environment to adequately protect IP and the prospect of currency appreciation all contributed to a fair level of uncertainty in ABC's market space.

Based on these factors and the company's financial condition, we then plotted ABC's overall risk tolerance (Figure 8.18). After much discussion, the group agreed that ABC's position was precariously close to the danger zone. Therefore, they needed to be both very nimble and resilient in their investment approach.

FIGURE 8.18: ABC's RISK TOLERANCE LEVEL

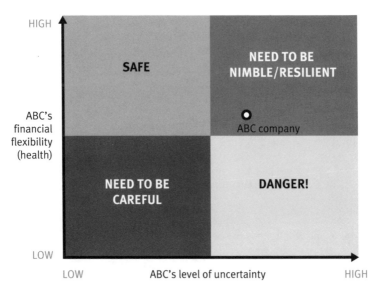

Expectations on returns: Our consideration of ABC's expectations on returns consistently followed the line of discussion as on the other financial indicators. As a publicly traded company, ABC would have defined expectations for the return of a China investment: The initiative could not drag down quarterly performance. Additionally, since a major motivation for ABC to consider China was a reduction in operating costs, management needed to calculate a very real—and believable—ROI on the initiative. As mentioned before, ABC management disagreed on the confidence of their financial projections. One executive was more certain, saying, "I think we are conservative in our financial planning and yet look for creative opportunities," while another was decidedly guarded: "Based on past experiences doing these kinds of things, I think we should double the costs and halve the benefits. That is probably where we are going to end up."

This disagreement was a red flag for us: If the pilots of the airplane cannot agree on which instruments to trust while flying through the clouds, they should consider staying on the ground until they do! The key is transparency in the analysis so that a proforma financial outlook can be accurately weighed against the benefits and risks of entering China, without inappropriate manipulation to make the deal pass muster. And every member of management needs to agree on how to keep score. ABC's managers had some work to do around this issue before they could confidently proceed.

FINANCIAL PREPAREDNESS SUMMARY PERSPECTIVE

ABC's overall financial preparedness was a mixed picture (Figure 8.19). Combined, the company's limited ability to absorb financial failure and the level of doubt around the China venture's investment return meant a moderate to high level of risk aversion. On the positive side, ABC management had a solid track record of investing properly in the exploration and due diligence phases of any new project.

FIGURE 8.19: ABC'S OVERALL FINANCIAL PREPAREDNESS

F1	Financial health
F2	Ability and willingness to spend
F3	Level of risk aversion
F4	Expectations on returns

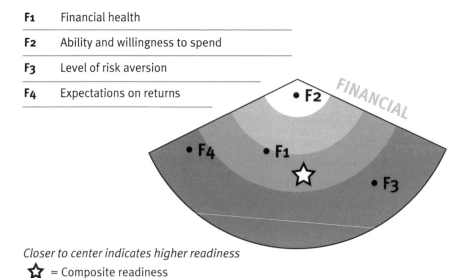

Closer to center indicates higher readiness
☆ = Composite readiness

The final result was a relatively low overall financial preparedness level. Whatever investment strategy ABC pursued, the "acrobatic trick" would need to be modest or the pile of Buddhas could collapse.

RESOLUTION—GO OR NO GO?

When we completed our discussions of all the dimensions and indicators of the China Readiness Assessment, a fundamental and strategically critical change had evolved. ABC's overall readiness position had shifted left and "crossed the line": The company was not ready for China—at least not ready to support a full-scale manufacturing facility. The balance of risk-reward had altered, and it would be imprudent to pursue a facility investment in China under the current circumstances. From an initial assumption by the group that they would have a green light to move ahead, they now saw a cautionary signal.

FIGURE 8.20: ABC'S OVERALL READINESS POSITIONING, BEFORE AND AFTER

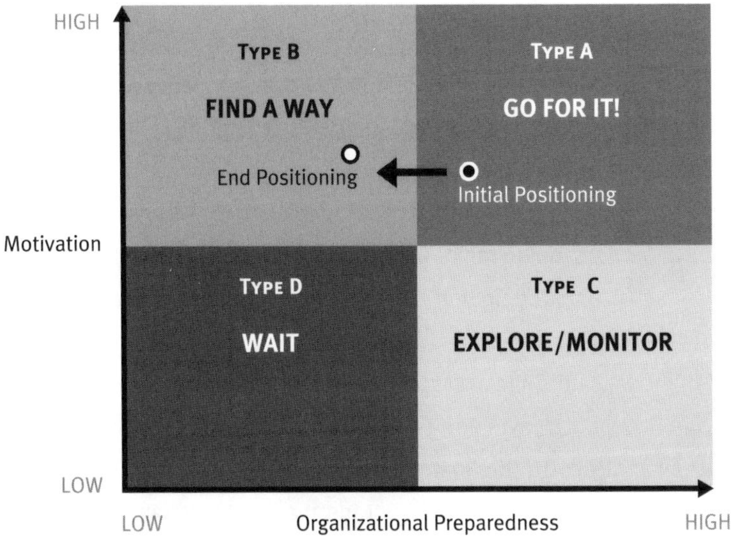

While there was a shift on the horizontal axis, ABC's position on the vertical Motivation axis inched upward. The process had substantiated the need to do something meaningful in response to these tangible drivers to be in China. The urgency level had not abated and it had become more complex as the combination of drivers to become increasingly active in China was exposed. Cost pressures still existed, customer pull appeared to have some teeth to it and competitive threat had risen from the shadows to add another key driver to the mix.

FIGURE 8.21: ABC'S FINAL MOTIVATION TO PURSUE CHINA

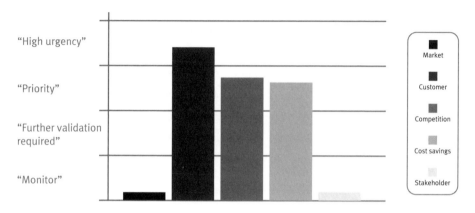

As the quadrant name states, ABC had *to find a way* to address these motivations while at the same time recognizing the gaps in its readiness to do so. Its main challenges were a combination of variables on the organizational side that suggested a high level of risk. To lower costs substantially enough to make a difference, ABC needed to set up a full-fledged facility. But a review of the technical plausibility of transferring the right assets to capture the "magic" of ABC's value proposition indicated a host of barriers, not to mention significant IP exposure. And ABC's strong DNA to do things itself prohibited finding an acceptable solution via an alliance.

The company's delicate financial health and short leash by Wall Street combined to create a relatively high aversion to risk with little room for error in performance. Adding these handicaps to the limitations ABC had in operational areas resulted in a prohibitively tough challenge. ABC's strong management team and deep human resources, while an effective support to a China initiative, would not be enough to overcome these hurdles.

When the time came to articulate this conclusion, there was a pregnant pause in the room as team members sat stoically looking at each other. They knew what to do, they just couldn't believe it enough to say it. Finally the CEO articulated what everyone was thinking. "What this is telling me is that we can't do over there what we do here; if we tried to manufacture our product there we would no longer be us and that won't work in our market. Therefore, we shouldn't do it. Right?" There was a collective sigh of relief and all heads began nodding in agreement.

FIGURE 8.22: ABC'S OVERALL ORGANIZATIONAL READINESS PROFILE

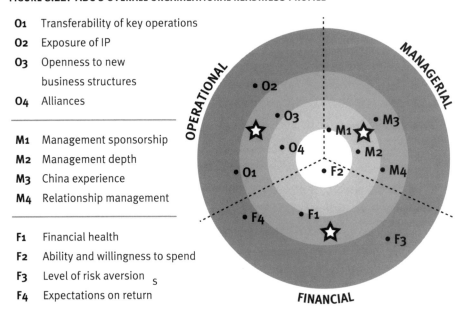

O1	Transferability of key operations
O2	Exposure of IP
O3	Openness to new business structures
O4	Alliances

M1	Management sponsorship
M2	Management depth
M3	China experience
M4	Relationship management

F1	Financial health
F2	Ability and willingness to spend
F3	Level of risk aversion s
F4	Expectations on return

Closer to center indicates higher readiness
☆ = Composite readiness

What came as a surprise to the group was that ABC was actually not ready to invest in a direct China manufacturing presence. After four years deliberating on the decision, most executives just assumed that ABC would eventually pull the trigger on China manufacturing—but it was now clear that this was not the right path forward, at least not for now.

The challenge, of course, was to determine what was the right path. "Seems like just moving manufacturing over there would be the easiest thing to do," one executive said. "We know we still need to do something to address the issues there. But what?" We then reviewed the key outcomes of the process we had toiled through. In the findings on each dimension of the China Readiness Assessment and how ABC fared on its specific set of indicators, the team found the ingredients to fashion a supportable response. ABC Company's management team learned that the results of the China Readiness Assessment do not reveal a simple yes-or-no answer or a concise, fool-proof plan on which to proceed. A China strategy is much more complicated than that. As H.L. Mencken said, "For every complex problem, there is a solution that is simple, neat, and wrong." Rather, the process is meant to support the executives who say, "I am feeling this pressure from customers to locate in China and need to respond somehow. Is this really a good action for my company to take? Realistically, what are my options?"

ABC management decided that their response to China should follow three basic principles: control, service and perception. They must consistently position themselves to have direct control over their operations, wherever the location. They needed to focus on the details of customer service, exceeding expectations at every point and foiling competitors' abilities to keep up. Finally, they needed to manage the perception from customers, Wall Street—and even internally—that they "had to be manufacturing in China."

Control: Our discussions in the workshops clearly pointed out that ABC management was committed to controlling all key aspects of their business. They designed their own technology, built their own products and managed their own sales team—and anything short of this full control would be going against the company's DNA. The Operational Preparedness indicators showed that it would be very difficult to transfer ABC's manufacturing operations to China and nearly impossible to mirror U.S. processes exactly. ABC's core differentiator was its ability to build high-quality product using leading technology, and this did not appear possible in China.

Service: ABC committed instead to focus more on service, becoming even better at supporting its customers. The China Readiness Assessment highlighted the fact that there were significant pressures from customers to meet specific needs including delivery, price, technology and technical support, and those needs would not go away. ABC decided to pursue two key initiatives:

- Open customer support centers in China, housing design, technical sales and after-sales support and logistics. The charter of these offices was to "delight the customer." The Singapore office was expanded to support the new offices in the same time zone and to link other customers in Southeast Asia.

- Understand the detailed capabilities and strategies of the competition. To provide the industry's best customer service, ABC had to better understand where the bar was being set and how its competitors might beat it. Uncovering the details of competitor strengths and weaknesses in China would enable ABC management to construct a China strategy to win at key points.

Perception: Finally, ABC's greatest battle might be to fight the perception from a number of fronts that it should be manufacturing in China because the industry seemed to be moving in that direction. To address low price, timely delivery and proximity to customers, the expectation was that ABC would eventually give in and move its manufacturing. To conclude that they should *not* do this was gutsy of ABC management, but they still had to deal with the perception that they should be manufacturing in China. The perception issue was fought on three fronts.

First, although ABC was already considered a technology leader in the industry, management decided to seek ways to widen the gap between it and the rest of the pack. If the perception was that ABC should be manufacturing in China because "everyone was doing it," ABC chose to position itself as "not like everyone." Rather than invest in establishing China manufacturing, ABC invested in more R&D, pushing the technology envelope and setting the bar higher for the competition. The goal was to be able to say, "We continue to spend the extra money and effort to manufacture in the U.S. because we are the technology leader and that's where state-of-the-art product needs to be made. We are not like the other guys." In the computer and consumer electronics industries, where cost is king, this was a hard sell.

Second, ABC had to combat perceptions among customers that because it kept manufacturing in the U.S., it would be more expensive and logistically cumbersome to work with. ABC first pursued detailed discussions with customers, probing for the price threshold that would meet their needs. It discovered that this price was not as low as originally imagined; the stereotypical "China price" had worked its power as a business myth, setting low-price expectations that even the customer did not believe were achievable. In fact, further probing revealed a growing concern about quality levels and yield, looking at price from a total cost standpoint and not per-piece cost. Customers feared that the quest for low price might compromise quality and reliability. These were not easy discussions to have, but when combined with the commitment to put more service resources in the region and to invest more in technology, customers were open to what ABC had to say about the best price at best quality and using best technology.

Finally, the battle for perception had to be fought on the shareholder front. The internal and external PR staff at ABC was tasked with telling the new China Story, a unique spin from its competition, which was picked up by major news media. "When the world says turn left and you choose to turn right, that is news," the CEO said. "And we want to make the right kind of news." Wall Street was somewhat pacified; analysts applauded ABC's decision to take it slow with respect to China and do the hard work of finding out what the China market really demanded before investing.

Epilogue
The Fight Goes On

 To get profit without risk, experience without danger, and reward without work, is as impossible as it is to live without being born.

A. P. Gouthey

Certainly, the story doesn't end here. ABC is still wrestling with the China challenge and fighting battles. But like a couple who has successfully gone through premarital counseling, ABC invested in the upfront work and dialogue to enable management to constructively respond to the challenges that will come. The company's early years in its "China marriage" have not been without difficulties and disappointments. China, like life, is throwing unpredictable challenges its way. The difference today for ABC is that management will not be caught off guard when these difficulties come. They now have a framework and process to deal effectively with them.

In reviewing the work completed during and after the China Readiness Assessment, one manager's response summed it up well: "The Readiness Assessment didn't tell us *what* to think about our challenges in China; rather, it told us *how* to think about them. It did not give us specific, step-by-step instructions; it gave us options and approaches that we had never before explored and we took it from there."

As ABC management experienced, a China Readiness Assessment will help you ask the right questions and provide a framework on which to organize the answers. If we have learned one thing about working in China for more than 20 years, it is to expect change—generally, the unexpected kind. In fact, new problems will crop up every day. The important thing is how you face these changes. The China Readiness Assessment was designed to give you the process to deal with China's challenges honestly and productively by putting handles on a seemingly unmanageable topic.

My aim has been to provide you with the necessary insights and tools to success-fully address China. First, I've described the dynamics of China's market landscape and key aspects of doing business there to give you a context for considering a China initiative. Second, I've reviewed the lessons learned by other Western companies to help keep you from making the same mistakes. And, third, I've detailed an overall process and practical diagnostic exercises to assist your management team in getting to the truth as well as reaching consensus on a path forward.

Let me close by going back to the beginning and the metaphor of a gold rush.

This is the law of the Yukon, and ever she makes it plain:
Send not your foolish and feeble; send me your strong and your sane—
This is the Law of the Yukon, that only the Strong shall thrive;
That surely the Weak shall perish, and only the Fit survive.

'The Law of the Yukon' by Robert W. Service

It is my sincere hope that this book has helped you become a little bit stronger, saner and fitter to thrive in China.

Appendix A: On-line China Readiness Assessment

In order to get you started on your own China Readiness Assessment, we have setup a web-site, **www.chinareadycompany.com** , which provides the following:

- An on-line questionnaire which can be used to generate an initial positioning of your company's state of China readiness
- Background on the methodology, structure and output of the China Readiness Assessment
- A review of your company's results to the on-line version of the assessment
- Suggestions for using these results in a workshop format

By completing the on-line questionnaire, you will be able to see an initial view of your company's readiness for China. We encourage you to complete multiple questionnaires by different managers to provide a more inclusive view of management's perspective on your company's readiness position. If you are like most companies, the results will show varying and often conflicting views. This output provides fertile ingredients for your workshop and will be a catalyst to productive discussion of the key issues that need further probing and resolution as you address China.

The overall goals of a China Readiness Workshop are to:

- Discuss the results of the online China Readiness Assessment, getting input from all management.
- Refine the results—process the results to find consensus among the management team. Work through the various exercises outlined in this book and reposition the indicators on the charts to best reflect your perceived position. Identify areas needing further follow up and develop initiatives to address them.
- Take action on the results—for each indicator that falls in a critical zone, discuss ways that your team might take action to make your company more ready for China.

- Determine impact on your China strategy—discuss the implications of your readiness position and review their impact on your strategic alternatives.

Let me remind you that the readiness process is an art, not a science, and its results should be used as "indications", not conclusions. The China Readiness Assessment is a means to an end—the end being a decision on whether or not to take the next step to seriously explore a China expansion. The China Readiness Assessment is ideally done through personal, probing interviews with management. This on-line version should be viewed as the beginning of a more comprehensive and ongoing process.

Appendix B: List of Figures

CHAPTER 1

CHAPTER 2

CHAPTER 3

CHAPTER 4

Index